Sex Matters

Sex Matters

Essays in Gender-Critical Philosophy

HOLLY LAWFORD-SMITH

OXFORD
UNIVERSITY PRESS

Great Clarendon Street, Oxford, OX2 6DP,
United Kingdom

Oxford University Press is a department of the University of Oxford.
It furthers the University's objective of excellence in research, scholarship,
and education by publishing worldwide. Oxford is a registered trade mark of
Oxford University Press in the UK and in certain other countries

© Holly Lawford-Smith 2023

The moral rights of the author have been asserted

All rights reserved. No part of this publication may be reproduced, stored in
a retrieval system, or transmitted, in any form or by any means, without the
prior permission in writing of Oxford University Press, or as expressly permitted
by law, by licence or under terms agreed with the appropriate reprographics
rights organization. Enquiries concerning reproduction outside the scope of the
above should be sent to the Rights Department, Oxford University Press, at the
address above

You must not circulate this work in any other form
and you must impose this same condition on any acquirer

Published in the United States of America by Oxford University Press
198 Madison Avenue, New York, NY 10016, United States of America

British Library Cataloguing in Publication Data

Data available

Library of Congress Control Number: 2023933555

ISBN 978-0-19-289613-1

Printed and bound in the UK by
Clays Ltd, Elcograf S.p.A.

Links to third party websites are provided by Oxford in good faith and
for information only. Oxford disclaims any responsibility for the materials
contained in any third party website referenced in this work.

Contents

Acknowledgements — vi
Preface — ix
Some Notes on Language — xii

I. THEORY

1. Ending Sex-Based Oppression: Transitional Pathways — 3
2. Gender: What is it, and What Do They Want it to Be? — 30
3. Do Arguments for 'Trans Women are Women' Succeed? — 53

II. POLICY

4. Women-Only Spaces and the Right to Exclude — 79
5. Sex Self-Identification and Costly Signals of Assurance — 102
6. The Never-Ending Dispute over Public Bathrooms — 123

III. SPEECH

7. Is 'TERF' a Slur? — 149
8. Is Gender-Critical Speech Hate Speech? — 172
9. Is Gender-Critical Speech Harmful Speech? — 194

Index — 219

Acknowledgements

I've had so many conversations with so many people since 2018—when I started writing the first of what would eventually be the chapters of this book—that I've lost track. So I apologize to anyone left off the following list! But at the very least, I am grateful to Kate Phelan, Emily Vicendese, William Tuckwell, Sun Liu, Rene Rejon, Stephanie Collins, Cordelia Fine, Jess Megarry, Caroline Norma, Katie Steele, Christian Barry, Colin Klein, Luara Ferracioli, Kieran Oberman, Wolfgang Schwarz, Frank Hindriks, Arto Laitinen, Olle Blomberg, David Schweikard, Nin Kirkham, Rosa Freedman, Kathleen Stock, Mary Leng, Sophie Allen, Elizabeth Finneron-Burns, Rebecca Reilly-Cooper, Miriam Ronzoni, Anca Gheaus, Alex Byrne, Tomas Bogardus, and Callie Burt.

I also benefited from discussions with many audiences in presenting one or the other of these chapters, including at the Australian Association of Philosophy conference in Wollongong in 2019, the Conference on Sex and Gender in Manchester in 2019, and the Legal and Political Theory Seminar at University College London in 2021; at the public events 'What Is A Woman?' at the University of Reading in 2019 and *Philosophie Mittenmang* at the University of Flensburg in 2019; as well as in departmental seminars at the Australian National University, the University of Auckland, Victoria University of Wellington, the University of Sydney, Murdoch University, the University of Western Australia, the University of Melbourne, York University, Lund University, Pepperdine University, Hong Kong University, and the University of West England between 2018 and 2020.

A huge thank you, too, to all the real-name and anonymous radical feminist and gender-critical women of Twitter and Facebook who shared their thoughts with me and provided such vigorous debate when I was new to these issues (and before I was banned from Twitter). Chapter 4, in particular, was written with a lot of input from those women.

Finally, I'd like to acknowledge the work of the women who have published on the conflict of interests between gender identity activism and feminism before me, and whose work has helped to shift the public conversation to taking feminist interests more seriously. Among the first were Gloria Steinem ([1977] 1983, pp. 224-228), Mary Daly (1978, pp. 67-69 & pp. 71-72), Janice Raymond (1979), Germaine Greer (1989; 1999, pp. 80-93 & p. 422), and Julie Bindel (2004); and more recently Sheila Jeffreys (2014), Ruth Barrett (Ed.) and contributing authors (2016), Michelle-Moore and Heather Brunskell-Evans (Eds.) and contributing authors (2018; 2019), Abigail Shrier (2020), Lisa Selin Davis (2020), Sarah Pedersen (2020), Kathleen Stock (2021), Julie Bindel (2021), Helen Joyce (2021), and Kara Dansky (2021).[1]

Permissions

'Ending sex-based oppression: Transitional pathways', reprinted by permission from Springer Nature Customer Service Centre GmbH: Springer Nature *Philosophia* 49, pp. 1021–41, Holly Lawford-Smith, © 2021.

References

Barrett, Ruth (Ed.). *Female Erasure* (California: Tidal Time Publishing, 2016).
Bindel, Julie. 'Gender benders, beware', *The Guardian*, 31st January 2004. Online at <https://www.theguardian.com/world/2004/jan/31/gender.weekend7>
Bindel, Julie. *Feminism for Women* (London: Constable, 2021).
Daly, Mary. *Gyn/Ecology: The Metaethics of Radical Feminism* (London: The Women's Press, 1978).
Davis, Lisa Selin. *Tomboy* (New York: Legacy Literature, 2020).
Dansky, Kara. *The Abolition of Sex* (New York: Bombardier Books, 2021).
Greer, Germaine. 'On why sex-change is a lie', *The Independent Magazine*, 22nd July 1989, archived at <https://twitter.com/terfcitations/status/1550465693073567744>
Greer, Germaine. *The Whole Woman* (London: Black Swan, 1999).
Jeffreys, Sheila. *Gender Hurts* (Abingdon: Routledge, 2014).
Joyce, Helen. *Trans: When Ideology Meets Reality* (London: Oneworld, 2021).
Moore, Michele, and Brunskell-Evans, Heather. *Transgender Children and Young People: Born in Your Own Body* (Newcastle upon Tyne: Cambridge Scholars Publishing, 2018).
Moore, Michele, and Brunskell-Evans, Heather. *Inventing Transgender Children and Young People* (Newcastle upon Tyne: Cambridge Scholars Publishing, 2019).
Pedersen, Sarah. *The Politicization of Mumsnet* (Bingley: Emerald Publishing, 2020).
Raymond, Janice. *The Transsexual Empire* (New York: Teachers College Press, [1979] 1994).
Shrier, Abigail. *Irreversible Damage* (New Jersey: Regnery Publishing, 2020).
Steinem, Gloria. *Outrageous Acts and Everyday Rebellions* (New York: Henry Holt, 1983).
Stock, Kathleen. *Material Girls* (Great Britain: Fleet, 2021).

---

[1] For a list of recent journal articles in philosophy and related disciplines, see <https://hollylawford-smith.org/gcf-bibliography/>

Preface

At the time this book goes to press in 2023, there are already thriving grassroots social movements of women reclaiming their sex-based rights in many countries of the world. The most prominent, and most successful, sex-based rights movement is in the United Kingdom, but movements elsewhere are growing in strength. I wrote about how I understand the theory and activism of this movement in my book *Gender-Critical Feminism* (2022). In that book I noted that this movement for sex-based rights, popularly known as gender-critical feminism, has a disagreement with mainstream or socially dominant conceptions of feminism in multiple areas, including about prostitution and pornography, about transgender issues, and about intersectionality. One of my arguments in that book was that while gender-critical feminism is ceaselessly positioned by its detractors as being about trans issues—indeed, as being essentially 'anti-trans'—gender-critical feminism's disagreement with gender identity activism (the activism of some members of the trans community and their allies) is actually just an implication of its core commitments to a sex-based feminism, and not its central preoccupation. I predicted that that preoccupation will pass when the urgency of the disagreement passes, hopefully because a reasonable compromise has been reached rather than because women's interests have simply lost out. I have pursued those three main areas of gender-critical feminism's disagreement with mainstream feminism into separate work (on intersectionality see Lawford-Smith and Phelan 2022; on prostitution and pornography see Lawford-Smith and Pepper, manuscript; on trans issues see Lawford-Smith 2021 (republished here as Chapter 1), and Hauskeller and Lawford-Smith 2022). In this book I pursue in greater detail what I see as the conflict of interests between gender identity activism and gender-critical feminism, in particular in the areas of disagreement about what gender is, disagreement over access to women-only spaces and (relatedly) to the legal status of being a woman, and disagreement over the status of gender-critical speech (especially where it asserts that core commitments of gender identity activism are false).

Each chapter of this book is an independent essay, so there is no need to read in order, or to read everything. I have organized the chapters into three parts: the first about theory, the second about issues in law and policy, and the third about speech. Most of these chapters are defensive. A newer understanding of gender as identity is displacing the older understanding of gender as caste, to the detriment of radical and gender-critical feminists, for whom gender as caste is a key political concept. Chapters 1 and 2 address competing understandings of gender and visions for gender-related liberation. Radical and gender-critical feminists have been told that 'trans women are women!' and that it is wrong-headed, exclusionary, hateful, or bigoted to deny that, or to deny transwomen entry into women-only spaces. Chapter 3 takes up whether it is wrong-headed to deny it; Chapters 4, 5, and 6 take up whether it is exclusionary, hateful, or bigoted to deny transwomen entry into women-only spaces. Chapter 4 focuses on the question of women-only spaces broadly construed (all/any such spaces), while Chapter 6 focuses on bathrooms in particular. Chapter 5 is about the social and legal means that might be deployed to moderate access to women-only spaces. Finally, radical and gender-critical feminist theory and activism has been accused by its detractors of being hateful and/or harmful, in particular to transgender and nonbinary people. Chapters 8 and 9 take up those accusations directly, working through whether gender-critical speech is plausibly either hate speech, or harmful speech. Chapter 7 takes up the term 'TERF', routinely used against radical and gender-critical feminists, and asks whether it counts as a slur.

These chapters do not cover all the interesting points of conflict between gender identity activism and feminism. To cover all of these would require a very big book. In the section on speech, I could have talked about the current practice of replacing sex-specific language with gender-neutral language, and I could have talked about the ethics and politics of neo-pronouns and 'misgendering'. In the section on policy, I could have talked about ways of protecting trans and gender-diverse people from discrimination and unequal treatment that don't infringe on the interests of women and lesbian, gay, and bisexual people, for example legal protection of gender-expression and third spaces. I could have talked more about the harmfulness of medically and surgically transitioning children and adolescents, expanding on my arguments in (Lawford-Smith 2022, Chapter 5). In addition to, or instead of, talking about bathrooms in particular in Chapter 6, I could have talked about women's prisons (Biggs 2022), or women's sports (Devine 2021; Pike 2021; Hilton and Lundberg 2021; Pike et al. 2021; Imbrisevic 2022), or women's drug and alcohol addiction or sexual trauma recovery groups, or women-only hospital wards, or any other of the important women-only spaces. I could have had a section on the ethics of transition, and talked about 'trans widows', women whose marriages are ended and children impacted when their husbands transition, or about the balance of interests between those males who wish to transition to live as women, and the women whose feminist politics are best served by a sex-based understanding of what a woman is. In short, there are many interesting things to talk about in this area, and the fact that I chose the things I did should not be taken to suggest that these other topics aren't equally important. Luckily, more people are managing to publish in this area in the last couple of years,[1] so it is my hope that in the coming years there will be discussion of all these issues.

---

[1] See the last paragraph of the Acknowledgements for references.

References

Biggs, Michael. 'Queer theory and the transition from sex to gender in English prisons', *Journal of Controversial Ideas* 2/1 (2022), pp. 1–21.

Devine, Cathy. 'Female sports participation, gender identity and the British 2010 Equality Act' *Sport, Ethics and Philosophy*, 15 (2021), pp. 1–23.

Hauskeller, Michael, and Lawford-Smith, Holly. 'Gender', in Michael Hauskeller (Ed.) *The Things That Really Matter: Philosophical Conversations on the Cornerstones of Life* (London: UCL Press, 2022).

Hilton, Emma, and Lundberg, Tommy. 'Transgender women in the female category of sport: Perspectives on testosterone suppression and performance advantage', *Sports Medicine* 51 (2021), pp. 199–214.

Imbrisevic, Miroslav. 'Patriarchy in disguise: Burke on Pike and world rugby', *Sports, Ethics and Philosophy*, 16 (2022), pp. 1–19.

Lawford-Smith, Holly. *Gender-Critical Feminism* (Oxford: Oxford University Press, 2022).

Lawford-Smith, Holly. 'Ending sex-based oppression: transitional pathways', *Philosophia* 49 (2021), pp. 1021–41.

Lawford-Smith, Holly, and Phelan, Kate. 'The metaphysics of intersectionality revisited', *Journal of Political Philosophy* 30/1 (2022), pp. 166–87.

Lawford-Smith, Holly, and Pepper, Angie. *Is It Wrong to Buy Sex?* Manuscript, as at April 25th 2023.

Pike, Jon. 'Safety, fairness, and inclusion: transgender athletes and the essence of rugby', *Journal of the Philosophy of Sport* 48/2 (2021), pp. 155–68.

Pike, Jon, Hilton, Emma, and Howe, Leslie. 'Faster, higher, stronger: The biological and ethical challenges to including transgender athletes in women's sports', Macdonald-Laurier Institute, December 2021. Online at <https://macdonaldlaurier.ca/biology-fairness-trans-inclusion-sport-paper/>

Some Notes on Language

In this book, 'male' and 'female' will be used in the standard way, to refer to (biological) sex. I take male to be the sex that, all going well, produces small mobile gametes (sperm), and female to be the sex that, all going well, produces large immobile gametes (ova/eggs). 'All going well' here means something like, bracketing certain issues like endometriosis that can create problems for typical reproductive functioning. This is not the only way to understand sex, but I think it is the best way. Some people contest the meaning of 'male' and 'female', and prefer to use them interchangeably with 'man' and 'woman' to refer to one or more of gender identity, gender role, or position in a social hierarchy. I won't be using them in that way, for the primary reason that there are no other sex terms available, and a sex-based feminism needs terms to refer to sex.

I'll try to be as clear as possible throughout the book that the question of which terms we should use to refer to sex and gender is separate from the question of what the correct understandings of sex and gender are. I am assuming an understanding of sex, but one of the things at issue in this book is what the correct understanding of gender is. We could have that argument, and settle it, without settling what the existing sex and/or gender terms should refer to. For example, perhaps the gender-critical feminists are right and gender is a caste system that uses sex to sort people, but it's best to refer to as a woman anyone who feels that the word 'woman' describes them. Or, perhaps the gender identity activists are right and gender is one's subjective sense of oneself in terms of masculinity or femininity (or neither, or both), but it's best to reserve the word 'woman' for those who have been treated in a particular way since birth because of their sex. There might not be enough words for all the things we care about. I am primarily interested in the world, not the words we use to talk about the world, although I am concerned that we have some words rather than no words for that project. For that reason, I'm not assuming in this book that 'woman' means 'adult human female'. I'll be clear in each chapter whether I'm using the terms 'female' and 'woman' interchangeably, or whether I'm considering 'woman' as having alternative meanings.

There's a more subtle disagreement over what 'woman' means that is separate from the issue of whether transwomen are women. That is the issue of whether 'woman' is a success term. Because I'm interested in this book in the differential socialization of the sexes, we'll need a way to refer to a female *as she really is* (or could be), compared to a female person *as she has been made to be*. One way to mark this distinction doesn't involve the word 'woman' at all: we can use 'sex' for the way she really is and 'feminine' for the way she has been made to be (or at least, has been subject to attempts to make her be). This is one version of a sex/gender distinction in which 'female' tracks sex and 'woman' tracks gender. 'Feminine' is appropriate because it's an adjective; it describes a way that female people can be (made to be). But some feminists instead use 'woman' where I have used 'feminine', so that a female person successfully made feminine becomes a woman. When Simone de Beauvoir said that one is not born, but becomes, woman, this is what she meant.

Even more confusingly, some feminists think sex itself (at least as we currently understand it) is a way that human individuals are made to be, rather than a way they really are, in which case we should just use 'human' or 'person' for her as she really is (or could be), and all/any of 'feminine', 'woman', or 'female', for ways she has been made to be. The extension of each term is the same, picking out female people. But their intensions are different. If 'woman' names the class of people made feminine, and we stop making people feminine, there will be no women. Similarly, if 'female' names the humans made into one of the two socially constructed sex kinds, and we stop socially constructing sexes, there will be no females. I'll try to be clear when we're dealing with an account that uses 'woman' as a success term in this way.

'Transgender' is often used as an umbrella term to include both (binary) trans and nonbinary identities. I find it conceptually unhelpful to use as an umbrella term one of the identities that the umbrella covers, so I'll generally use 'transgender' to mean a male person who identifies as either or both of female/woman, or a female person who identifies as either or both of male/man. (Some gender identity activists prefer to say 'person born male', or 'person assigned male at birth', either because they countenance the possibility of changing sex, or because they use 'male' and 'female' interchangeably with 'man' and 'woman' for current identity. I won't be doing that, because I don't countenance the possibility of changing sex, and because as already noted, we need terms to refer to sex). In one chapter I say 'observed male at birth' or 'observed female at birth', but that is because I'm talking about the option of changing one's legal sex, and this is something that an intersex person, observed as being one sex but in fact another, might want to do. So we need the distinction there between being a sex, and being observed to be a sex (where observation can, occasionally, be mistaken).

'Transwoman', then, refers to a male who identifies as either or both of female/woman, 'transman' refers to a female who identifies as either or both of male/man. There is a political issue about a space in these words, namely, the difference between 'trans woman' and 'transwoman'. The first suggests that 'trans' is a way for someone born male to be a woman, like 'tall' woman or 'angry' woman. (The qualification is necessary, because 'trans' is clearly a way to be a woman, one way or the other. If it's not a way for someone born male to be a woman, then it's a way for someone born female to be a man). The second suggests that 'transwoman' is its own distinct category. Gender identity activists prefer the former, and radical and gender-critical feminists prefer the latter. Both beg the question when *whether* transwomen are women is at issue, which it sometimes will be in this book. If the question has to be begged one way or the other, I'll beg it in the direction I think is correct. So I use 'trans women' when quoting or referring to the claims of gender identity activists, and 'transwoman' otherwise.

'Nonbinary' in my usage means a person of either sex who identifies as neither man nor woman, and in some (but not all) cases also as neither male nor female. Sometimes I will need to specify the sex of the nonbinary person, so I will say 'female nonbinary person' or 'male nonbinary person'.

I will often talk in terms of gender identity rather than in terms of being trans, taking gender identity to be the trait or protected attribute of interest that trans people have.

I will occasionally be using 'woman' in a way that is neutral about disagreements over who is included in this category, and in that case when I need to refer to women-by-way-of-femaleness and women-by-way-of-identity I will use 'natal women' to refer to women-by-way-of-femaleness.

Finally, intersex conditions are not at issue in this book (they are mentioned only very briefly in Chapter 5 to make clear that my arguments against change of legal sex on the basis of gender identity are not intended to prevent change of legal sex in cases where an intersex person's sex has been incorrectly recorded). There are a number of plausible ways to understand sex, and most of them have no difficulty in classifying intersex people, and moreover, in classifying intersex people as the sex they understand themselves to be. There are very rare cases where a theory of sex may classify someone as other than they were 'assigned at birth' and/or understand themselves to be. It makes no difference, for my purposes in this book, whether we understand the 'sex' in 'sex-separated spaces' to be the all-going-well production of large or small gametes; progress down a developmental pathway to producing large or small gametes; having a 'Y' chromosome or not; or a homeostatic property cluster of primary sex characteristics (on the last three see Stock 2021). It also wouldn't matter, for my purposes in this book, to add the disjunct 'or assigned ____ (male/female) at birth' every time I mention a sex (so e.g. 'female or assigned female at birth'), to ensure that those with the very rare intersex conditions that would cause a plausible theory of sex to misclassify them by their own lights were included within the appropriate sex category. At issue is *not* whether intersex people assigned female at birth but technically male can use women-only spaces. At issue is males with 'woman' gender identities, and they don't tend to be intersex. Intersex issues are a red herring when it comes to the issues of Chapters 4–6 of this book.

References

Stock, Kathleen. *Material Girls* (London: Fleet, 2021).

I
THEORY

1
Ending Sex-Based Oppression
Transitional Pathways[1]

1.1 Gender norms

From a radical feminist perspective, gender is a cage.[2] Or to be more precise, it's two cages. The cages trap people with the biological sex 'male' and 'female' respectively. Those of the male sex are trapped by one set of gender norms—norms of masculinity—and those of the female sex are trapped by another—norms of femininity. Influential feminists have used the metaphor of a cage in connection with gender, including Marilyn Frye in her famous essay 'Oppression', as well as Mary Wollstonecraft and Shulamith Firestone (Frye 1983; Wollstonecraft [1792] 2017, p. 77; Firestone 1970, p. 25).[3] The metaphor helps to express that gender is something external, and confining.

Gender—which for the rest of this chapter means gender norms—is social expectations about a person's behaviour applied to their sex. Such expectations constrain the things that people can do and the ways that they can be, from who they date, how they present themselves, the way they move, the way they relate to other persons, the kinds of jobs they have, their passions and pursuits, the sports they play, and so on. For example, the gender norms applied to female people include androphilia (attraction to males), feminine presentation, contained movements, being warm and nurturing toward others, working in care- and people-focused jobs, pursuing e.g. dance or theatre rather than e.g. model-building or astronomy, playing e.g. netball rather than e.g. rugby, and so on.

Gender norms are one kind of social norm. Social norms are marked by the fact that conformity is dependent upon others' expectations. Non-conformity can be expected to bring social sanctions (Bicchieri 2016, pp. 35–40). The cage metaphor is appropriate, because gender norms are heavily policed compared to some other types of social norms. Compare queuing: when you push to the front of a

---

[1] This essay was first published in *Philosophia* 49 (2021), pp. 1021–42, and is reprinted here (with minor edits) with the permission of the journal.

[2] The aim of this chapter is not to defend the conception of gender as norms against the alternatives (on which more in Chapter 2), but to use one plausible conception of gender to explore the issue of ending sex-based oppression.

[3] Frye would likely resist my application of the metaphor to men, given that men are not oppressed. Individual men, and sub-groups of men, may be oppressed as members of other social groups, but men are not oppressed *as men*.

queue, you may hear some muttering from those behind you; someone may even demand that you go to the back of the line. The social sanctions associated with violations of the queuing norm are minor. When you are a boy who wears girls' clothing, however, you may be harassed, verbally abused, and even physically assaulted.

It would be bad enough if these norms only pushed people into gender roles—the social roles resulting from conformity to gender norms—that were 'equal but different'. But they do more than that. They push people into roles that are unequal. Men dominate, subordinate, and oppress women. Femininity is constructed in a way that legitimates and facilitates sexual violence (MacKinnon 1987, pp. 85–92). Science is wheeled in to justify sex inequality (e.g. talk of sexed brains, or the difference testosterone makes—see discussion in Fine 2010; 2017), and violence and other forms of social policing work to maintain it (Manne 2017).

If genders are cages, then surely we want to let people out. Being less constrained in our choices is something we all have reason to want. Many normative theorists in recent years have emphasized the importance of the capability to do and be many different things (see e.g. Nussbaum 2011; 2000). At the very least, we should want an end to sex-based oppression. While female people are the largest group to benefit from an end to sex-based oppression, other groups benefit too, including gay, lesbian and bisexual people (because the gender norm of heterosexuality disappear); gender non-conforming people (because the gender norms of female people presenting in a feminine way and male people presenting in a masculine way disappears); and trans and nonbinary people (because if there are no gender norms, then there is no 'incongruence' between sexed bodies and gender expressions).[4] But what is the best route to ending sex-based oppression?

Answering that question is the aim of this chapter. I'll compare four candidate 'transitional pathways'—*from* the world as it actually is *to* a world with substantially less, or no, sex-based oppression—with a view to considering how each relates to the ultimate end of eliminating sex-based oppression. Should we open the doors to the cages, so that people can move freely between them, but leave the cages themselves in place? Should we add more cages? Should we make the cages bigger, so that people have a lot more room to move around inside them? Or should we dismantle the cages, so there are no more gender norms at all?

These are questions in non-ideal theory, about the pathways from the actual world as it is currently, where genders are cages, to the ideal world, whether that is gender abolitionist or merely gender revisionist (for a useful overview of ideal and non-ideal theory, see Valentini 2012). But because ideal worlds include their

---

[4] For a critical discussion of 'incongruence' as used in medical definitions of being trans, see (Vincent and Jane, forthcoming), and the collection of commentaries in the same issue of *Australasian Philosophical Review*.

histories, the question of which pathway to take is crucial to establishing which is the ideal world. It also helps to make clear that the gender abolitionist pathway is *high ambition*, leading to liberation for many more people, while the gender revisionist pathways, particularly the nonbinary pathway, are *low ambition*, leading only to minor changes to the status quo.

This discussion should be of interest to radical and gender-critical feminists (and their allies) committed to gender abolitionism; to transgender people (and their allies) committed to revision of the existing gender binary without abolishment; to nonbinary people (and their allies) committed to resisting the gender binary; and indeed to all gender-conforming and gender non-conforming people who have thought about possible tensions between sex-based oppression and identities that depend on the existence of gender norms in some form or other.

1.2 A world without sex-based oppression, and transitional pathways

Let's return to the metaphor of gender as two cages. It's easy enough to imagine ways to make things better. Here are four possibilities, some of which I've already mentioned:

(1) Open the cage doors
(2) Add a new cage
(3) Add escape hatches to the cages
(4) Make the cages bigger

A world where the cage doors are open would be better, because then at least people would have a choice about which cage to be in. They could choose to move from the one cage to the other, and perhaps even to move freely between them. In the world where gender is two cages but the cage doors are open, sex and femininity/masculinity will have been fully decoupled. At the moment to be female is to be put in the 'feminine' cage; in a world with open cage doors, a female person would get the choice whether to be put in the 'feminine' cage or the 'masculine' cage.

A world where there's an additional cage, which people from either of the two other cages are free to enter, would also be better, because again this would give them a choice about which cage to be in. In principle one could add in any number here, although at a certain point, the question of whether these additional cages are still *gender*, rather than e.g. personality, will emerge. At the moment to be male is to be put in the 'masculine' cage; in a world with a third cage, the male could opt out of the cage of 'masculinity' and into the new cage.

A world where the cages had escape hatches would also be better, because then anyone who wasn't comfortable in the cage they were in could leave it. The difference between (1) and (3) is that (1) would let male people leave the 'masculine' cage and join the 'feminine' cage, let female people leave the 'feminine' cage and join the 'masculine' cage, and in principle let both male and female people go back and forwards between the cages; while (3) would only let female people leave the 'feminine' cage, and masculine people leave the 'masculine' cage. By escaping, they come to be in no cage, rather than the other cage (as in (1)), or a new cage (as in (2)). This gives some people more freedom, and it transforms the status of the cages: if it's viable for everyone to take the escape hatch, and people choose to remain in the cage of their own volition, they are not accurately described as 'trapped' or 'constrained' or 'imprisoned'. The cages become mere options.

A world where the cage doors remain shut but the cages are bigger would also be better, because there would be fewer constraints on the ways that people of a particular sex could be, or the things that people of a particular sex could do. The bigger the cage, the more ways there are of being a man, or a woman. There may be as many ways—or more—of being a man as there are men; as many ways—or more—of being a woman as there are women. If there are many ways to be a woman, but they overlap either not at all, or only in part, with the ways there are to be a man, and *vice versa*, then there's a lot more freedom, but there are still gender norms.

There are versions of (3) and (4) which amount to the same thing: getting rid of the cages entirely. If *everyone* takes the escape hatch then no one is caged, and if it's viable for everyone to take it then some people remain in the cage but are not technically 'caged' (because they are free to leave). If the two cages become so big that they overlap perfectly, then being caged is equivalent to not being caged. (Building a wall around the whole world wouldn't make it a prison). The ways of being a woman would overlap perfectly with the ways of being a man. A world where there are simply no cages would be better than the world where there are two but it's possible for some to escape, *and* the world where there are cages that are bigger (less constraining) than they are now, but still constraining. No cages at all means maximal freedom: male and female people are free to do and be whatever they want to be. The world without cages achieves the radical feminist goal of gender abolitionism (sometimes also called 'gender annihilation') (see e.g. Atkinson 1974, pp. 42–3; Firestone 1970, pp. 184–7; Frye 1983, pp. 35–7; The Feminists [1973]).

So we have four transitional pathways, all of which would take us to a world that is better than the actual world, at least when it comes to sex-based oppression. We don't yet know which of these would be the *best* pathway. So long as the best pathway is accessible to us, we should take it (if it were inaccessible, and we knew that, then we would be justified in taking another). One way we can start to think about which is the best is by thinking about the tradeoffs each pathway involves compared against the others.

Before I get onto that, let me note emphatically that nothing I say below is intended as a criticism of *current* gender norm-violating (or 'gender non-conforming') people. This is a speculative chapter about pathways to a world without sex-based oppression, and its observations depend on substantial numbers of people taking up the proposed strategies. In the actual world, people have their own reasons for violating gender norms, including being gay, being transgender or nonbinary, alleviating gender dysphoria, alleviating discomfort with aspects of one's physical sex, expressing opposition to gender norms, expressing opposition to 'the gender binary' (Dembroff 2018), and self-expression. In addition, some people may simply violate gender norms without any intention.

Most of these reasons would not be undermined by a philosophical discussion concluding that widespread adoption of transgender, third gender, or nonbinary identities is not the best pathway to a world without sex-based oppression. (The political reasons, however, would be undermined.) But all such reasons might be *bolstered* by a philosophical discussion concluding that transgender, third gender, or nonbinary identities are part of the best pathway. (Wouldn't it be satisfying for a gender identity activist to be able to say to a so-called 'trans-exclusionary' radical feminist, 'I'm doing my part in bringing about the world that *you* want?')

To translate the metaphorical cages into real strategies for political change, we have: changing between the two genders ('transgender pathway'); opting into a third (fourth, etc.) gender category ('third gender pathway');[5] opting out of binary gender ('nonbinary pathway') without opting into a third gender category; and rejecting gender without repudiating being a female/woman, or male/man ('gender abolition pathway'). Which of these is the best strategy? Which is the transitional pathway to the *best* world? Here is the list, so we can keep track:

(1) Open the cage doors → Transgender pathway
(2) Add a new cage → Third gender pathway
(3) Add escape hatches to the cages → Nonbinary pathway
(4) Make the cages bigger → Gender abolition pathway

What are the 'limit cases' for each pathway? I'll assume that for the transgender pathway, it is when half of all female people are subjected to norms of masculinity, and half of all male people are subject to the norms of femininity.[6] For the

---

[5] I'll use 'third' in the rest of the paper, but this should be taken to mean any number of genders greater than two.
[6] B. R. George and R. A. Briggs (manuscript) make a similar assumption when they explore the 'liberalization' of gender categories on trans twin earth: 'Through all these changes the [gender] roles themselves remain largely intact, but the demographics of the two worlds shift until there is no

third gender pathway it is when there are sufficiently many gender categories that no one feels trapped, and membership in these categories is freely chosen. For the nonbinary pathway, it is when everyone has repudiated being either female/women or male/men, so there are no people left for gender norms to be applied *to*. For the gender abolition pathway, it is when no one has repudiated being female/women or male/men, and yet gender norms are not applied to anyone. Some people may still choose the behaviours historically associated with their sex, but they would not do so because of gender norms. What we currently describe as gender non-conformity would just be normal variation between persons, and there would be a lot more of it.

The pathways introduced above are not mutually exclusive. In the actual world, they are all in play. But as political strategies to end sex-based oppression, they will be most effective if there is momentum around one in particular. That is because if the non-binary pathway is successful it pulls the rug out from under the transgender pathway; if the transgender pathway is successful it precludes the gender abolition pathway. (Still, in Section 1.3 I will briefly consider hybrid pathways). Each pathway comes with costs, and these costs impact upon different groups.

I think that these differential costs partly explain some of the heat around debates over proposed (and in some cases actual) changes to the recognition of sex/gender under the law, for example the 2018 consultation over the Gender Recognition Act (2004) in the UK, debate over the Human Rights (Gender Identity) Amendment Bill in New Zealand in 2019, and the quiet passing of the Births Deaths and Marriages Registration Amendment Act (2019) in Victoria, Australia, in 2019.[7] Gender-critical feminists[8] have argued that there's a tension, brought out by these proposed (and actual) legal changes, between advancing the interests of transgender, third gender, and nonbinary people, on the one hand, and advancing the interests of females/women on the other (Burt 2020; Asteriti and Bull 2020; Murray and Hunter-Blackburn 2019; Stock 2018a; 2018b; Reilly-Cooper 2016a; Lawford-Smith 2019a; 2019b; 2019c). Comparing these differential costs can help in figuring out which is the best pathway, and whether any pathway allows us to escape sex-based oppression entirely.

I'll take them in reverse order, starting with the gender abolition pathway, then moving on to the nonbinary pathway, the third gender pathway, and finally the

---

correlation at all between gender role and biological sex characteristics. [...] roughly half of all blokes and half of all grrrls possess typically female biology' (George and Briggs, manuscript., p. 18). ('Blokes' is the name they give to the previously male-associated gender category, 'grrrls' to the previously female-associated category).

[7] The latter, which came into force in May 2020, makes legal sex a matter of statutorily declared belief.

[8] Gender-critical feminists, following radical feminists, believe in a sex-based analysis of women's oppression; and in contrast to some radical feminists, also take a sex-based approach to her liberation. See further discussion in (Lawford-Smith 2022, Chapter 3).

transgender pathway. The gender abolition pathway is, as its name suggests, gender *abolitionist*, while the nonbinary, third gender, and transgender pathways are merely gender *revisionist*. This means that in assessing them, we have to think not only about what gender *is*, but what gender *should be* (if anything at all).

1.2.1 The gender abolition pathway

Along the gender abolition pathway, *everyone* repudiates their gender, understood as the set of norms they are subject to on the basis of their sex (masculinity for males/men, femininity for females/women). But no one repudiates their sex. No female/woman claims that she is not female/woman, and no male/man claims that he is not male/man. People do whatever they like, which means many women violate the norms of femininity and many men violate the norms of masculinity. This does not require that *everyone* violate *all* such norms. Feminine is a way to be female just as much as it is a way to be male, and the same is true for masculinity. So there will remain some feminine women and some masculine men. But these combinations will not be seen as normative. At the 'end' of this pathway, when we map the full spectrum of human behaviour, we will find substantially less clustering according to sex than we see now.

This does not require accepting a 'blank slate' view, presuming that in the debate over nature/nurture/nature-via-nurture the correct diagnosis of all sex differences is 'nurture'. It requires only to say that *whatever* proportion of 'femininity' and 'masculinity' have been constructed through early childhood socialization, culture, and social sanctions/rewards, *that* will disappear—and the interests previously gendered will be distributed more evenly across the population. This is compatible with there remaining some interests that relate more directly to sex, for example things to do with reproductive function, the specifics of sexed bodies, and sexual orientation/attraction.[9]

So far this is just the familiar feminist distinction between sex and gender,[10] where we get rid of gender by getting rid of sexist assumptions about how persons of one or the other sex should be and what they should do. It is distinctive because of its focus on ways of doing and being, rather than on identity labels. By violating gender norms, it hopes to erode and dismantle those norms, to leave people to be however they would be without them.

Which social groups does the gender abolition pathway involve costs for? Understanding this will allow us to assess the desirability of the pathway on its

---

[9] As Marilyn Frye put it: 'we do not know whether human behaviour patterns would be dimorphic along lines of chromosomal sex if we were not threatened and bullied; nor do we know, if we assume that they would be dimorphous, *what* they would be, that is, *what* constellations of traits and tendencies would fall out along that genetic line' (Frye 1983, p. 36).

[10] Cf. Bogardus (2020) on whether there really is such a distinction.

own merits, and then later to make tradeoffs between the four pathways. The first group who there are costs for will be those who wish to repudiate their sex. Because the violation of gender norms must be undertaken *without* repudiation of one's sex, we'll need to know how many of the people who currently repudiate their sex would still want to do that when their sex did not constrain them in any way. All those who are transgender, nonbinary, or third gender because of a gender dysphoria that is specifically about their *bodies* are likely to still want to reject their sex.

Those who are transgender, nonbinary, or third gender for reasons not specifically connected to their bodies are *not* likely to still want to reject their sex. It strikes me as plausible—although it's ultimately an empirical question—that the wider the scope of what it *means* to be a female person, or a male person, the less people would feel the need to repudiate their sex.

This is a point that many people critical of surgical transitioning (the undergoing of sex reassignment surgery) have made: we should change society so that it's more accommodating of difference, rather than change physically healthy individuals so that they can fit into the other of the small cages society currently has to offer (see e.g. discussion in Raymond 1979; Vincent and Jane, forthcoming). (Again, this is not intended as a criticism of people who undergo such surgery; it's intended as a criticism of gender norms, and the extent to which such people may not feel the need to *have* surgery if we managed to dissolve those norms).

This pathway will also be costly for transgender people who feel strongly that they are, or ought to be, subject to the gender norms of the other sex. Here's transwoman Andrea Long Chu, in an interview with Anastasia Berg for *The Point Magazine*:

> The TERF position that I would through transition be solidifying and reproducing normative gender roles—I find that argument *completely convincing*. I mean I think it's completely right, because I *know* that it's right, because it's the thing that I *want*! Like, I'm not interested, actually, not at all interested in dismantling gender (Long Chu and Berg 2018).

(The acronym 'TERF' that Chu uses in referring to 'the TERF position' is one gender identity activists use to refer to radical feminists, the '—RF' in the acronym, who acknowledge transwomen to be male and thus justifiably excludable from female-only spaces (the 'TE—' stands for 'trans-exclusionary'). Radical feminists themselves do not self-describe with this term, and many consider it to be a slur (Allen et al., manuscript; see also Chapter 7 of this volume)).

Normative gender roles are built out of conformity to gender norms, so there cannot be roles without norms. The fulfillment of Long Chu's desires *depends* on gender norms. So the abolition of gender frustrates those desires.

Costs to a third social group depend on the implications, in the early stages of the pathway, of others' violation of gender norms. Consider two female people, and imagine that one conforms to gender norms while the other violates gender norms without denying her membership in the class to whom the norms apply. The fact that the second violates gender norms may be taken to imply that the first (and all of those who conform) accepts her subjection to gender norms. But she may not; she may conform because she cannot afford the sanctions of nonconformity; she may conform because she happens to prefer to be as the norms direct her to be, while wishing there were no such norms. Given that these costs relate only to a person's actions being interpreted correctly by others, I give them little (but not no) weight (cf. Jenkins 2018, p. 732).

The gender abolition pathway comes with costs for one final social group: those social conservatives who think that conformity to gender norms is morally good, and that the gender roles that result from conformity to gender norms structure society in a positive and meaningful way.

In 1963, Helen Andelin wrote *Fascinating Womanhood*, directing women to be good wives to their husbands by reverting to traditional gender roles. She advocated 'girlishness, tenderness, and sweetness of character', and advised letting 'him be the guide, protector, and provider' (Smith 2017; see also Neuffer 2015 and Andelin 1963). There are conservative women (and indeed, some liberal women too) who enjoy gender role differentiation within a heterosexual relationship, and do not feel *all* gender norms to be constraining (e.g. they may be happy enough to be expected to be homemakers while their husbands work, even if they would rather not be expected to respond positively to catcalling).

It is tempting, of course, to dismiss these beliefs as adaptive: 'traditional husbands' have become accustomed to their privilege and 'traditional wives' have become resigned to their subordination. But it's dangerous territory to start assuming the ability to distinguish adaptive from non-adaptive beliefs (such distinctions are sometimes warranted, but they should be used sparingly). Any social change that will reduce the wellbeing of a particular social group should be factored in. So this cost counts.

In summary, there are four social groups for whom the gender abolition pathway comes with a cost. These are (i) the transgender, third gender, and nonbinary people who would still want to reject their sex even when that sex came with no particular expectations; (ii) the transgender people whose identities depend upon the existence of gender norms; (iii) those along the early stages of the pathway who do not violate gender norms; and (iv) the gender traditionalists, who would be unhappy to lose the sense of purpose, and social scaffolding, that comes from gender norms and the roles that come from conformity. For everyone else, the gender abolition pathway is liberating.

How do these internal costs and benefits pan out? While the costs to the transgender, third gender, and nonbinary people in (i) and the transgender people in (ii) are high, both groups are very small;[11] and while the group of those who are not gender norm-violating early on is large, the costs to individuals in that group are minimal. The costs to gender traditionalists may appear to be high; after all, they are a large group, so this pathway may risk a substantial loss of wellbeing. But this risk is partly mitigated when we remember that gender abolition means gender norms not being applied to anyone. That doesn't mean there can be no femininity (or masculinity), only that there can be no *enforcing* of femininity onto females (masculinity onto males). Those of the gender traditionalists whose preferences remained firmly in place even as social incentives around presentation, behaviour, and roles changed would be free to remain as they were. Thus the loss of wellbeing is not individual, about any particular woman having to do other than she prefers, but social, about the fact that she can no longer conceive herself as fulfilling a woman's destiny, or doing what women ought to do. Abolishing gender means there is no such thing. But it is not clear how much wellbeing there is in that.

The remaining group of people for whom this pathway would be liberating (which includes those who are norm-conforming in the early stage) is extremely large. Women, who stand to benefit the most from gender abolition (although men will benefit too), make up roughly half the population. (And this includes gender traditionalist women, who will benefit in other ways). Once we add in gender non-conforming men, we have an even bigger group. So unless the interests of gender norm-dependent trans people or gender traditionalists are *so important as to be considered to trump the interests of everyone else*, there are no internal reasons not to pursue the norm-violation pathway. (The comparison between the four pathways must be left until the end of this section).

1.2.2 The nonbinary pathway

One straightforward way to understand the difference between the gender abolition pathway and the nonbinary pathway is the matter of *how* to violate gender

---

[11] The closest group to (i) for which there is a population estimate is transsexuals, people who have had sex reassignment surgery. On one estimate, there were between 2,400 and 10,500 transsexual people in the UK (Equality and Human Rights Commission 2009, p. 33). The total population of the UK in that year was 62 million, which means transsexual people were less than 0.02% of the population. The closest group to (ii) for which there is a population estimate is what the UK Equality and Human Rights Commission calls 'the trans population'. This will be an overestimate relative to the understanding of transgender I am using here, because it will count nonbinary people, and other people too (see discussion in Equality and Human Rights Commission, pp. 10–19). The estimated size of the trans population in the UK was between 65,000 and 300,000 (Equality and Human Rights Commission, p. 33). That is 0.48% of the population.

norms. According to the gender abolition strategy, no female person denies that she is female/woman, but she might violate the norms of femininity. According to the nonbinary strategy, female nonbinary people *do* deny that they are female/women (this is not necessarily the case in the actual world, where there is diversity among nonbinary people in whether they deny only that they are women, or deny both that they are women and that they are female). Whether or not they also violate other gender norms, this denial of sex/gender category is front and centre in the nonbinary strategy.

On the radical feminist understanding of gender, where gender is a set of norms applied on the basis of sex, it is hard to understand what the point of denying these categorizations would be. There is a fact of the matter about a person's sex, and there is a fact of the matter about which set of norms they are subjected to on the basis of that sex (with some exceptions for people who are perceived by others to be the opposite sex). Is the strategy here to deny these facts?

We can avoid this conclusion by shifting to an alternative conception of gender, rather than insisting that gender is (only) norms. The term 'gender' is polysemous, at least in the academic literature if not beyond. It might refer to any of 'gender role, gender identity, gender expression' (Barnes 2020, p. 723), gendered social position (p. 706), or as we have been discussing, gender norms. If we take gender to be gender expression, then androgynous or masculine-presenting female nonbinary people may claim to 'escape the cage' of (binary) gender by expressing themselves in non-feminine ways. (Still, they would have to answer the question of why *they* are not female/women, while other androgynous or masculine-presenting female people are; or, alternatively, bite the bullet on a lot of women being mistaken that they are female/women).

The two main 'types' of theory of gender are social position theories, and identity theories (Barnes 2020, pp. 706–11, and exceptions in fn. 11). Social position theories are 'externalist'. They take gender to be a position in a social structure, a matter of how others perceive you, treat you, expect you to behave, etc. (see e.g. Ásta 2013, 2019; Witt 2011; Haslanger 2012; and discussion in Barnes 2020). Identity theories are 'internalist'. They take gender to be a matter of how you feel, how you see yourself, which group you take yourself to belong to (see e.g. Appiah 1990; McKitrick 2015, Bettcher 2009, 2013; Jenkins 2016; 2018; and discussion in Barnes 2020). The radical feminist view of gender as norms is externalist; perhaps an internalist view would make better sense of the nonbinary strategy.

While proponents of gender identity theories have accused externalist social position theorists of having an exclusion problem (specifically, failing to include all self-identified transwomen as women), gender identity theories face an exclusion problem of their own (specifically, failing to include some natal women as women) (Barnes 2020). The most worked-out theory of gender identity on offer actually understands gender identity as taking norms to apply to you; for example, a male person has the gender identity 'female/woman' when he takes more of the norms applied to female people than the norms applied to male people to apply to him (Jenkins 2018, pp. 728–36, esp. p. 731). That means gender as gender identity depends on a prior understanding of gender as gender norms.

But Jenkins' account fails on the grounds that this is not how norms work. Others apply norms to you, and sanction you for non-conformity. You can *take norms to apply to you* all you like, but if you won't be sanctioned for non-conformity, then you're simply making a mistake. Most male people with 'female/woman' gender identities will be subjected to the norms of masculinity (there are some exceptions for males who are perceived by others to be female). So internalist theories are largely unpersuasive. They have going for them that they are 'inclusive' and vindicate the self-understandings of some people who are marginalized. But they have against them that they capture virtually nothing of the empirical fact of sex-based oppression, and offer little contribution to dismantling it.

Returning to the externalist understanding of gender as norms, then, can we understand the nonbinary strategy as a version of the gender abolition strategy focused specifically on rejecting the norm *that* everyone is either a male/man or a female/woman? Nonbinary people attempt to escape gender norms by denying that those norms are correctly applied to *them*. Robin Dembroff, who is nonbinary, insists that this need not involve denial of one's sex or gendered socialization, writing 'most nonbinary persons do not claim they are (or were) not marked with a binary sex, or socialized according to that assigned sex. Whatever these persons mean by claiming nonbinary identities, it is not a lack of gendered socialization' (Dembroff 2018).

Terminological differences lead to the appearance of more disagreement than there really is between the gender abolition strategy and the nonbinary strategy, I think. Radical feminists[12] tend to refer to the gender norms as 'masculinity' and 'femininity'. On this view, a female person who violates gender norms may not be feminine, but she is still a woman. But some refer to the *social role* of those to whom gender norms are (successfully) applied as 'woman' and 'man', so a female person who violates gender norms is *not* a 'woman'. If we use the latter terminology, then we can accept Dembroff's point that nonbinary people need not deny their sex or sexed socialization, compatible with the point that they protest gender by denying *that they are women*, or *that they are men*.[13]

---

[12] Radical feminists, preceding gender-critical feminists, believe in a sex-based analysis of women's oppression. For a historical overview see (Lawford-Smith 2022, Chapter 2).
[13] It has been common in recent feminist history to take this view, that 'man' and 'woman' refer to social roles. But this creates a contradiction with ordinary linguistic usage, in implying that all female people who don't occupy the social role don't count as 'women' (for a discussion about the ordinary

But there isn't any real difference here. Nonbinary people are just male and female people who oppose the application of gender norms to persons (or at least, to themselves). They attempt to sidestep the application of gender norms by sidestepping sex/gender classification.

If what it is to be 'neither a male/man nor a female/woman' is to be a third gender, then the nonbinary strategy is a version of the third gender pathway. If it is no gender, or a rejection of gender, then it is a version of the gender abolition pathway. In either case, it remains distinctive, because of the *way* it articulates that third gender, or the specific *kind* of norm violation it focuses on.

There is a question about the likely efficacy of this pathway. There really are gender norms, and they really are applied on the basis of sex (including on the basis of assumptions about sex that are mistaken). So unless nonbinary people successfully confound sex classification, it is unlikely that they would escape subjection to gender norms. A child bride cannot escape being married off to a life of domestic and sexual servitude by claiming that she is neither a woman nor a man. So there is a risk that this pathway actually does little to challenge the status quo. That creates a large group for whom there are high costs: all the people suffering sex-based oppression that have been mentioned already.

If nonbinary people *do not* confound sex classification, but violate the gender norms applied to people of their sex in other ways, then they will be advancing the gender abolition project (through non-conformity) rather than the specifically non-binary project (through increasing the size of the group of people not subject to either set of gender norms). If nonbinary people *do* confound sex classification, there is a risk of new norms evolving for the policing of nonbinary as a third gender category, rather than no gender. So they themselves are the second group for whom this pathway may involve costs.

Which other social groups would be harmed by the nonbinary strategy? In the early stages of the pathway, before it reaches its conceptual limit, the nonbinary strategy involves costs for those people who do not deny that they are female/women or male/men. Consider two female people, one who conforms to feminine gender norms and doesn't claim to be nonbinary, and another who violates feminine gender norms *by* denying that they apply to her, because she is nonbinary. The fact that the second denies the norms apply to her may suggest they *do* apply to the woman who does not claim to be nonbinary, and thereby reinforce feminine gender norms for other women (Reilly-Cooper 2016*b*; Cox 2016; cf. Skylar 2016). This is a comparative cost: in a straightforward choice between being a female/woman astrophysicist, and being a nonbinary astrophysicist, the

---

understanding of 'woman' see Byrne 2020). On the understanding of gender as gender norms, a female nonbinary person is a woman, *because* (or, as long as) the norms of femininity that are applied to female people are still applied to her. For an argument against 'woman' as a social role, see Stock (manuscript).

former does more to challenge gender norms and contribute to the dismantling of sex-based oppression than the latter. The former is a positive representation of a woman doing something that is atypical for women; the latter leaves women to their feminine jobs and casts an astrophysicist as 'not a woman'.

At the end of the pathway, as mentioned already in Section 1.2.1, there are also costs for anyone who *liked* the sex/gender binary and doesn't want a world of nonbinary humans. This includes the gender traditionalists and the transgender people who depended upon the gender norms (i.e. who wanted to *swap* categories, not for the categories to be eliminated). Given the risk of inefficacy, the size and seriousness of the potential harms, and the fact that nonbinary people who don't confound sex classification will actually be contributing to the gender abolition pathway, the nonbinary pathway doesn't look to have a lot going for it.

1.2.3 The third gender pathway

Along this pathway, increasing numbers of male and female people start declaring themselves to be members of third gender categories. This means more freedom: the more gender categories there are the more choices people have, and the less constrained they are.

There are already third gender categories in many countries, including Australia (among some Aboriginal peoples), Samoa, India, Pakistan, and the United States (among some Native American peoples).[14] Some people already conceive of gender as a 'spectrum', which contains as many categories as there are personalities (for criticism see Reilly-Cooper 2016*b*).

One advantage of this pathway compared to the transgender pathway—yet to be discussed—is that it avoids a conflict between transwomen and women. When we *add* genders, people can opt out of one of the traditional two without that entailing they must opt into the other. When we merely liberalize membership of the two traditional gender categories, a male person's opting out of maleness, manhood, masculinity means his opting into femaleness, womanhood, femininity. For those female people who have been subordinated by male people on the basis of their sex, this can seem a bitter pill to swallow—at least if it means accepting such people in female-only spaces, as mothers, as lesbians, etc. The third gender pathway sidesteps such conflicts.

One problem with this pathway is the same as that raised already for nonbinary people, which is that if gender norms are applied on the basis of sex, and it's difficult to confound sex classification, then this pathway won't actually result in an escape from gender, at least not in the sense I'm understanding it in this

---

[14] For an interactive map of countries and third gender categories, see: https://www.pbs.org/independentlens/content/two-spirits_map-html/

chapter. If we take this pathway, we might still end up in a world with oppressive social norms applied on the basis of a person's sex. That means there's a serious cost for all people who are oppressed on the basis of their sex, i.e. all female people, because this pathway does nothing to mitigate their oppression.

I said earlier that the third gender pathway and the transgender pathway were merely gender revisionist. At this point it matters a lot *how* revisionary they are.

If the gender norms applied to a female person on the basis of her sex are the same as they are now, regardless of the proliferation of new gender categories, then we still have sex-based oppression, and this world is not better than the one we are in now. (The 'pathway' to the ideal is no pathway at all). If, however, the gender norms applied to a person on the basis of her sex are *replaced* by norms applied to a person on the basis of her third gender category membership, and there are many such categories membership in which is freely chosen, then there may be little or no sex-based oppression at all.

This pathway comes with costs for transgender people who do not see themselves as 'third gender', but rather as one of the existing two genders. If third gender categories translate into third gender spaces, this may be felt as a further cost by people who society classifies as third gender but who would themselves prefer to use the spaces of one of the existing two genders. It also comes with costs for anyone who would still feel constrained by the gender categories, no matter the options. (Imagine that there are three gender categories, and a person feels that none fit her; imagine there are twenty categories, and a person feels that none fit her).

It's difficult to assess the internal tradeoffs here, because much depends on whether binary gender norms (norms that apply to sex category membership) are replaced at some point along the pathway by third gender norms (norms that apply to membership in one of the new plurality of categories).

In terms of the costs to transgender people the tradeoff is the same as for *i.*, namely that while the costs are high, the number of people affected is small, so unless their interests trump everyone else's, there are no internal reasons not to pursue the third gender pathway. Because this pathway comes with a risk of failing to mitigate sex-based oppression while the gender abolition pathway doesn't, the gender abolition pathway looks to be ahead in terms of overall cost-benefit tradeoffs.

1.2.4 The transgender pathway

Along the transgender pathway, increasing numbers of male people start being subjected to the norms of femininity, and increasing numbers of female people start being subjected to the norms of masculinity.[15] It's important to make a distinction here between conforming to norms that are applied to you, and acting in a way that is congruent with the norms that are applied to others. On my conception of gender, specific norms are applied to the members of the female sex class. If a person is a member of the male sex category, but either chooses or feels compelled to act in a way congruent with the norms applied to the members of the female sex class, that does not mean that person shares a gender with female people. Gender is *subjection to* specific norms, whether you conform to those norms or not.[16]

Some people who are transgender change some of their primary sex characteristics (via sex reassignment surgery) or secondary sex characteristics (via cross-sex hormones) *so that* they may be perceived by others as members of the sex category to which the norms are applied. Such people may more accurately be said to 'conform' to the norms rather than simply act in a way congruent with the norms. People who are transgender but choose not to take steps to be perceived by others as members of the sex category to which the norms are applied (or are unsuccessful in the steps they do take) merely act in a way congruent with the norms. For the transgender pathway to be a pathway at all, it will need to be that people *conform* to the norms of the opposite sex category, not merely act consonantly with them. (Otherwise there is no challenge to gender, because there is no shift in the makeup of the population to which the norms are applied).

Transgender author Julia Serano (2007) argues that transgender activism is a feminist movement. For Serano, the problem we have with gender, as a society, is *not* that gender roles oppress those who occupy them, but that femininity is constantly devalued relative to masculinity. On this view, to remove much, if not all, gender injustice, we need to do two things. The first is to decouple sex and gender (which on my understanding of gender would mean making it the case that people can choose which set of norms applies to them). This removes one major constraint, which is that one's gender is not chosen. The second is to improve the status of femininity, pushing against 'the belief that maleness and masculinity are superior to femaleness and femininity' (Serano 2007; see also Pandian 2018). This maintains the two traditional gender categories, but it equalizes them and gives people a choice.

---

[15] Note that because the numbers of people with gender dysphoria are too small to make this pathway successful, we have to imagine people *without* gender dysphoria nonetheless taking it up.

[16] If we understood this pathway in a weaker way as requiring only action congruent with gender norms, it would seem to become a version of the gender abolition pathway—people of each sex violating gender norms *by* acting in accordance with the other sex's norms. The problem with how that is working in the actual world is that by claiming to actually *be* the opposite sex/gender, the behaviour is not necessarily interpreted as norm-violating.

At the end of this pathway, we have the same gender categories—masculine and feminine (or what some others call 'man' and 'woman')—but they are composed differently in terms of sex, with male and female in each, and they are valued equally. This is unlike the end of the gender abolition pathway and the nonbinary pathway, where there will be no genders. (For the former, there will be female/women and male/men but no gender; for the latter there will be female and male but no gender—in the sense that if everyone is nonbinary then no one is). And it is unlike the end of the third gender pathway, where there will be sexes and many different genders.

Which social groups does the transgender pathway involve costs for? It comes with serious costs for female people, at least in the beginning of the shift. We currently live in a sexist and misogynistic society, where men have advantage over women, and women have disadvantage relative to men and suffer violence at the hands of men. If we want to get to a society without sex hierarchy, we need to mitigate the historical oppression of women and women's ongoing disadvantage, and that means *keeping track of* who has in the past suffered sex-based oppression, and who continues to suffer sex-based disadvantage. In a society in which people of either sex identify into and out of each other's categories, it will be hard to keep track of sex-based privilege and oppression. At least, this will be true if the law fails to keep track of 'original' sex category membership after sex category membership has been liberalized. (This problem is in large part an artifact of many countries' failure to keep sex and gender separate in the law—working to protect transgender rights by replacing sex with gender identity, rather than adding distinct protections for gender identity or gender expression).

Consider an analogy: a person who lives in a racist society pronounces herself to be 'colourblind'. That is, she says she doesn't see race, she just sees people. That's all very well, we might tell her, but if you don't see race then you don't see *racism*, and that means you're not able to do anything to help its victims. We don't want colourblindness in a racist society, because we want to be able to mitigate racist oppression, in order to eventually get to a non-racist society.

Ditto for sex-blindness in a sexist and misogynistic society. By the time each gender category is occupied by 50% female and 50% male people, it will be impossible to make provisions for the amelioration of sex-based oppression[17]—or at least, not without catching a whole lot of people who don't need it, and missing a whole lot of people that do. But there will be a lot of unfairness along the pathway if we lose the ability to recognize, and therefore mitigate, the historical and ongoing oppression and disadvantage of female people.

In case this seems like a merely hypothetical worry, note that in the UK, transwomen have taken positions on political party shortlists reserved for

---

[17] Similarly, we would lose the ability to track violence and discrimination against trans people.

women in an attempt to improve women's participation in politics; in the US, Australia, and New Zealand, transwomen have competed in and won at women's elite sports; in the UK, a transwoman was invited to speak at a women's film festival, put together to work against the exclusion of women from the film industry; and so on.

This might seem like a strange thing to articulate as a cost. There are many differences within the class of women: black women, brown women, white women; poor women, rich women; lesbian women, bisexual women, straight women; able-bodied women, disabled women; neurotypical women, neuro-atypical women; young women, old women; and so on. If positions reserved for women (as a measure to combat historical injustice against women by men and equalize relations between the sexes) were filled with white, rich, straight, able-bodied, neurotypical women, other women could complain, because these are the most privileged of the class of women. If such positions were filled with black, lesbian, disabled women, no one could complain, because they're not a privileged group within the class. This is why it's so important to consider the intersection of different identities (Crenshaw 1989). But transwomen are not a privileged group within the class, so why isn't that analogous?

Bracketing for the sake of argument the more controversial question of whether they are appropriately understood as a group within the class at all, there's an interesting question about whether we should expect to see them *become* the privileged group within the class once the sex composition of the class has changed. Transwomen who are assumed by others to be female, but in the past were assumed by others to be male, will have the historical advantage of male socialization (for example they may be more confident) and the future disadvantages of being treated as female (for example they may experience more sexual harassment). (Gendered socialization is influential, and much of the conditioning effect that it has will be invisible to its subjects; see e.g. Fine 2010, and the discussion in Chapter 2 of this volume). This undermines the claim sometimes made that people who experience gender dysphoria will simply reject their gender socialization—see e.g. Finlayson et al. 2018).

Transwomen who were in the past, and continue to be, assumed by others to be male (i.e. are consistently 'misgendered') will have historical male privilege *and* future male privilege (which is compatible with their also being disadvantaged in virtue of being trans, which is a distinct, and significant, cause of disadvantage). To the extent that some transwomen will have experienced male socialization, we should actually expect to see them come to be privileged within the class, because males are socialized to be bold, ambitious, dominant, self-confident, etc. (This point about the 'male privilege' that many transwomen have is acknowledged in the 'The Transfeminist Manifesto'—see discussion in Koyama 2003). This is something that we should take seriously as a cost to women, not because it's bad for one type of woman[18] to be dominant (although it is), but because males are *already* so dominant outside the class.

One response here is to emphasize the fact that these costs only arise if the shift between gender categories is accompanied by a shift between legal sex categories. If it isn't, and sex continues to be a legally protected characteristic,[19] then we could continue to track the oppressed group by tracking the female *sex* rather than the woman/female gender, at least until such a time as the gender revolution is complete and sex-based oppression has disappeared. This will still mean making some mistakes, because transmen will count as female but may lose status as oppressed the longer they spend being assumed by others to be male, and symmetrically, transwomen will count as male but may lose status as privileged the longer they spend being assumed by others to be female. But these mistakes involve smaller numbers of people.

If we are to avoid one of the serious costs of this strategy by legally protecting sex regardless of what is happening with gender, then that will mean applying strict conditions to a person's capacity to change their legal sex. For example, we might want to make change of legal sex impossible, or possible only when a genuine mistake was made in the recording. At the very least, we will need to keep legal records of birth sex. This will count as yet another cost for people in the trans community who want to change their sex on official documentation and not just change their gender category membership. If sex continues to be legally protected, and the protection of gender category membership—on a conception of gender that is not 'the norms applied on the basis of sex', obviously—is kept distinct, then the conflict of interest between transwomen and women is largely resolved.

This pathway is extremely costly for everyone who would prefer to challenge gender norms *without* conforming to the norms applied to people of the opposite sex (which means taking steps to be perceived as a member of the opposite sex). People with gender dysphoria may be happy to challenge gender norms in this way, but there are only small numbers of people with gender dysphoria, certainly not enough to make this strategy successful by themselves.[20] What about everyone else? Confounding accurate sex perception is demanding, and many people

---

[18] Note that this is a revised understanding of 'woman' as a class for the purposes of discussion in this section, and is at odds with the usage synonymous with 'female' used throughout the rest of the chapter.

[19] Or sex *and* gender could be legally protected characteristics (as they are in the UK, where a person can get a Gender Recognition Certificate, but there are specific exemptions for where sex and legally recognized gender come apart). In this case there would be need to be clear guidelines allowing the exclusion of all male people from female-specific rights and legal protections regardless of gender.

[20] In the DSM-5 prevalence in males was 0.015–0.014% and in females 0.002–0.003%, and they conclude that it is 'rare' or 'uncommon'. For discussion of the various issues involved with getting an accurate estimation of the prevalence of gender dysphoria and transgender identity (which can come apart) see discussion in (Zucker 2017).

will not accept that demand. People should not have to undergo medical and surgical interventions with long-term health implications in order to eventually free themselves and others of oppressive gender norms. That would be too high a price to pay even if it were the only strategy available; and it isn't the only strategy available.

Assessing these internal costs, there seem to be good reasons not to take the transgender pathway. With the very small numbers who actually suffer gender dysphoria, it won't be efficacious; and with bigger numbers incorporating those who don't suffer gender dysphoria, it will be over-demanding. Furthermore, the costs to women of sacrificing the legal protection of sex may be so high as to be a trumping concern.

1.2.5 Tradeoffs between pathways

I've already considered each pathway's internal tradeoffs. I said that there are no good reasons not to pursue the gender abolition pathway, some good reasons to be sceptical about the efficacy of the nonbinary and third gender pathways, and some good reasons not to pursue the transgender pathway. The third gender pathway and the nonbinary pathway (interpreted as a version of the gender abolition pathway) both come with the practical problem that if we can't successfully confound sex identification, and if binary gender norms don't turn into third gender norms along the pathways, then we'll end up in a world that is still marked by sex-based oppression.

This suggests a comparative ranking on which the transgender pathway should be the least preferred, with the gender abolition pathway most preferred. It is not clear how to rank the nonbinary against the third gender pathways (especially given that on one interpretation, the former collapses into the latter). But these conclusions are necessarily highly speculative, and depend on details about how gender norms might evolve and erode, and how their subjects might shift as we move along each pathway.

1.3 Falling short of the limit cases, and hybrid pathways

In the previous section I suggested four transitional pathways from the actual world to a world without sex-based oppression, and talked about tradeoffs between them. But it's not clear why we should assume that there's substantial uptake of one and only one pathway. So in this section I relax some of the simplifying assumptions that helped us to make progress in the previous section (i.e. exclusive uptake of one pathway), and think about some of the interaction effects.

It might be that despite coming from different angles and having different commitments, the presence of trans, nonbinary, third gender, and norm-violating people all have the combined effect of challenging society's ideas about gender, in a way that has positive effects on those who are most constrained by gender roles.

The gender abolition pathway and the third gender pathway are good candidates for a hybrid pathway.[21] At a certain point, when there are enough third gender categories and membership is entirely voluntary (at least when third gender norms have replaced binary gender norms), the third gender world is actually gender abolitionist. We might still use the word 'gender', but the norms wouldn't be creating the problems they are today, especially for women. This hybrid pathway would combine the costs and the advantages of the two.

Whether the transgender pathway sits as easily with these two depends a lot on the difference between the limit case and all of the many steps along that pathway that involve smaller numbers of people. This means it's important to consider whether one male, or a small number of males, taking up the social position of women would create any of the same conflicts of interest that I mentioned already when discussing the limit case of that pathway.

For every case where gains for female people are zero-sum, there's a conflict. One male in a women-only sports team, one male in a women-only political party shortlist or serving as a political party's 'women's officer', even one male as a keynote speaker at a women's film festival, one male 'lesbian' as an advisor to a major non-governmental LGBTQI+ charity, one male on the 'Top-100 Women in Business' list, one male in a women-only prison, one male in a women's shelter (there are real examples of all of these) makes a difference. It has a negative impact on the woman who misses out, or the women who are adversely affected by the presence of males, and it sends a message to all women that their interests are secondary to male interests.

Having a women-only football team that has one male player and the rest female players is still better than having a women-only football team that has *all* male players, but even one male player means that one female player is missing out on a spot in that team. If the women on the team are prohibited from speaking out against that male's inclusion (there are real examples of this as well), this has the further negative impact of silencing women's legitimate resistance. Males, unlike females, have not been historically excluded from or under-represented in football (and sports more generally, as well as politics, filmmaking, business. etc.). So even just one female football player losing her spot is bad.

---

[21] On some readings, nonbinary *is* a third gender category (some nonbinary people report being sanctioned within their communities for not appearing androgynous enough). To the extent that's true, all three can be combined, in virtue of nonbinary being collapsed into third gender.

This might also be true for cases where the gains for females are not so clearly zero-sum. For example, it is important for oppressed groups to have spaces of their own, to organize politically, and to experience solidarity with other members, and to simply have time that is free from interaction with members of the oppressor group and their socialized behaviours (for a discussion of this need in the context of people of colour needing spaces without white people, see Blackwell 2018; or watch the 2014 film and/or 2017 Netflix series *Dear White People*).

Olivia Blackwell gives the following as reasons for spaces free of white people:

> We need places in which we can gather and be free from the mainstream stereotypes and marginalization that permeate every other societal space we occupy. We need spaces where we can be our authentic selves without white people's judgement and insecurity muzzling that expression. We need spaces where we can simply be—where we can get off the treadmill of making white people comfortable and finally realize just how tired we are. [...] In integrated spaces, patterns of white dominance are inevitable. These patterns include things like being legitimized for using academic language, an expectation of "getting it right" (e.g. perfectionism), fear of open conflict, scapegoating those who cause discomfort, and a sense of urgency that takes precedence over inclusion. [...] These spaces aren't acts of oppression, but rather responses to it. They are our opportunity to be with each other away from the abuses of racism and patterns of white dominance (Blackwell 2018).

Simply having one white person in a space like that can undermine the important gains to people of colour of having a space of their own, and likewise simply having one male in a women-only space can undermine the important gains to women of having a space of their own (on the parallels between race and gender transitioning see discussion in Tuvel 2017; see also discussion at Singal 2017). So long as this organization is informal, or is formalized as a club, it is possible to achieve these ends (as the hybrid pathway gets started, individuals could choose to organize on the basis of biological sex alone). But as soon as the group formalizes in any other way, it would be at risk of being made to be 'inclusive' of those males who have made themselves subject to the opposite sex's gender norms, as a matter of non-discrimination laws that conflate sex and gender. This puts the goods achievable in those spaces at risk.

So even when transition pathways are hybrid and partial, rather than singular and at the limit case, there is still reason to prefer the gender abolition and third gender pathways to the transgender pathway. If we are going to persist with the transgender pathway (in particular if we are going to move to an understanding of gender as identity that we wish to protect under the law) then it is imperative that we protect biologically female people too, by clarifying the interaction between sex and gender (gender identity, gender reassignment, etc.) in law so that sex-based rights and protections remain sex-based, and by resisting the attempt by some gender identity activists to erase sex as a meaningful category (both socially and legally).

1.4 Conclusion

None of the pathways explored here should be reserved for women, or for people with gender dysphoria, because these are not the only people for whom gender causes problems, and these are not the only people who have a capacity to contribute to positive change. People for whom the stakes aren't nearly so high should also consider taking on some of the social costs associated with the abolition or revision of gender norms and roles. The more flexibility there is around gender, the less pressure both male and female people will face in light of non-conformity, and the more that *all of us* will be free to do and be whatever we want to be.

But the costs to each group of different ways of changing the world should be carefully assessed. Female people are still oppressed on the basis of their biological sex and should both have continued access to legal protection on that basis, and continued access to provisions to mitigate that oppression (without being expected to share these with other oppressed or disadvantaged groups).

Trans people still suffer high levels of harassment and discrimination and should have access to legal protection on that basis (or on a broader basis like gender expression), and should be granted special provisions to mitigate any disadvantage (without that coming at a cost to other oppressed or disadvantaged groups—third spaces and anti-discrimination legislation are a way to accomplish this).

Biological females and trans people are both vulnerable groups (which partly overlap, by way of transmen), and both need to be protected along the way to achieving a world where gender isn't constraining for anyone. On these grounds, the exclusive pathways should be ranked from best to worst: gender abolition; third gender; nonbinary; transgender. The partial/hybrid pathways should be ranked from best to worst: gender abolition and third gender; gender abolition and third gender and transgender.

References

Allen, Sophie, Finneron-Burns, Elizabeth, Leng, Mary, Lawford-Smith, Holly, Jones, Jane Clare, Reilly-Cooper, Rebecca, and Simpson, R. J. 'On an alleged case of propaganda: Reply to McKinnon', manuscript, archived at <https://philpapers.org> 23rd September 2018.

Andelin, Helen. *Fascinating Womanhood* (New York: Random House, 1963).

Appiah, Anthony. '"But would that still be me?" Notes on gender, "race", ethnicity as sources of "identity"', *Journal of Philosophy* 87/10 (1990), pp. 75–81.

Ásta. 'The social construction of human kinds', *Hypatia* 28/4 (2013), 716–32.

Ásta. *Categories We Live By* (Oxford: Oxford University Press, 2019).

Asteriti, Alessandra, and Bull, Rebecca. 'Gender self-declaration and women's rights: How self-identification undermines women's rights and will lead to an increase in harms: A reply to Alex Sharpe, "Will gender self-declaration undermine women's rights and lead to an increase in harms?"' *Modern Law Review* 83/3 (2020), #539.

Atkinson, Ti-Grace. *Amazon Odyssey* (New York: Links Books, 1974).

Barnes, Elizabeth. 'Gender and gender terms', *Nous* 54/3 (2020), pp. 704–30.

Bettcher, Talia Mae. 'Trans women and the meaning of "woman"', in A. Soble, N. Power, and R. Halwani (eds.) *Philosophy of Sex: Contemporary Readings* 6th Ed. (Maryland: Rowman and Littlefield, 2013), pp. 233–50.

Bettcher, Talia Mae. 'Trans identities and first-person authority', in Laurie Shrage (Ed.) *You've Changed: Sex Reassignment and Personal Identity* (Oxford: Oxford University Press, 2009).

Bicchieri, Christina. *Norms in the Wild* (Oxford: Oxford University Press, 2016).

Blackwell, Kelsey. 'Why people of colour need spaces without white people', *The Arrow*, 9th August 2018. Online at <https://arrow-journal.org/why-people-of-color-need-spaces-without-white-people/> accessed 26th September 2018.

Bogardus, Tomas. 'Evaluating arguments for the sex/gender distinction', *Philosophia* 48 (2020), pp. 873–92.

Burt, Callie H. 'Scrutinizing the US Equality Act 2019: A feminist examination of definitional challenges and sociolegal ramifications', *Feminist Criminology* 15/4 (2020) [early view].

Byrne, Alex. 'Are women adult human females?' *Philosophical Studies* 177 (2020), pp. 3783–803.

Cox, Susan. 'Coming out as "non-binary" throws other women under the bus', *Feminist Current*, 10th August 2016. Online at <https://www.feministcurrent.com/2016/08/10/coming-non-binary-throws-women-bus/>, accessed 10th September 2018.

Crenshaw, Kimberle. 'Demarginalizing the intersection of race and sex: A black feminist critique of antidiscrimination doctrine, feminist theory and antiracist politics', *University of Chicago Legal Forum* 8/1 (1989), pp. 139–67.

Dembroff, Robin. 'Why be nonbinary?' *Aeon*, 30th October 2018. Online at <https://aeon.co/essays/nonbinary-identity-is-a-radical-stance-against-gender-segregation> accessed 4th November 2018.

Equality and Human Rights Commission. 'Research Report 27: Trans Research Review', 7th October 2009. Online at <https://www.equalityhumanrights.com/en/publication-download/research-report-27-trans-research-review> accessed 5th November 2020.

Fine, Cordelia. *Delusions of Gender* (New York: Norton, 2010).

Fine, Cordelia. *Testosterone Rex* (New South Wales: Allen and Unwin, 2017).

Finlayson, Lorna, Jenkins, Katharine, and Worsdale, Rosie. ' "I'm not transphobic, but…": A feminist case against the feminist case against trans inclusivity', *Verso*, 17th October 2018.

Firestone, Shulamith. *The Dialectic of Sex* (New York: William Morrow, 1970).

Frye, Marilyn. *The Politics of Reality* (New York: Crossing Press, 1983).

George, B. R., and Briggs, R. A. 'Science fiction double feature: Trans liberation on Twin Earth', manuscript, archived at <https://philpapers.org/rec/GEOSFD> 26th October 2016.

Haslanger, Sally. 'Gender and race: (What) are they? (What) do we want them to be?' in *Resisting Reality* (Oxford: Oxford University Press, 2012), pp. 221–47.

Jenkins, Katharine. 'Amelioration and inclusion: Gender identity and the concept of woman', *Ethics* 126/2 (2016), pp. 394–421.

Jenkins, Katharine. 'Toward an account of gender identity', *Ergo* 5/21 (2018), 713–44.

Koyama, Emi. 'The transfeminist manifesto', in Rory Dicker and Alison Piepmeier (Eds.) *Catching a Wave: Reclaiming Feminism for the Twenty-First Century* (Northeastern University Press, 2003).

Lawford-Smith, Holly. 'If anyone can choose to be female, what happens to women's rights?' *The Australian*, February 27th 2019a.

Lawford-Smith, Holly. 'Implications of sex-change act amendment have not been fully explored', *The Age*, 6th July 2019b.

Lawford-Smith, Holly. 'Why some feminists oppose allowing people to choose their sex on birth certificates', *The Conversation*, 23rd August 2019c.

Lawford-Smith, Holly. *Gender-Critical Feminism* (Oxford: Oxford University Press, 2022).

Long Chu, Andrea, and Berg, Anastasia. 'Wanting bad things', *The Point*, 2018. Online at <https://thepointmag.com/2018/dialogue/wanting-bad-things-andrea-long-chu-responds-amia-srinivasan> accessed 6th September 2018.

MacKinnon, Catharine. *Feminism Unmodified* (Massachusetts: Harvard University Press, 1987).

Manne, Kate. *Down Girl: The Logic of Misogyny* (Oxford: Oxford University Press, 2017).

McKitrick, Jennifer. 'A dispositional account of gender', *Philosophical Studies* 172/10 (2015), pp. 2575–89.

Murray, Kath, and Hunter-Blackburn, Lucy. 'Losing sight of women's rights: the unregulated introduction of gender self-identification as a case study of policy capture in Scotland', *Scottish Affairs* 28/3 (2019), pp. 262–89.

Neuffer, Julie Debra. *Helen Andelin and the Fascinating Womanhood Movement* (Utah: University of Utah Press, 2015).

Nussbaum, Martha. *Creating Capabilities* (Cambridge, MA: Harvard University Press, 2011).

Nussbaum, Martha. *Women and Human Development: The Capabilities Approach* (Cambridge: Cambridge University Press, 2000).

Pandian, Sharad. 'Whipping girl: A transsexual woman on sexism and the scapegoating of femininity', *GoodReads,* 25th June 2018. Online at <https://www.goodreads.com/review/show/2435403536> accessed 10th September 2018.

Raymond, Janice. *The Transsexual Empire* (Boston: Beacon Press, 1979).

Reilly-Cooper, Rebecca. 'Equality for trans people must not come at the expense of women's safety', <http://wwwpolitics.co.uk>, 26th January 2016*a*. Online at <http://www.politics.co.uk/comment-analysis/2016/01/26/equality-for-trans-people-must-not-come-at-the-expense-of-wo> accessed 6th September 2018.

Reilly-Cooper, Rebecca. 'Gender is not a spectrum', *Aeon,* 28th June 2016*b*. Online at <https://aeon.co/essays/the-idea-that-gender-is-a-spectrum-is-a-new-gender-prison>, accessed 4th October 2018.

Serano, Julia. *Whipping Girl: A Transsexual Woman on Sexism and the Scapegoating of Femininity* (Berkeley: Seal Press, 2007).

Skylar. 'No, coming out at non-binary does not throw other women under the bus', 2nd December 2016. Online at <http://itequals.com/gender/no-coming-out-as-non-binary-does-not-throw-women-under-the-bus/> accessed 10th September 2018.

Smith, Laura. 'This book is the marriage bible for "alt-right" women, and it was written in 1963', *Timeline,* 18th August 2017. Online at <https://timeline.com/fascinating-womanhood-andelin-feminism-509dfe538de7> accessed 25th September.

Stock, Kathleen. 'Why self-identification should not legally make you a woman', *The Conversation,* 1st October 2018*a*.

Stock, Kathleen. 'Changing the concept of woman will cause unintended harms', *The Economist,* 6th July 2018*b*.

Stock, Kathleen. 'Not the social kind: Anti-naturalist mistakes in the philosophical history of womanhood', manuscript, as at 24th February 2020. Online at <https://philpapers.org/rec/STONTS>

Singal, Jesse. 'This is what a modern-day witch hunt looks like', *Daily Intelligencer,* 2nd May 2017. Online at <http://nymag.com/daily/intelligencer/2017/05/transracialism-article-controversy.html> accessed 26th September 2018.

The Feminists. 'The Feminists: A political organization to annihilate sex roles', in Anne Koedt, Ellen Levine, and Anita Rapone (Eds.) *Radical Feminism* (New York: Quadrangle, 1973), pp. 368–78.

Tuvel, Rebecca. 'In defence of transracialism', *Hypatia* 32/2 (2017), pp. 263–78.

Valentini, Laura. 'Ideal vs. non-ideal theory: A conceptual map', *Philosophy Compass* 7/9 (2012), pp. 654–64.

Vincent, Nicole, and Jane, Emma. 'Interrogating incongruence: Conceptual and normative problems with the ICD-11's and DSM-5's diagnostic categories for transgender people', *Australasian Philosophical Review*, forthcoming.

Witt, Charlotte. *The Metaphysics of Gender* (USA: Oxford University Press, 2011).

Wollstonecraft, Mary. *A Vindication of the Rights of Woman* (London: Arcturus, [1792] 2017).

Zucker, Kenneth. 'Epidemiology of gender dysphoria and transgender identity', *Sexual Health* 14 (2017), pp. 404–11.

2

Gender

What is it, and What Do They Want it to Be?

I teach an undergraduate philosophy class in feminism. I can talk to the students about the way that women have been treated throughout history, the way that ideals of womanhood create constraints that make it harder for women to realize their potential, and the way that women have been excluded from, or discriminated against in, certain domains. Little of this is considered controversial. But there is always confusion at the point that any of this is named as 'gender'. Isn't gender *identity*?—they ask each other, or their tutor. It seems that there is a generational divide over the concept of gender, with older people generally understanding gender as a system of external constraints, and younger people generally understanding gender as a subjective identity. But it is not the case that the people on both sides of this divide understand each other and their disagreement. Rather, many of my students seem to be unaware of the alternative understanding of gender. This chapter is for them, and anyone else whose primary concept of gender is about identity. The chapter aims to explain what gender was, and still is, to many people, and to provide the resources for a more productive conversation across the conceptual divide.

2.1 What gender has been

In 1405 in *The Book of the City of Ladies*, Christine de Pizan wrote of herself in a study surrounded by books, a woman with a passion for the pursuit of knowledge.[1] As she reads, she becomes frustrated, wondering 'why on earth it was that so many men, both clerks and others, have said and continue to say and write such awful, damning things about women and their ways' (Pizan [1405] 1999, pp. 5–6). She notes that 'It is not just a handful of writers who do this...It is all manner of philosophers, poets and orators too numerous to mention, who all seem to speak with one voice and are unanimous in their view that female nature is wholly given up to vice' (p. 6). But these men's view of women doesn't fit well with all the women Christine actually knows. Still, she reasons, given that *so*

---

[1] Rosalind Brown-Grant writes: 'Christine's catalogue of illustrious heroines appears within the framework of an allegorical dream-vision in which she herself is the chief protagonist' (Pizan [1405] 1999, p. xvii).

many men have this view of women, and these are men with 'such great intelligence and insight into all things', surely it must be they, and not she, who are getting it right (p. 6). Christine begins to despise herself and all women ('the whole of my sex') as an aberration (p. 7).

In 1792 in *A Vindication of the Rights of Woman*, Mary Wollstonecraft drew an ingenious parallel between women and the rich, in order to argue that women's inferiority was caused by her situation, not anything intrinsic to her nature. She saw women's situation as containing a surplus of pleasure, and wrote rather scathingly: 'Confined then in cages like the feathered race, they have nothing to do but plume themselves, and stalk with mock majesty from perch to perch' (Wollstonecraft [1792] 2017, p. 77). In this respect, women are like the rich; greatness does not emerge from excessive pleasure and idleness.[2] Wollstonecraft noted that members of the nobility are admired for traits like 'gracefulness', 'majestic beauty', and 'deportment', rather than more substantial traits like talent, virtue, justice, heroism, knowledge, or judgement (Wollstonecraft [1792] 2017, p. 83). She does not blame men alone for women's situation, declaring that women have 'chosen rather to be short-lived queens than labour to obtain the sober pleasures that arise from equality' (p. 76). Ultimately, Wollstonecraft denied that woman was 'created merely to be the solace of man', and argued that changes to her situation—particularly, providing women with an education—would transform her (p. 74).

These are two important insights that would come to inform the explosion of feminist thinking from the 1960s onwards.[3] First, women are up against serious amounts of propaganda that attempts to convince them of their own inferiority and their 'natural' role in relation to men. Second, the social context women find themselves in can itself *produce* a version of womanhood that looks to vindicate the male propaganda. But how women are at a time and in a context is not sufficient to reveal a woman's 'true nature', for how she is may itself be *created* by that context.[4] Early feminists pointed at differences in women's opportunities and

---

[2] Wollstonecraft is best understood as talking about middle- and upper-class women, given that many women in that period were engaged in domestic labour; some took on additional work inside the home e.g. childcare, textile work, or farm work; and some worked outside the home e.g. as domestic servants, nannies, or laundry workers.

[3] The start of the second wave of feminism in the United States is generally thought to be Betty Friedan's book *The Feminine Mystique* (1963), with the first specifically radical feminist books emerging in 1970—including Kate Millett's *Sexual Politics*, Shulamith Firestone's *The Dialectic of Sex*, and Germaine Greer's *The Female Eunuch*.

[4] For the social version of this claim see (Mackinnon 1989, p. 122; Haslanger 1995, p. 103), for the developmental version of the claim see (Jordan-Young 2010, Chapter 10). Kate Phelan writes that if ideology creates reality, then 'we stand before those who claim to suffer a moral wrong with no sense at all of whether they do, of whether they are the oppressed speaking a truth that ideology makes incredible or the deluded speaking nonsense' (Phelan, 2022, p. 20). If a sexist ideology *causally constructs* women's inferiority, then woman really is inferior, and we will not know until we have rejected her inferiority and tested the possibilities for her equality whether she *really was* equal all along and subject to ideology, or *really was* inferior all along and feminism was subject to delusion. Phelan

treatment relative to men, as potential explanations for the differences between men and women that were observed. This was the start of a long, and ongoing, debate about sex differences. Are men and women fundamentally the same, but *made* different by society and culture? Or are men and women fundamentally different, in ways that society and culture are merely able to do better or worse at accommodating? And—to the extent that women are made different—what is the relationship between the making of women as feminine, and the *treatment* of women as subordinate? The fact of being made to be a certain way might be a violation of autonomy; if the way women are made to be serves men's interests it might be a form of exploitation. But *that* women are made to be a certain way might also justify *treating* her in a particular way, and depending on the treatment that might be oppressive. Catharine MacKinnon, for example, saw pornography as propaganda, presenting a view of women as objects which in turn legitimated men's *treatment* of women as objects.[5] The making, and what it justifies, are two distinct things.

These questions are at the heart of what gender is and what we should want it to be. Consider one of the upper-class women Wollstonecraft wrote about, preoccupied with her own adornment. Second-wave feminists used the terminology of 'sex' and 'gender' to mark the difference between what she *is* ('sex': she is female) and what she has been *made to be* ('gender': she is feminine).[6] Making a sex/gender distinction allowed feminists to decouple femininity from woman herself, and to challenge and work to eliminate the making of women into feminine beings.[7] And this paved the way for a number of important feminist projects, such as articulating the content of femininity, identifying the most harmful

---

argues that imagining her equality is an act of faith, not reason; and that this has implications for what we can demand from others in terms of acceptance.

[5] She writes: 'Men treat women as whom they see women as being. Pornography constructs who that is' (MacKinnon 1989, p. 197).

[6] As explained in the note on language at the start of the book, 'feminine' is helpful because it's an adjective, a description attached to a noun (she, the woman, is feminine). But some people prefer to use the noun 'woman' as a success term here, as in, those female people who are made feminine *are* women. If 'woman' names the class, and the class is characterized by subordination/oppression, then 'oppressed woman' (as in the Rubin quote in fn. 7) is redundant. We need to pay close attention to how each feminist is using these particular terms and how they fit in with her conception of what woman really is, and what she has been made to be.

[7] For example, Gayle Rubin wrote: 'A woman is a woman. She only becomes a domestic, a wife, a chattel, a playboy bunny, a prostitute, or a human dictaphone in certain relations. Torn from these relationships, she is no more the helpmate of man than gold in itself is money... What then are these relationships by which a female becomes an oppressed woman?... one begins to have a sense of a systematic social apparatus which takes up females as raw materials and fashions domesticated women as products.... I call that part of social life the "sex/gender system", for lack of a more elegant term. As a preliminary definition, a "sex/gender system" is the set of arrangements by which a society transforms biological sexuality into products of human activity, and in which these transformed sexual needs are satisfied' (Rubin 1975, pp. 157–210). Rubin refines her understanding of this system throughout her essay, describing gender as 'a socially imposed division of the sexes' (p. 179), and saying that we should aim for 'the elimination of the social system which creates sexism and gender' (p. 204), a 'genderless (though not sexless) society' (p. 204).

aspects of femininity, identifying the mechanisms through which femininity is taught and reproduced, and opening up new ways of being for women—relating to her capacities, her aspirations, her skills, her behaviour, her sexuality, her dress, her body language, and more. 'Gender', here, refers to everything that woman is made to be, and which generally works in the interests of men by producing a class of support persons *for* men.[8]

Radical feminists in particular made substantial contributions to understanding these mechanisms through which femininity is taught, and their impacts on women's lives. They wrote about the historical origins of ideas about male superiority (Lerner 1986; Eisler 1987), and the way they became entrenched through religion and philosophy (Lerner 1986; Daly 1973). They wrote about historical injustices against women as a caste (Dworkin 1974, pp. 91–150). They analysed popular literature to reveal its view of women (Millett [1970] 1977). They wrote about love (Firestone 1970, pp. 113–19; Atkinson 1974, pp. 41–5; Greer 1970, pp. 157–275); the family (Firestone 1970, pp. 65–94); sexual intercourse (Atkinson 1974, pp. 5–7 and 13–23; Koedt 1973, pp. 198–207; Dworkin 1987); prostitution (Pateman 1988, pp. 189–218); pornography (MacKinnon 1989, pp. 195–214); (MacKinnon1987, pp. 127–213); (MacKinnon [2005] 2006, pp. 247–58); (Dworkin 1974, pp. 51–90); rape (Brownmiller 1976); abortion (Firestone 1968); (Atkinson 1974, pp. 1–3); religion (Daly 1968); marriage (Cronan 1973, pp. 213–21); (Pateman 1988, pp. 116–88); women's domestic, sexual, and emotional servicing of men (Frye 1983, pp. 1–16); and more. Once the nature of these practices and institutions has been explained, it becomes less tenable to think that what women are like, and how women are treated, is just a natural expression of sex difference. If it were, why would it need so much institutionalization and enforcement?

I'll refer to this understanding of gender as 'gender as sex caste'.[9] In the second part of the chapter, I'll say more about the empirical evidence we have for this

---

[8] This is narrower than taking 'gender' to refer to the social meaning of sex, whatever it is. Whatever real sex differences exist between men and women, they may come to have social meaning, and that is not necessarily social meaning that feminists have particular reason to be concerned about (I'm grateful to Kathleen Stock for discussion on this point). There would be reason for concern, however, if such social meaning would inevitably expand into something oppressive. Rubin, following Lévi-Strauss, suggests that a division of labour based on sex creates gender (Rubin 1975, p. 178). Cailin O'Connor suggests that some such divisions of labour are simply efficient solutions to coordination problems, given physiological sex differences, and provides evidence that some such divisions are chosen in virtually every society (O'Connor 2019, pp. 17–18 and 97).

[9] For a discussion of the aptness of the term 'caste', and speculation as to why some resist it, see (Daly 1973, pp. 2–3). Readers may wonder about the relation between the 'gender as sex caste' of this chapter and the 'gender as norms' of the previous. These concepts are related, but have a different emphasis. Gender norms—specifically norms of femininity applied to females—are a central mechanism by which females are made feminine (some would say, made into women). Once females are made feminine, there is sex caste: not just a social group, but a socially subordinated group. The previous chapter explored ways of making the world better by challenging those mechanisms, while this chapter is more interested in explaining what those mechanisms (and perhaps others) bring about.

understanding of gender. In the third part of the essay, I'll explain how this motivated the feminist project of gender abolitionism, and the disagreement between some feminists over whether we should abolish gender while leaving sex in place, or attempt to abolish sex itself, thereby making 'gendering' impossible. In the fourth and final part of the chapter I'll explain the newer view of gender that some feminists have taken up, and assess whether it offers any improvement on the older understanding.

2.2 What gender still is (whether or not it is also other things)

Before I say more about the empirical evidence, let me be clear about exactly what I'm trying to establish here. One question we might be interested in is, *what accounts for femininity*? That is an explanatory question. Supposing that there is something that accounts for it, it wouldn't really matter what we called it; we could stop calling it 'gender' and start calling it something else. Another question we might be interested in is, when we use the word 'gender', what phenomenon are we picking out? It might be that at one point in time the term was picking out the same phenomenon that accounts for femininity, but that at another point in time it started picking out something else. The meanings of words can change over time. In this chapter I'm *not* interested in what the word 'gender' picks out in the world. What I'm interested in is what phenomenon accounts for sex-differentiated behaviour and treatment, particularly the behaviour and treatment that casts women as the support persons for men, and what oppression and injustice there is in the vicinity of sex.

There are two ways to argue that gender—or to be more precise, at least some of what we think of as gender[10]—is socially enforced. One is to argue that it is *not* a result of sex differences in the brain, or otherwise biological. If it's not biological, then it's not biological-via-social (nature via nurture); it can only be social. The other is to argue that there are differences in how the sexes are treated, that could be creating the sex differences we see. This does not establish that such differences are in fact socially enforced, but the *more* that differences track differential treatment, the less tenable it becomes to suppose that there's no causal connection between the two. (Conversely, if it can be established that there is no differential treatment, then that can be eliminated as the explanation of the differences we see). We can draw on evidence within a particular context at a time, such as modern-day Australia, and also on evidence that makes comparisons between cultures and historical periods. There are many books on these subjects, which I don't have a chance of covering here, so instead I'll just mention some highlights.

---

[10] This caveat makes room for the possibility that *some* of what we currently think of as femininity and *some* of what we currently think of as masculinity is socially enforced, but not all of it.

In *Delusions of Gender*, Cordelia Fine takes both of the approaches just mentioned, systematically working through the research that declares gender to be biological and revealing its weaknesses, and surveying the evidence for differential social treatment (Fine 2010, esp. Parts 1 and 2). I'll focus on the latter. Included in her survey is data from interviews with the parents of young children, studies of birth announcements, a study of baby names, a study on the home environments of children, a study on the impact of body language on children's attitudes, interviews with children on parents' approval of gender non-conforming play, work from developmental psychologists on the way that sex can be used to create tribes; a report from parents who went to great lengths to provide their children with a gender-neutral upbringing; observations of gender norm policing in pre-schoolers; and studies on the representation of the sexes in popular children's picture books and in educational readers. The overwhelming impression from all of this is that sex stereotypes are virtually invisible to us, they start being enforced before a child is even born, they show up all through a child's developmental environment, they are reinforced by peers, and anyone who thinks they tried 'gender-neutral parenting' but it didn't work probably didn't *really* try, because it's hugely difficult to pull off, if not entirely impossible.

Parents interviewed about whether they wanted girls or boys and why revealed sex stereotypes, e.g. that boys would be good to teach sports, and girls would be good for emotional connections (Kane 2009, p. 373; in Fine 2010, p. 192). Pregnant women who knew the sex of their babies described the babies' movements differently to pregnant women who did not know the babies' sex; boys were 'vigorous' and 'strong' while girls were 'not violent', 'not excessively energetic', 'not terribly active' (Rothman 1988, p. 130; in Fine 2010, pp. 192–3). An analysis of birth announcements revealed more *pride* about boys, and *happiness* about girls (Gonzalez and Koestner 2005, p. 407; in Fine 2010, pp. 194–5). There were also slightly more birth announcements for boys than girls, and boys were more likely to be given names that started with the same letter as their father's (Jost, Pelham. smd Carvallo 2002, p. 597; in Fine 2010, p. 196). A study looking at the toys of boy and girl children found that boys tended to have more vehicles and machines, while girls tended to have more dolls and housekeeping toys, and that was true even for babies aged 6–12 months (Nash and Krawczyk 2007; in Fine 2010, p. 198). Another set of studies found that mothers conversed more with their girl babies and toddlers (Clearfield and Nelson 2006; in Fine 2010, pp. 198–9), were more sensitive to changes in the facial expressions of what they thought were girl babies (Donovan, Taylor, smd Leavitt 2007; in Fine 2010, pp. 198–9), and had different perceptions of babies' (same) crawling and risk-taking abilities (Mondschein, Adolph, and Tamis-LeMonda 2000; in Fine 2010, pp. 198–9). Mothers have also been found to talk about emotions in different ways with boy and girl children (Dunn, Bretherton and Munn 1987; in Fine 2010, p. 199).

Another great source of evidence for differential treatment on the basis of sex is meta-analyses, which survey findings from a number of different research papers. One such meta-study—the first 'quantitative review of studies of sex-differentiated socialization...to our knowledge' (Lytton and Romney 1991, p. 268)—analysed 172 separate studies, with the goal of discovering 'whether parents make systematic differences in their rearing of boys and girls'.[11] The authors hypothesized that parents' differential treatment of boys and girls would increase with the children's age; that greater effects would be found from observations and experiments than from interviews, because parents could be expected to minimize their own differential treatment in interview answers; and that earlier studies would show more significant effects, because a commitment to sex equality could be expected to produce less sex-differentiated parenting.

The authors of the meta-study assessed existing studies for parental socialization effects in a range of areas (Lytton and Romney 1991, p. 270).[12] Many areas showed only small, non-significant differences. But some significant differences did emerge. For example, the authors found that in North American studies there was a significant effect for the 'encouragement of sex-typed activities and perceptions of sex-stereotyped characteristics', with fathers doing this more than mothers (Lytton and Romney 1991, p. 283). (They class the magnitude of the effect as 'fairly modest'). In studies from other Western countries, a significant effect of parents' encouraging achievement more in boys than girls was found, although the researchers suggest that this result is driven by a single anomalous study (pp. 283–4). There was a significant effect for parents of both sexes in other Western countries inflicting more physical punishment on boys than girls, although this finding was based on a small number of studies (p. 283).

The hypothesis that parental sex-differential treatment would increase with the child's age was not supported, and the researchers suggest (albeit cautiously, because there were few studies on older children in the meta-study) that the opposite might be true, 'that parents treat older children less differentially than younger children' (Lytton and Romney 1991, p. 285). The hypothesis that studies

---

[11] Note that this is specifically about the role of parents, rather than the broader question of whether sex differences can plausibly be explained by differential social treatment, so a negative answer to these researchers' question wouldn't entail a negative answer to the socialization question. They say 'Null results would stimulate the theoretical and empirical search for other possible influences that may account for behavioural differences between the sexes' (Lytton and Romney 1991, p. 269).

[12] These areas were amount of interaction (including physical, verbal, and play); encouragement of achievement; care (including warmth, nurturance, responsiveness, and praise); material rewards; encouragement of dependency; restriction or low encouragement of independence; discipline (including physical punishment, non-physical strictness, and discouragement of aggression); encouragement of sex-typed activities and perceptions; encouragement of sex-typed activities in boys more than girls; and clear communication/reasoning.

based on observation and experiment would show greater effects was only weakly supported, with a non-significant effect (p. 286). Finally, the hypothesis that earlier studies would show more significant effects because of social trends toward sex equality was not supported (p. 286). The authors say 'the effect sizes in different socialization areas over the years seem to fluctuate almost randomly' (p. 287).

The finding on parents' encouragement of sex-typed activity drew on twenty-one studies from between 1956 and 1986. (More recent studies show similar results).[13] In one such study from 1985, researchers filmed play between 19–27-month-olds and their parents, in the family's home. Types of play (e.g. rough-and-tumble) and types of toys (e.g. dolls, kitchen toys, trucks, hammers, books, and board games) were categorized as masculine, feminine, or neutral in accordance with previous studies' classifications. Most children played with masculine toys if they were available; few children engaged with feminine toys. Nearly all parents brought neutral toys to the play sessions. Boys played with both neutral and masculine toys more than with feminine toys, and girls played more with neutral toys than either feminine or masculine toys. Parents did not give positive reinforcement in accordance with sex-typed play or toy choices, but children's choices about how to play/what to play with were related to what the parents brought to the session. The children who played more with feminine toys were the children whose parents brought more feminine toys to the session (either in number, or in proportion). The authors conclude that 'apparently, in the home, parents exert influence over their young children's play primarily via their selection of available toys' (Eisenberg et al. 1985, p. 1512). They say 'parents picked toys that were consistent with the child's sex (especially for boys). Parents of boys chose neutral and masculine toys more than feminine toys; parents of girls picked neutral toys more than masculine or feminine toys. Thus, merely by means of the process of selecting play items, parents "channelled" their children away from opposite-sex toys and, for boys, toward same-sex toys' (although they acknowledge that parents' choices could be partly due to their children's preferences) (Eisenberg et al. 1985, p. 1511).

In another of the twenty-one studies surveyed, researchers looked specifically at fathers' interactions with their male and female children. They observed father–child pairs in a 'waiting room' in which there were sex-typed toys (dolls, trucks) and also objects with the potential to produce disaster (ashtray, vase with flowers in it, jug of water). They found that fathers and daughters remained in closer proximity, fathers were more likely to give toys to girls than boys, were equally likely to give trucks to boys and girls, and were significantly less likely to give dolls to boys than girls. (They gave boys dolls less often than trucks, but gave girls both dolls and trucks the same amount). Boys were more likely to attempt to

---

[13] See e.g. Erden and Altun (2014), looking at Turkish parents and children, and Kollmayer et al. (2018), looking at Austrian parents and children.

touch the disaster-producing objects, and in response fathers were more likely to use verbal and physical prohibitions with boy children (Snow et al. 1983, p. 230).

What are the implications of parents' encouragement of sex-typed activities? This includes both play activities and household chores. The authors follow earlier research in suggesting that 'boys' toys provide more opportunity for manipulation and inventiveness, and that girls' preferred play activities contribute to a more structured world that elicits less creativity and more compliance', and that 'masculine sex-typed play may also afford an opportunity for practicing visuospatial skills' (Lytton and Romney 1991, p. 287). They note a lack of research on the connection between parental pressures in these areas, and the later sex differences we see in choices about occupation and interests in adolescence and adulthood (p. 287).

Michael Bailey's work on feminine boys is also instructive. In *The Man Who Would Be Queen*, Bailey writes about Danny Ryan, who as a 1-year-old would dress in his mother's shoes. His father disapproved and would verbally prohibit the behaviour. His sister told him that her things were not for him to play with. His mother was tolerant, and considered it a phase. When Danny got older he was bullied, especially by other boys. There are a number of boys like Danny, who are feminine in their boyhoods. Psychiatrist Richard Green followed sixty-six feminine boys in a longitudinal study, starting from an average age of 7 years old. These boys—compared to a control group of typically masculine boys—cross-dressed (nearly 70% of the feminine boys did this regularly, and none of the control group did); played with dolls (more than 50% of the feminine boys did this, and less than 5% of the control group did); took female roles in games (nearly 60% of the feminine boys did this, and none of the control group did); related better to girl peers than boy peers (true for about 80% of the feminine boys, and less than 5% of the control group); wished to be girls (80% of the feminine boys occasionally stated this wish, compared to less than 10% of the control group); and were less interested in rough-and-tumble play and playing sports (true for nearly 80% of the feminine boys, but only 20% of the control group) (discussed in Bailey 2003, pp. 17–18).

75% of the cohort of feminine boys, who were on average 19 years old at the final interview, were same-sex attracted. Only one of the cohort of masculine boys used as the control group grew up to be same-sex attracted. Bailey thinks 'it is conceivable that every one of the feminine boys grew up to be attracted to men' (Bailey 2003, p. 19) (contact was lost over time with about a third of the feminine boys in Green's cohort). The experiences that feminine boys report, from disapproval through to physical bullying, from a range of people including parents, siblings, peers, teachers, doctors, and more give us insight into the 'other side' of gender socialization—not the socialization of females into femininity, but of males into masculinity, and the weight of social pressure, including both rewards and punishments, brought to push people into the right boxes. A recent study looking at 829 young Australian males associated their higher suicide risk with non-conformity to norms of masculinity, finding that 'greater conformity to heterosexual norms was associated with reduced odds of reporting suicidal ideation' (King et al. 2020).[14] If 'masculine' were just a way that boys were by nature, and 'feminine' a way females were by nature, it is hard to see why there would be such policing of non-conformity to norms (or why there would need to be norms at all). As Marilyn Frye put it: 'The fact that there are such penalties threatened for deviations from these patterns strongly suggests that the patterns would not be there but for the threats' (Frye 1983, p. 36).

Of course, these are just small peeks into the empirical evidence supporting the view that gender is socially enforced—that gender is sex caste. It's not just parenting that may make a difference, but peers, schools, television, advertising, history, social attitudes, social institutions, and much more. To fully assess the weight of the evidence we would have to go through all of these, which couldn't be done in a single book, let alone a single chapter. But we should, at least, be in a position to see that it is highly likely that differential socialization, broadly understood, is a strong candidate explanation of 'gender'; that is, the correlation of femaleness and femininity, and maleness and masculinity, that we see all across the world today.[15] And if it is, then it is indispensable to feminist theory and activism that we have the language to talk about it, and that we do indeed keep talking about it and working to reveal, critique, and ultimately dissolve it. As we will see in Section 2.4, though, there has been a shift in the conceptualization of gender that risks undermining this project.

2.3 What they want gender to be

One of the most influential and most-cited papers in feminist philosophy is Sally Haslanger's 'Gender and Race: (What) Are They? (What) Do We Want Them To Be?' (Haslanger 2000).[16] Haslanger starts with the observation that among some academics, 'not only is it unclear what gender is and how we should go about

---

[14] The authors write: 'Such results do not indicate that being heterosexual is protective, but rather, highlight: firstly, the broader buffering effect of conforming to heterosexual masculine norms; and secondly, the potential to avoid the penalties that arise if deviating from socially accepted norms' (p. 6).

[15] For a contemporary presentation of gender as an external process that makes (or tries to make) female people feminine, and male people masculine, see Manne (2017). Manne focuses in particular on the imposition of gender onto women, with sexism working to justify our belief in women's inferiority and misogyny working to keep women in their place (especially through sanctions for non-compliance). In a footnote, Manne pays lip service to the idea of gender as identity, but she provides no indication of how a social system that treats people differently on the basis of sex could make exceptions on the basis of how some people subjectively identify.

[16] As of October 2022, Google Scholar showed its 'cited by' number as 1010.

understanding it, but whether it is anything at all' (p. 32). She explains that she takes an analytical approach to answering the question of what gender is, which means we ask why we have the concept, what cognitive or practical tasks the concept helps us with, and whether the concept does the job or some other concept would do it better (p. 33). Answering these questions might result in revision; we replace inadequate concepts with other ones. Hence the title of her paper: not only what gender *is*, but what *we want it to be*.[17]

There is an assumed 'we' throughout Haslanger's paper: '…on an analytical approach, the questions "What is gender?" or "What is race?" require us to consider what work *we* want these concepts to do for *us*; why do *we* need them at all? The responsibility is *ours* to define them for *our* purposes' (p. 34, my emphasis). She continues, 'On this approach, the world by itself can't tell *us* what gender is, or what race is; it is up to *us* to decide what in the world, if anything, they are' (p. 34, my emphasis). These words—'we', 'our', 'us'—suggest a single heterodoxy, taking a critical approach to widespread assumptions about what gender is, and/or to what, and *whether*, we want it to be. Even if we grant, for the sake of argument, the idea that there was a single heterodoxy at Haslanger's time of writing, her approach has since been embraced by one camp of *multiple* heterodoxies about gender today, the camp who prefer to see gender as a subjective, internal identity (whether or not it is also other things).[18]

Haslanger herself identified her task as being to develop a concept of gender that would be an effective tool in fighting against injustice (p. 36). This requires a concept able to explain sex inequalities, including 'to identify how social forces, often under the guise of biological forces, work to perpetuate such inequalities'; able to track sex differences *and* similarities (which will allow us to identify 'interlocking oppressions'); able to track how gender is implicated in broader social phenomena, like religion or science; and able to take women's agency seriously (p. 36). Haslanger took gender to be social class, following in the tradition of materialist feminism (p. 37). It is a matter of social position: how one is viewed, treated, and how one's life is structured. She also acknowledges that sexual difference is the marker used to distinguish the two groups that are then sorted into social classes. Her by-now familiar account is that someone is a woman if and only if they are 'systematically subordinated along some dimension (economic, political, legal, social, etc.)' and are '"marked" as a target for this treatment by observed or imagined bodily features presumed to be evidence of a female's biological role in reproduction' (p. 39). The social classes men and women stand in a

---

[17] This approach has come to be known as 'ameliorative analysis', a specific kind of conceptual engineering. For an excellent critique see Sankaran (2020).
[18] Things are further complicated by the fact that Haslanger herself now seems to agree with the gender identity camp, even though the paper whose method this camp seem to be following is, on its own terms, in the gender as sex caste/class camp (more on this below).

hierarchy; women are subordinate (p. 42). This view is not identical to the gender as sex caste view, mainly because it is worded in a way that allows that sex itself may be constructed ('...presumed to be evidence of...'). But it is close enough to be treated together with it for our purposes. Both see gender as something external to the individual, *done to* her: the female (or, *the human we think of as female*) is made feminine. Because Haslanger uses the word 'woman' to name the social position, she is thereby a 'woman abolitionist'.

A number of more significant changes to the understanding of gender—and so both the intension and extension of 'woman', at least for those feminists who paired that term with their gender concept—would follow in later years. One of these was an attempted revision of Haslanger's account, offered by Katharine Jenkins in 2016. While Haslanger followed Catharine MacKinnon and other feminists of the second wave (1960s–1980s), Jenkins appears to have been influenced by third wave feminism. Claire Snyder-Hall wrote that third wave feminism is 'a form of inclusiveness' (Snyder 2008; quoted in Stock 2021, p. 244).[19] Inclusiveness is a central preoccupation of Jenkins' throughout her work on the concept 'woman'. To her credit, Jenkins doesn't throw out gender as sex caste (unlike some activists who seek to supersede sex and sex caste with gender identity), but supplements it with gender as identity, revising an understanding of gender to be disjunctive: 'woman' picks out *both* gender as identity and gender as sex caste.[20]

She writes that 'it will be my contention that feminism needs both senses of gender and that a truly inclusive ameliorative inquiry into the concept of *woman* is only possible when gender as class and gender as identity are given equal consideration' (Jenkins 2016, p. 407). She accepts Haslanger's understanding of gender as class, but not gender as identity.[21] On Jenkins' account (which borrows from Haslanger's account of *racial* identity), gender as identity refers to 'the way that gendered subject positions are taken up by individuals' (p. 408). But what does this mean? She explains it in psychological and metaphorical terms, as

---

[19] Snyder-Hall was then publishing as R. Claire Snyder.

[20] As this makes clear, Jenkins follows Haslanger in using 'woman' as a term for the class rather than the people in it. It's not clear whether this make her a woman-abolitionist, like it did Haslanger. If gender identity has independent value, then it shouldn't. We'd be working to abolish *part* of the class 'woman' but not the whole class. The goal would be no-more-women-by-way-of-the-sex-caste-disjunct, leaving only women-by-way-of-the-gender-identity-disjunct. Eliminating sex caste would leave only female people and transwomen (who would just be called 'women'). If gender identity *doesn't* have independent value, then it might. Perhaps it is coherent for some male people to identify with women, and so to *be* women by way of the gender identity disjunct. But once we have eliminated sex caste, there will be no women left to identify *with*: only female people. Insofar as having a 'woman' gender identity is parasitic on there being women, gender identity will disappear when women disappear. On Stock's account of gender identity, which I think is the most promising currently on offer, it is parasitic in this way (see discussion in Stock 2021, Chapter 4). So then it would make sense for Jenkins to be a woman-abolitionist.

[21] Haslanger had earlier defined gender identity as 'a broad psychological orientation to the world', which is not particularly clear or precise (Haslanger 2000, p. 228; quoted in Jenkins 2016, p. 403).

someone having an 'internal map' of the type that guides people classed as women (or men) through particular social or material realities (p. 410).[22] There are ways that women are expected to behave, and these expectations cause people to form 'maps' that tell them how to navigate social space; for example. to use women's bathrooms rather than men's bathrooms. But while these 'maps' may be followed and thus result in public expressions of gender identity, they need not. Jenkins writes: 'some trans women make their gender identity public through the use of feminine pronouns, names, or forms of presentation, while others choose to keep their gender identification private' (p. 399). On this account, gender as identity refers to something internal, subjective, and private, which *can* be signalled in various more public ways if the person with the gender identity chooses to do so. But they need not. All transwomen have 'woman' gender identities, but these can have different content for different transwomen, because different 'maps' can pick up on different 'aspects of existence' (p. 413).

Jenkins' revised concept was operationalized in the publicity materials for a women's march she was involved in organizing. They advertised it in the following way: 'The march is open to all self-defining women. If you do not define as a woman but experience discrimination because you are perceived as female, you are also welcome to attend' (Jenkins 2016, p. 420). The march was a protest against violence against women. The publicity materials put gender as identity first: 'the march is open to all *self-defining women*'. It doesn't include gender as sex caste as the second disjunct, but something closer to Haslanger's gender as class: 'discrimination because you are *perceived as* female'. Both disjuncts are trans-inclusive, but the first is inclusive on the basis of gender identity alone, while the second is inclusive on the basis of passing as female. Because it is gender as identity that is at the fore in this statement, female people become an afterthought *in the women's march*, in the interests of being 'inclusive'.

What justification does Jenkins offer for the addition (and, as I see it, prioritization) of gender identity in the concept 'woman'? She stipulates early on that 'trans gender identities are entirely valid', and that it will be 'a foundational premise of my argument'... 'that trans women are women and trans men are men' (Jenkins 2016, p. 396). She claims that 'trans people...are a severely disadvantaged and marginalized group', and links 'Failure to respect the gender identifications of trans people' to 'transphobic oppression and even violence', and states that on these grounds, feminist analysis of gender concepts must include trans people in the categories they identify with (p. 396). There are three distinct claims being made here: we should include transwomen as women because they *are* in fact women (trans identities are valid); and because they are marginalized; and

---

[22] In a later paper, she presents a slightly different account, in terms of taking particular norms to be relevant. For example, a transwoman would take the norms that are imposed upon women to be relevant, and may choose to act in accordance with them (Jenkins 2018).

because if we don't, that might cause oppression and violence. But gender identities can be 'valid' (whatever that means) without making the person who has them a member of a different sex caste; we have been offered no reason to accept Jenkins' understanding of the terms 'men' and 'women' such that it is coherent for gender identities to determine who they apply to; the fact of being marginalized alone does not justify the classification practice; and there is no evidence that feminists continuing to theorize gender as caste will cause oppression or violence against trans people.

Even if we were concerned to ensure that 'women who are members of other oppressed social groups' were not excluded or marginalized from the concept 'woman' (Jenkins 2016, p. 394), that doesn't provide any justification for expanding to include people who are not women at all. If gender is sex caste, then men's gender identities are irrelevant to the concept of women, to feminism, and to protesting violence against women on a women's march. If someone doesn't already accept the importance of 'inclusion', or does but doesn't think it takes precedence in any conflict of values, then they have no reason to accept Jenkins' revision of the concept. Concepts track phenomena in the world, they're not decided on the basis of who wants to be picked out by them. They are tools that help us to do particular jobs (see also discussion in Stock 2021, Chapter 5). Even if that job is normative rather than descriptive, it will be about finding the concept of 'woman' that is likely to do the best job of eliminating sex/gender injustice. That's very different to the concept being inclusive for inclusiveness' sake.

Even those who value inclusion highly would surely agree that the imperative to be inclusive stops somewhere. If it doesn't, that undercuts the possibility of having social definitions at all. To put this in terms of another example, if there is no limit to inclusivity about blackness, then anyone at all might be black, and if our inclusive concept forces us to count enough people as black who would not have counted on a narrower concept, we may no longer be able to use the concept to talk about race, or to do anti-racism activism. Social definitions are useful to social groups, especially those pursuing a politics based on their shared situation (see also discussion in Barker 1997). Jenkins' reconciliation of gender as class and gender as identity in a disjunctive concept of 'woman' is *ad hoc*. There appears to be no theoretical justification for it; only a political motivation.

Jenkins' disjunctive revision of the concept 'woman' is a radical revision relative to gender as sex caste, because it no longer means that women as a social group are subordinated. Jenkins says 'a woman who is not subordinated at all and therefore does not count as a woman in the class sense may still count as a woman in the gender identity sense. This ensures that if there are any prima facie women, trans or cis, who are not subordinated at all and who are not classed as women for this reason, their gender identities will still be respected by the account' (Jenkins 2016, p. 416, fn. 48). She seems to count it as a positive that she has produced an account that can respect gender identities, rather than a negative that she has produced an account that cedes the very feature feminists were trying to explain—women's subordination to men. If women need not be subordinated, then it cannot be an essential feature of woman that she is subordinated, and so we ought not be woman-abolitionists. (Or for those who talk instead in the language of femininity, if the social group contains some people who are female-made-feminine, and other people who are male with a particular identity, why does *that group* need a politics?)

One way to attempt to justify Jenkins' revision is to argue that including males with 'woman' gender identities as women[23] (or as part of the constituency of feminism, or in women's spaces) will not undermine any important political, social, legal, or economic interests women have. If inclusion isn't bad for women, and is good for some men, then we have a reason to include and no reason to exclude.[24] Whether some individual males with 'woman' gender identities are in fact 'the same' as women in the relevant respects, so that including them would be no worse than including any woman, and excluding them would be as bad as excluding any woman, depends on a slew of empirical questions about which there isn't much, if any, evidence yet.[25]

For example, some people are gender non-conforming, despite the fact that femininity and masculinity are socially enforced. What explains why some people are conforming, and others are non-conforming? If a girl can grow up to be a butch lesbian, despite all her socialization toward femininity and heterosexuality, why can't a man grow up to be relevantly woman-like, despite all his? One possible explanation, which does not depend on making an exception for people with gender identities, is simply that some people are what Cristina Bicchieri calls 'trendsetters'; relatively immune to social sanctioning, and so the kind of people who will often pose an early challenge to particular social norms (Bicchieri 2017). This is an intriguing idea in that it has broad explanatory power. It would predict that there are some people in *all* domains of life who are prepared to go against social norms, and many people who are not. Gender is no exception, and the fact that there are gender non-conforming people does not alone establish that there must be 'gender identities', internal feelings that are so strong that people are willing to take on substantial social costs to live in accordance with them (which is the parallel of a narrative that is often given for being gay) (Lawford-Smith 2022, pp. 110–11).

---

[23] As Jenkins rightly points out, a male person can identify as a woman but not with femininity, so it would be misleading to use 'feminine' in place of 'woman' to signal the type of gender identity here (Jenkins 2016, p. 409).
[24] I think this route is a non-starter, for the reasons given elsewhere in this volume: inclusion *is* bad for women. See Chapters 4, 5, and 6.
[25] See also discussion in Lawford-Smith (2022, Chapter 5).

Still, for this explanation to justify treating males with 'woman' gender identities *as women* for the purposes of feminist theory and activism, or for all purposes, it would have to be the case that: i) all trans people are trendsetters; and ii) being a trans trendsetter indicates that gender socialization didn't have any influence on you, rather than that it did, but you were nonetheless willing to reject some component of it. Again, these are empirical matters. But recent work suggests that at least some people who adopt trans identities are *following* trends, rather than setting them (Marchiano 2017; Littman 2018; Schrier 2020), and given the pervasiveness of gender socialization, simply being willing to declare a 'woman' gender identity doesn't seem to be a secure guarantee that a person has not internalized or been shaped by male socialization at all. That a male should identify as a man is only one small part of how males are made to be masculine. The visibility of transwomen in the trans movement compared to transmen, the sexual entitlement demonstrated by some transwomen,[26] and the confidence of the trans movement in asserting its political demands, are all anecdotal evidence that masculine socialization is still very much present.

Regardless of what the empirical evidence eventually shows, however, including transwomen as women may still be misguided. Even if it turns out to be the case that there are some males with 'woman' gender identities who are 'the same' as women in all relevant respects, so long as they are still *visibly male*, there is reason to include them in a blanket exclusion of males from the subject of feminist theory and activism, and from women-only spaces. Women cannot know whether *this particular male* is 'the same' as women in this way, or what the details of his precise socialization are. Blanket exclusions overgeneralize; they exclude many males who would be unlikely to undermine particular feminist interests, not only transwomen. If we want to include the relevantly socialized transwomen *who look like women*, then we're not in the domain of gender identities any more, we're in the domain of appearance/expression. So that would not be an argument for adding gender as identity to gender as sex caste, it would be an argument for extending the conception of gender as sex caste from female people to female and female-appearing people. But that is not what those interested in gender as identity are trying to do. It is certainly not what Jenkins is trying to do.

Gender as sex caste is the primary conception of gender that should interest feminists. It captures the target phenomena that feminists are interested to explain and dissolve, namely, women's subordination to men. It picks out a very large

---

[26] I'm thinking particularly of the claim made by some transwomen that it is 'transphobic' or involves being a 'genital fetishist' to have a sexual orientation, e.g. for lesbians to be unwilling to sleep with transwomen with penises (which is the great majority of transwomen—88% according to James et al. 2016). This is despite the fact that lesbians are actually *more* willing to date trans than straight men or women are (Blair and Hoskin 2018). For examples of those making the 'transphobia' claim in relation to sexual orientation see discussion in (Stock 2021, pp. 89–98, esp. 96–7).

marginalized constituency, where that constituency is clear and unified.[27] Subordination may look different for different women in different times and places, but it is always on the basis of, or ultimately explained by, sex. Even when it misfires and impacts some people who are not female, the ultimate explanation of their treatment is (assumptions about) sex. That doesn't mean there isn't closely related subordination and marginalization. In fact gender as sex caste helps to explain other types of marginalization, like the marginalization of femininity. Because women are subordinated, if there's an association between being a woman and being feminine, femininity will come to have negative associations, and these associations can explain why femininity is penalized in men. That doesn't make feminine men women, and it doesn't mean feminism has to be about men's femininity.

2.4 Is reconciliation possible?

Haslanger's use of 'we' created a false impression of consensus about what feminists (and more specifically feminist philosophers) want when it comes to gender and gender terms. Feminism is in fact marked by disagreement on this point. Some think gender is sex caste, some think gender is identity, and some think it is both at once. I am a gender-critical feminist: *we* think gender is sex caste. Jenkins, and many other feminist philosophers besides, are not gender-critical: *they* think gender is identity (or, gender is *also* identity).[28] We should be careful not to confuse what *they* want it to be with what it really is. We should also be careful not to confuse what *they* want it to be with what it should be. For the gender-critical feminist, gender should be abolished, not merely transformed.

Many feminist philosophers today seem to feel the pull of both understandings of gender. The pull of understanding gender as identity seems to come less from the inherent plausibility of the concept of gender identity,[29] and more from

---

[27] Opponents are likely to point out that the constituency for gender as sex caste is not in fact 'clear and unified' because it assumes that everyone in the caste is female, but intersex people complicate unambiguous 'femaleness'. Intersex people do complicate this; some people who appear physiologically female externally nonetheless have a Y chromosome (and appear male internally in at least some respects). But there are hard cases for every definition and concept, and most importantly, the complexities some intersex people pose for understandings of femaleness do not establish anything at all for non-intersex people of the opposite sex who have a 'woman' gender identity.

[28] I have focused on the detail of Haslanger and Jenkins here, but as Elizabeth Barnes notes: 'Contemporary gender metaphysics can be (roughly) divided into two main camps: social position accounts and identity-based accounts' (Barnes 2020, p. 706). Gender as class/caste is a social position account; gender as identity is, obviously, an identity-based account. So the detailed disagreement I've presented here is representative of a more general division between feminist philosophers over what gender is.

[29] See critical discussion in Gheaus (forthcoming).

worrying about 'exclusion'.[30] Some proponents of gender as identity seem less concerned to displace gender as sex caste (or at least gender as class) with gender as identity, and more concerned that we simply include everyone with a gender identity *as if* the gender as caste/class analysis applied to them. For example, Kate Manne presents misogyny as the policing of women in accordance with norms of femininity. But she acknowledges that 'Perhaps the biggest omission...in this book' is 'a discussion of transmisogyny' (Manne 2017, pp. 24–5), and talks about the vulnerability of transwomen. Norms of femininity are not applied to most transwomen, so it is hard to see why Manne would consider this an omission. If there's an intersectional issue connecting misogyny to transphobia, it would appear to be about trans*men*, not trans*women*, for those are the people who are both subject to norms of femininity and also contending with biases against trans people. Manne does note that 'trans men are also highly vulnerable', but this comes *after* the discussion of transwomen.[31] Intellectually, this is baffling. Politically, it is not.

Or to give another example, in a recent piece for *Boston Review*, Robin Dembroff and Dee Payton seem to accept gender as caste/class when they say 'gender inequality is rooted in historical and continuing manifestations of sexism and misogyny, from policies that economically exploit women and undermine their reproductive autonomy to social practices like sexual harassment and rape culture.' So far so good, except that they go on to say 'Young girls inherit the same sexism and misogyny that their mothers faced as young girls, *regardless of whether they are transgender or cisgender*' (Dembroff and Payton 2020, my emphasis). Suddenly young people are facing sexism depending on how they identify, rather than how they appear or in fact are. The authors partially justify this claim by assuming a wide understanding of misogyny, following Julia Serano, as 'rooted in the deeply entrenched social assumption that "femaleness and femininity are

---

[30] It's worth distinguishing exclusion from the *male concept* of woman, which feminists should not be concerned with, from exclusion from the *feminists' concept of woman*, which they should. But it is less obvious that the latter is a genuine worry; tropes about 'exclusionary white feminism' are often overstated for political effect.

[31] (Manne 2017, pp. 24–5). In a footnote, she says 'whether or not the transphobia to which trans men are subject counts as transmisogyny will depend on whose definition of transmisogyny one is working with' (p. 30). She seems herself to assume that it obviously counts for transwomen and only maybe counts for trans men. It seems much more consistent with her analysis to say that it obviously counts for trans men (at least for all those who don't pass as male) and only maybe counts for transwomen (e.g. it counts only for transwomen who pass as female). Julia Serano, alternatively, thinks misogyny is the devaluing of femininity, so following Serano *can* generate an understanding of transmisogyny that applies to transwomen. But if Manne followed Serano, her analysis would fail at crucial points. Manne wants to be able to explain misogyny as the enforcement branch of patriarchy, and that means women's non-conformity with femininity is sanctioned in order to bring women into line. Her account predicts that a masculine woman (e.g. a butch lesbian) will be sanctioned for failing to be feminine. Serano's understanding of misogyny would predict that such a woman is not subject to policing, because she is not feminine, and so her traits are not devalued. Thus Manne cannot simply buy into Serano's understanding of misogyny and transmisogyny, at least not without losing a lot of what was useful about her own account.

inferior"' (Dembroff and Payton 2020, quoting Serano in Carstensen 2017). But they offer no evidence to substantiate the claim that transgirls are systematically subject to the same norms and treatment as girls are. Some transgirls may be subject to this treatment, namely those who are considered by sexists to be girls, but other transgirls will not be subject to this treatment, including all those who are considered by sexists to be boys. It's not one's private gender identity as a 'girl' or 'woman' that causes sexist treatment, it's one's expression of that identity (whether through femininity or in public claims to be a girl).

There is also a sleight of hand in Serano's presentation of misogyny, putting femaleness together with femininity. If we assume that misogyny is exclusively about femininity (in either sex) rather than femaleness, then we can talk about it in a way that accommodates most transwomen's self-conceptions. Everyone who is detectably feminine is subject to misogyny; we get to retain one of the crucial parts of the gender as caste/class approach, as something that is imposed externally upon people, while also vindicating transwomen's self-understandings. For people who place a high value on inclusion, this will be appealing. The problem, of course, is that not all women are feminine. Some women are visibly female, but identify as men, or as nonbinary, or as 'genderfree' (having a sex, but not having a gender identity). Some women are visibly female, but masculine in terms of presentation, whether in hairstyles, grooming, clothing, posture, gait, or body language.

On the gender as sex caste approach, how one is socialized depends on what sex one is. All visibly female people will be rewarded for femininity and sanctioned for masculinity. Sometimes they will also be sanctioned for femaleness regardless of femininity or masculinity, as with pregnancy and breastfeeding discrimination in the workplace, or put at risk because of femaleness regardless of femininity and masculinity, as with sexual violence. Serano's account of misogyny seems to give the wrong results: effeminate gay men are subject to misogyny; butch lesbians are not. Serano's addition of 'femaleness' was presumably meant to sidestep this problem. But what is the justification for having both? One can be female without being feminine, and feminine without being female. We cannot simply assume that the relevant social mistreatment targets one or the other or both, and especially not just because that assumption is convenient to transwomen.

Returning to an understanding of misogyny as being about femaleness can still account for the devaluing of femininity which Serano points to, because the sex caste system not only makes female people feminine, but also positions them as inferior. Because being feminine is a way for a boy to fail to be masculine, it is something that *he* will be sanctioned for. But this latter claim is not universal: *males* are sanctioned for femininity, because they are 'supposed to be' masculine, but *females* are rewarded for femininity, because they are 'supposed to be' feminine. If we lose sight of this, we lose explanatory and predictive power when it comes to how sex-based oppression works. And that is not just bad for women, it's bad for trans people too. If we have the wrong explanation of the mistreatment of transwomen, we are likely to come up with the wrong solutions to it. Rolling together the targeting of females for failing to be feminine (or, indeed, for being female/feminine—that's the double bind) with the targeting of males for failing to be masculine in the one concept 'misogyny' is not conceptually helpful.

In summary, gender *was* and *is* sex class (whether or not it is also other things). Gender identity activists want gender to be identity. (Some, like Jenkins, want it to be class *and* identity). But gender as identity means losses that are not justified or counterbalanced by the value of inclusiveness, which is the only thing that is gained by the revision. Feminism doesn't have to be kind or inclusive. Gender as sex class/caste is descriptively accurate, and normatively helpful. It answers a central concern of feminism, namely women's subordination, and it creates a unified constituency for feminist theory and activism. It picks up a large enough constituency of people who have serious enough problems that it has no reason to apologize for not extending its scope to more people, or more issues. Standing for women is enough. Unless empirical evidence can be furnished to substantiate the claim that any male who declares a 'woman' gender identity is like a woman in the relevant respects, and until such a time as women themselves can tell which males really have these gender identities and which don't (which is likely to be never), males with 'woman' gender identities have no place in feminism, and no place in women-only spaces or in accessing women-only services or provisions. The reconciliation of gender as sex caste and gender as identity fails. Gender *is* sex caste and gender as sex caste *should be* abolished.

References

Atkinson, Ti-Grace. *Amazon Odyssey* (New York: Links Books, 1974).

Bailey, J. Michael. *The Man Who Would Be Queen: The Science of Gender-Bending and Transsexualism* (Washington: Joseph Henry Press, 2003).

Barker, Victoria. 'Definition and the question of "woman"', *Hypatia* 12/2 (1997), pp. 185–215.

Barnes, Elizabeth. 'Gender and gender terms', *Nous* 54/3 (2020), pp. 704–30.

Bicchieri, Cristina. *Norms in the Wild* (Oxford: Oxford University Press, 2017).

Blair, Karen, and Hoskin, Rhea. 'Transgender exclusion from the world of dating: Patterns of acceptance and rejection of hypothetical trans dating partners as a function of sexual and gender identity', *Journal of Social and Personal Relationships* 36/7 (2018), pp. 2074–95.

Brownmiller, Susan. *Against Our Will: Men, Women and Rape* (New York: Bantam, 1976).

Carstensen, Jeanne. 'Julia Serano, transfeminist thinker, talks trans-misogyny', *The New York Times*, 22nd June 2017.

Clearfield, Melissa, and Nelson, Naree. 'Sex differences in mothers' speech and play behaviour with 6-, 9- and 14-month-old infants', *Sex Roles* 54 (2006), pp. 127–37.

Cronan, Sheila. 'Mariage', in Anne Keodt, Ellen Levine, and Anita Rapone (Eds.) *Radical Feminism* (New York: Quadrangle, 1973).

Daly, Mary. *The Church and the Second Sex* (Boston: Beacon Press, 1968).

Daly, Mary. *Beyond God The Father* (Boston: Beacon Press: 1973).

Dembroff, Robin. 'Real talk on the metaphysics of gender', *Philosophical Topics* 46/2 (2018), pp. 21–50.

Dembroff, Robin, and Payton, Dee. 'Why we shouldn't compare transracial to transgender identity', *Boston Review*, 18th November 2020.

Donovan, Wilbert, Taylor, Nicole, and Leavitt, Lewis. 'Maternal sensory sensitivity and response bias in detecting change in infant facial expressions: Maternal self-efficacy and infant gender labeling', in *Infant Behaviour and Development* 30/3 (2007), pp. 436–52.

Dunn, Judy, Bretherton, Inge, and Munn, Penny. 'Conversations about feeling states between mothers and their young children', *Developmental Psychology* 23/1 (1987), pp. 132–9.

Dworkin, Andrea. *Woman-Hating* (New York: E. P. Dutton & Co.: 1974).

Dworkin, Andrea. *Intercourse* (New York: Basic Books, 1987).

Eisenberg, Nancy, Wolchick, Sharlene, Hernandez, Robert, and Pasternack, Jeannette. 'Parental socialization of young children's play: A short-term longitudinal study', *Child Development* 56/6 (1985), pp. 1506–13.

Eisler, Riane. *The Chalice and the Blade* (New York: Harper & Row, 1987).

Erden, Feyza, and Altun, Dilek. 'Parents' toy preferences: Is gender still an issue?' in Jeanne Galbraith, Ozkan Ozgun, and Mustafar Yasar (Eds.), *Contemporary Perspectives and Research on Early Childhood Education* (Newcastle upon Tyne, Cambridge Scholars Publishing, 2014), Chapter 31.

Fine, Cordelia. *Delusions of Gender* (UK: Icon Books, 2010).

Firestone, Shulamith. *The Dialectic of Sex* (New York: William Morrow, 1970).

Firestone, Shulamith. 'On abortion', in *Notes from the First Year: Women's Liberation Movement* (New York: 1968).

Frye, Marilyn. *The Politics of Reality* (New York: Crossing Press, 1983).

Gheaus, Anca. 'Feminism without "gender identity"', *Politics, Philosophy & Economics* (2022), forthcoming.

Gonzalez, Alexei., & Koestner, Richard., 'Parental preference for sex of newborn as reflected in positive affect in birth announcements', *Sex Roles* 52(5/6) (2005), pp. 407–411.

Greer, Germaine. *The Female Eunuch* (London: MacGibbon & Kee, 1970).

Haslanger, Sally. 'Gender and race: (What) are they? (What) do we want them to be?' *Nous* 34/1 (2000), pp. 31–55.

Haslanger, Sally. 'Ontology and social construction', *Philosophical Topics* 23/1 (1995), pp. 95–105.

Jenkins, Katharine. 'Amelioration and inclusion: Gender identity and the concept of Woman*', *Ethics* 126 (2016), pp. 394–421.

Jenkins, Katharine. 'Toward an account of gender identity', *Ergo* 5/27 (2018), pp. 713–44.

Jordan-Young, Rebecca. *Brainstorm: The Flaws in the Science of Sex Differences* (Massachusetts: Harvard University Press, 2010).

Jost, John, Pelham, Brett, and Carvallo, Mauricio. 'Non-conscious forms of system justification: Implicit behavioural preferences for higher status groups', *Journal of Experimental Social Psychology* 38 (2002), pp. 586–602.

Kane, Emily. '"I wanted a soul mate": Gendered anticipation and frameworks of accountability in parents' preferences for sons and daughters', *Symbolic Interaction* 34/4 (2009), pp. 372–89.

King, Tania, Shields, Marissa, Sojo, Victor, Daraganova, Galina, Currier, Dianne, O'Neil, Adrienne, King, Kylie, and Milner, Allison. 'Expressions of masculinity and associations with suicidal ideation among young males' *BMC Psychiatry* 20/288 (2020), pp. 1–10.

Koedt, Anne, Levine, Ellen, and Rapone, Anita. (Eds.) *Radical Feminism* (New York: Quadrangle Books, 1973).

Kollmayer, Marlene, Schultes, Marie-Therese, Schober, Barbara, Hodosi, Tanja, and Spiel, Christiane. 'Parents' judgements about the desirability of toys for their children: Associations with gender role attitudes, gender-typing of toys, and demographics', *Sex Roles* 79 (2018), pp. 329–41.

Lawford-Smith, Holly. *Gender-Critical Feminism* (Oxford: Oxford University Press, 2022).

Lerner, Gerda. *The Creation of Patriarchy* (Oxford: Oxford University Press, 1986).

Littman, Lisa. 'Parent reports of adolescents and young adults perceived to show signs of a rapid onset of gender dysphoria', *PLOS One* 13/8 (2018), pp. 1–44.

Lytton, Hugh, and Romney, David. 'Parents' differential socialization of boys and girls: A meta-analysis', *Psychological Bulletin* 109/2 (1991), pp. 267–96.

MacKinnon, Catharine. *Feminism Unmodified* (Massachusetts: Harvard University Press, 1987).

MacKinnon, Catharine. *Toward a Feminist Theory of the State* (Massachusetts: Harvard University Press, 1989).

MacKinnon, Catharine. *Are Women Human?* (Massachusetts: The Belknap Press of Harvard University Press, 2006).

Manne, Kate. *Down Girl* (New York: Oxford University Press, 2017).

Marchiano, Lisa. 'Outbreak: On transgender teens and psychic epidemics', *Psychological Perspectives* 60/3 (2017), pp. 345–66.

Millett, Kate. *Sexual Politics* (London: Virago, [1970] 1977).

Mondschein, Emily, Adolph, Karen, and Tamis-LeMonda, Catherine. 'Gender bias in mothers' expectations about infant crawling', *Journal of Experimental Child Psychology* 77/4 (2000), pp. 304–16.

Nash, Alison, and Krawczyk, Rosemary. *Boys' and Girls' Rooms Revisited: The Contents of Boys' and Girls' Rooms in the 1990s*. Paper presented at the Conference on Human Development, Pittsburgh, Pennsylvania, 2007.

O'Connor, Cailin. 'The evolution of gender', in *The Origins of Unfairness* (Oxford: Oxford University Press, 2019), pp. 84–102.

Pateman, Carole. *The Sexual Contract* (Stanford: Stanford University Press, 1988).

Phelan, Kate. 'Ideology: The rejected true', *Inquiry* (2022) [early view].

Pizan, Christine de. *The Book of the City of Ladies*. Rosalind Brown-Grant (Trans.). (London: Penguin, [1405] 1999), Part I, pp. 5–11 and 78–80.

Rubin, Gayle. 'The traffic in women: Notes on the "political economy" of sex', in Rayna Reiter (Ed.) *Toward an Anthropology of Women* (New York: Monthly Review Press, 1975), pp. 157–210.

Rothman, Barbara. *The Tentative Pregnancy: Prenatal Diagnosis and the Future of Motherhood* (London: Pandora 1988).

Sankaran, Kirun. 'What's new in the new ideology critique?' *Philosophical Studies* 177/5 (2020), pp. 1441–62.

Schrier, Abigail. *Irreversible Damage: The Transgender Craze Seducing Our Daughters* (Washington: Regnery Publishing, 2020).

Snow, Margaret, Jacklin, Carol, and Maccoby, Eleanor. 'Sex-of-child differences in father–child interaction at one year of age', *Child Development* 54/1 (1983), pp. 227–32.

Snyder, R. 'What is third-wave feminism? A new directions essay', *Signs* 34/1 (2008), pp. 175–196.

Stock, Kathleen. *Material Girls: Why Reality Matters for Feminism* (Boston: Fleet Reads, 2021).

Wollstonecraft, Mary. 'Observations on the state of degradation to which woman is reduced by various causes', in *A Vindication of the Rights of Woman* (London: Arcturus [1792] 2017), Chapter IV, pp. 73–104.

3

Do Arguments for 'Trans Women are Women' Succeed?

The claim that 'trans women are women' is not always argued for. Katharine Jenkins, writing in *Ethics* in 2016, simply asserted it: 'The proposition that trans identities are entirely valid—that trans women are women and trans men are men—is a foundational premise of my argument, which I will not discuss further' (Jenkins 2016, p. 396). Talia Mae Bettcher asserts it in a more subtle way, writing in *Philosophy Compass* in 2017 that 'the invalidation of trans identities is a central issue in trans politics' (Bettcher 2017, p. 1). To invalidate transwomen's identity is to deny that they are what they say they are, that is, to deny that 'trans women are women'. Rachel McKinnon writes in *Philosophy and Phenomenological Research* in 2018 'I take it as now well-established that trans women *are women*. Full stop' (McKinnon 2018, p. 485). But McKinnon does not provide any references indicating where this was established, or by whom. Clearly, mere insistence upon the claim that 'trans women are women' is not an argument. Those who did not already accept the claim have no reason to get on board with anything that follows it.

But that the claim is so often simply asserted does not mean it is not possible to give arguments for it. Some arguments do exist, and I will invent some more. Some are metaphysical. They say that transwomen are women because whatever it takes to be a woman, transwomen have it. The gender identity argument is like this: what it takes to be a woman is to have a 'woman' gender identity; transwomen have a 'woman' gender identity; therefore transwomen are women.[1] Others are verbal. They say that we should *say* 'trans women are women', because doing so brings about good consequences. The violence argument is like this: transwomen experience public harassment and violence; they wouldn't experience public harassment and violence if people accepted them as women; saying that 'trans women are women' is a way of accepting, and encouraging others' acceptance, of them as women; therefore 'trans women are women'.

In the first section of this essay I will survey some of the existing arguments that can be found in the philosophical literature. These include what I will call

---

[1] I won't discuss this argument here, it having been a large part of Chapter 2. Those who are interested in that specific argument are encouraged to consult that chapter, and also the discussions in Stock (2021) and Joyce (2021).

'the moral/political not metaphysical argument', 'the hermeneutical injustice argument' (a narrower version of which is 'the ontological oppression argument'), 'the violence argument' (which can be generalized into 'the perlocutionary effects argument'), 'the libertarian self-determination argument', 'the first-personal authority argument', and the 'aspirational argument'. None of these succeed, for various reasons, although some are more promising than others. In the second section, I propose some further arguments. I call these 'the Star of David argument', 'the war argument', 'the recognition respect argument', and 'the womanizing argument'. Again, although some are more promising than others, none succeed.

Before we start, a brief note about terminology that is specific to this chapter. I explained already that there is a disagreement between gender-critical feminists and gender identity activists over whether one should write 'transwomen' (no space) or 'trans women' (space). The latter reads as a description of a woman, akin to 'tall' woman or 'angry' woman, while the former does not. Gender-critical feminists prefer the former, gender identity activists prefer the latter. Both beg the question in the context of this essay, where *whether* transwomen are women is at issue. I'll beg it in the direction I think is correct, so use 'trans women' when quoting others, and 'transwoman' otherwise.

3.1 Existing arguments

There are at least six different arguments given across the philosophical literature for 'trans women are women'. I'll explain each, and its weaknesses, in what follows.

The *'moral/political not metaphysical'* argument. Mari Mikkola writes in her book *The Wrong of Injustice* '[t]heory of gender that point-blank excludes trans* women from women's social kind is simply unacceptable. But just as I find it politically problematic to propose such an exclusionary theory, I find it problematic to propose a view that unquestionably includes trans* women. After all, not all trans* women want to be part of women's social kind. [...] *Political concerns are critical when deciding how to proceed*' (Mikkola 2016, pp. 114–15, my emphasis).[2] Robin Dembroff argues against a metaphysical approach to gender on which gender classifications should track facts about membership in current/dominant gender categories, and in favour of a moral approach: 'what, according

---

[2] Mikkola explains her use of 'trans*' instead of just 'trans' as being 'considered to be more inclusive', because 'trans' 'is taken to refer to medically or hormonally altered transsexual men and women' (Mikkola 2016, p. 23). This is a little confusing because 'transsexual' is usually reserved for those who have transitioned surgically, 'transgender' or just 'trans' for those who haven't (whether they've transitioned medically, or only socially). It is my understanding that 'trans' has the meaning that Mikkola thinks 'trans*' has.

to our best normative theory, seems to accommodate the interests of gender justice' (Dembroff 2018, p. 36). This argument is familiar from other subdisciplines. In 2006 Ron Mallon made the argument for race: against the view that racial terms or concepts refer to metaphysical features of the world, and in favour of the view that 'disputes over "race" talk should be resolved by a complex evaluation of a host of practical, normative considerations' (Mallon 2006, pp. 527–8).[3]

We take this approach by asking, what understanding of the moral/political category 'woman' would best serve gender justice? We might decide that gender justice requires voluntariness in gender categorization, so that people aren't simply 'assigned' to categories on the basis of sex, but get to choose which category to be in. Then we might decide that what it means to be a woman is to have decided to be a woman, which can be signalled most clearly from saying that you are one. Transwomen say that they are women, so transwomen are women, on this new understanding.

There is a problem with using this approach to vindicate the claim that 'trans women are women', and it is that neither moral nor political concerns can generally be limited to the interests of just one group, but they would have to be limited to trans people alone in order to vindicate an understanding of 'woman' that counted transwomen as women. That is not to say we can't take action for specific groups, but that when we think about what actions to take, we generally have to consider *all affected parties*, and possible opportunity costs and tradeoffs, rather than simply siloing one group off from all the others. But gender categories affect everyone, not just trans people, and they *particularly* affect female people, who have been long subjected to mistreatment on the basis of assumptions about female inferiority. Any moral/political considerations about how the category of woman should be changed and towards what end had better take female people's interests seriously.

It is not necessary for me to argue that an understanding of woman that counts transwomen as woman is *definitely* against female people's interests; I need only to establish that it is far from obvious that it is in female people's interests, which means it is far from obvious that the 'moral/political not metaphysical' argument would vindicate 'trans women are women'. The biggest reason to think it's against female people's interests is that it shifts 'women' from a unified group (all and only adult human females) to an *ad hoc* group, and this in turn puts feminism as a political project at risk. As Natalie Stoljar put it, diversity 'raises the issue of whether women constitute a genuine class and hence whether feminism can operate as a political movement on behalf of a unified group of women' (Stoljar

---

[3] Mallon does not 'eliminate' the metaphysical. He clarifies later in the paper that 'to say that debates about "race" talk are normative, not metaphysical, risks being misunderstood. What is normative is not what is in the world, but how, when, and where we decide to talk about what is in the world' (Mallon 2006, pp. 550–1).

1995, p. 262). Or as Theodore Bach put it, 'if there is no real group "women", then it is incoherent to make moral claims and advance political policies on behalf of women' (Bach 2012, p. 234).

The best candidate for a common feature among women is biological sex.[4] This creates a clear metaphysical category, and that category can be easily shown to have social significance (from the beginning of sex caste hierarchy through the effects of that hierarchy in the last several thousand years). It is far from obvious that it is in female people's interests, at least in the near term, to cede the metaphysical in favour of the moral/political.[5] But even if they did, any moral/political understanding of 'woman' that took more than just transwomen's interests into account is unlikely to vindicate the understanding of 'woman' that transwomen-inclusive feminist philosophers want. A revision that is good for women, for example, would be 'a biologically female adult human with any interests, any job, any sexual orientation, and any kind of presentation'. This revision is incompatible with the inclusion of male people, and could only be made compatible at the cost of giving 'woman' and 'man' the same meaning, thus defeating the whole point of having gender terms.

There are some exceptions to this rule about taking action in limited groups' interests. Prioritarians, for example, are concerned with improving the position of the least well-off. So if trans people could be shown to be the least well-off, then perhaps doing something to advance their interests, *even if* it set back the interests of other groups (so long as it didn't set them back far enough to make one such group the worst-off), could be justified. The problem is that it is unlikely that trans people are the least well-off social group. Sometimes they are assumed to be, on the basis of disproportionately high rates of murder or suicide, but the statistics frequently invoked appear to be overstated (on suicide see Biggs 2015; on murder see Reilly 2019).[6] Gender identity ideology can also distort applications of intersectionality in ways that create an inflated impression of disadvantage. Being male with a 'woman' gender identity is one thing about a person, but gender identity ideology sees it as transforming many other things about a person, including sexual orientation (a heterosexual male in an opposite-sex relationship becomes gay by identifying as a woman), and sex (a male becomes female by

---

[4] Understanding 'woman' as 'adult human female' gives *every* woman in the class something in common. There is no other feature that can capture anything like as many people who we intuitively think of as women (e.g. sexual subordination, capacity to reproduce, extraction of domestic labour, 'woman' gender identity, femininity).

[5] I say 'at least in the near term', because I can imagine a future in which, having paid attention to sex and sex-based injustice for long enough, we achieve sex equality and it becomes less important, or even entirely unimportant, to still care about it. At that time, women might happily cede the metaphysical. But to do so now, in the face of widespread global sex-based injustice, would be hugely premature (see e.g. Criado-Perez 2019 for a recent empirical overview of sex-based injustices created by androcentrism in research and policy-making).

[6] See also the details in fn. 19 and fn. 32.

identifying as a woman). A person who was not multiply disadvantaged, meaning, either not disadvantaged at all, or disadvantaged only along one dimension of identity, may become multiply, and potentially intersectionally,[7] disadvantaged (a black male who identifies as a woman becomes a 'trans woman of colour', someone impacted by the intersection of trans, race, and sex; a white heterosexual male who identifies as a woman becomes a 'trans lesbian woman', someone impacted by the intersection of trans, sexual orientation, and sex). (For a real-world example of this reasoning see Feng 2020).[8] If we reject the claim that gender identity transforms other things about a person, the impression of disadvantage reduces.

Thus revising the understanding of 'woman' by taking transwomen's interests into account *exclusively* is not likely to be justifiable on prioritarian grounds. One group of women with a *prima facie* strong claim to being the least well-off group of women is women in prison, who generally have suffered histories of abuse,[9] and who are vulnerable to the prison administration, with its attendant human rights abuses (see e.g. Balsamo and Sisak 2022; White 2019). These women's interests certainly aren't served by a revision of 'woman' to include male people, a revision implemented in law in multiple countries and already having the effect of sending male sex offenders into women's prisons.[10]

The hermeneutical injustice argument. 'Hermeneutical injustice' is a phrase coined by Miranda Fricker. She argued that because 'the powerful have an unfair advantage in structuring collective social understandings' (Fricker 2007, p. 148), there could be a specifically epistemic injustice involved in the absence of particular social terms or concepts. She was interested in the terms or concepts that allow (or would have allowed, had they existed) people to articulate disadvantage. The familiar example is 'sexual harassment': in a society in which women are considered to be primarily sexual/aesthetic objects *for* men's pleasure, it is difficult to articulate the wrong of being touched, looked at, or spoken to in an 'inappropriately sexualized' way.[11] Lacking the *concepts*, or *terms*, 'sexual harassment', 'sexual objectification',[12] or 'thingification' (MacKinnon 1982, p. 520), women were at a

---

[7] On the concept of intersectionality, see also discussion in Lawford-Smith and Phelan (2022) and Lawford-Smith (2022, Chapter 7).

[8] Feng quotes Jane Ussher, author of a report on sexual harassment and assault against transwomen, saying '[It's] because they are women, because they are trans, because they are a woman of colour and many of whom were bisexual, queer, or lesbian so these different multiple identities put them at high risk of sexual violence' (Ussher, in Feng 2020).

[9] According to a 2017 article in *Time*, 'the vast majority of women in prison are single mothers who have been victims of domestic and/or sexual violence' (Cox 2017).

[10] On prison transfers under sex self-identification in Canada, see Kay (2021). Kay reports the former Deputy Commissioner for Women saying in 2019 that 50% of requests for transfer from the male to the female estate were coming from male sex offenders.

[11] Other examples Fricker discusses are masturbation and post-partum depression (drawing on Brownmiller 1990), and negative constructions of homosexuality (Fricker 2007, pp. 149 and 165).

[12] For an early discussion of objectification, see (Beauvoir 1949, Volume II, Part 1, Chapter 2 'The girl', p. 360).

loss to articulate exactly *what* was happening to them in the workplace, and *why* it was wrong (Fricker 2007, p. 151). Women as a group are impacted by the absence of this concept: 'her hermeneutical disadvantage renders her unable to make sense of her ongoing mistreatment, and this in turn prevents her from protesting it, let alone securing effective measures to stop it' (p. 152).

We might make use of this idea in a direct argument for 'trans women are women'. The concept of a *biologically male woman* does not exist, or at least, does not exist outside of trans-friendly subcultures. Indeed, it would be considered a contradiction in terms outside of those subcultures. So we could say, this is an *absence* of a concept that renders transwomen unable to articulate their disadvantage. What is the disadvantage though? It is unlike that named by the concept of sexual harassment, because we already have the concepts to name the parallel mistreatment: transphobia, homophobia, femmephobia. So it must be something else, perhaps being subject to 'misrecognition': treated as men because male. Without the concept 'biologically male woman', transwomen cannot name that disadvantage, and so cannot protest it, or secure measures to stop it. Introducing the concept of a biologically male woman by insisting that 'transwomen are women' resolves the hermeneutical injustice.

Perhaps this was all true at some point in history, before the concept *transwoman* came into common understanding. But it is a matter of common usage now, and it is widely understood that transwomen are making a claim to being women while being biologically male (they might say, 'women assigned male at birth'). (There is a complication here because some transwomen are sex denialists, or collapse the sex/gender distinction into gender, and so assert that they are *female*.[13] In this case we would have to say something a bit different, like, there is a concept of being a 'woman/female with a penis and testicles', or in the case of sex reassignment surgery, being a 'woman/female who had gone some way down the developmental pathway to producing small gametes', or, being a 'woman/female with a Y chromosome').[14]

The problem is not the *lack* of the concept, but the *uptake* of the concept. Once 'sexual harassment' had a name, women took it up with a vengeance, because it named an experience so many of them had had, and the words together indicated

---

[13] Transwoman Rachael McKinnon, for example, wrote in *The New York Times* 'I am a woman, after all. I am female as well'; and 'Trans women are women. We are female' (McKinnon 2019).

[14] This latter expression of the concept is not particularly helpful, because it threatens to conflate the fact of having a specific intersex condition, namely CAIS (endogenous), with being transsexual (exogenous: accomplished through surgery). This difference is significant, for a CAIS 'woman/female with a Y chromosome' was assigned female at birth, raised female, grew up with/went through puberty with a female body, and socialized/treated as female for her whole life. A transsexual 'woman/female with a Y chromosome' may have 'sex reassignment surgery' late in life after having married and fathered children, which means having been observed male at birth, raised male, grown up with/gone through puberty with a male body, and socialized/treated as male throughout their life. So ideally we would have two different concepts for these two very different types of person.

something that it was easy for men to understand—precisely that this was a *form* of harassment. It became part of the stock of familiar concepts. But 'transwoman' has not had the same kind of uptake, because there is disagreement about whether *being biologically male* is a way one can be a woman. It is widely understood that there are biological male people who make a claim to being women; it is not clear that it is widely accepted that this claim is true. But this is not a hermeneutical injustice, it is a hermeneutical disagreement. That disagreement cannot be settled merely by stipulating that the lack of (uptake of) the concept is a disadvantage. If 'biologically male' is not a way to be a woman, then the lack of (uptake of) the concept is not a disadvantage.[15]

There is an indirect version of the hermeneutical injustice argument that is more interesting. Sexual subordination is central to the concept 'woman', whether or not it exhausts it. Suppose that transwomen experience sexual subordination, and that the best explanation for this is that they are seen as women. If 'woman' names the class of people who are treated a certain way, and transwomen are treated that way, then this is a reason to think that 'trans women are women'. Denying that 'trans women are women' would mean denying transwomen access to a concept that would help them understand their mistreatment. It would also mean feminists missing a crucial part of the story when it comes to understanding, and subsequently resolving, women's sexual subordination. Whether this argument goes through depends on whether in fact transwomen experience sexual subordination, and whether the best explanation for this is that they are seen as women. Some transwomen are explicit that their trans identification is motivated by a desire for sexual subordination (Chu 2019; see also testimonies in

---

[15] Robin Dembroff (2018) gives a more specific version of the hermeneutical injustice argument by claiming that it's an *ontological oppression* rather than a mere epistemic injustice when the concepts for social categories are lacking. Dembroff claims that our current gender kind concepts have oppressive membership conditions, because they don't count trans people as being what they say they are. Trans people are 'ontologically oppressed' because better gender kind concepts, with better (non-oppressive) member conditions, are absent. It is peculiar that Dembroff considers oppression to be gotten rid of in gender kind concepts when *trans* people, alone, get what they want. This sidelines female people, the primary historical victims of gender kind concepts and by far the largest constituency of people affected by them. It would be better for female people if pernicious stereotypes limiting their options on the basis of their sex were gotten rid of. Their situation is not remotely improved by making it the case that some biological males are intelligible as 'women' too. So the ontological oppression argument for 'trans women are women' doesn't go through either. As a side note, whether the ontological oppression argument is genuinely distinct from the hermeneutical injustice argument depends on what it takes for there to be a term/concept. If it has to have uptake, so that it can be communicated between people, then the absence of the ontological category looks to be the same thing as the absence of the concept. But if it's sufficient for one person to have the concept, or a small group to have it without it having more general uptake, or for everyone to know about it *but reject it* (say, because it's incoherent or undesirable), then it might be that hermeneutical injustice and so-called 'ontological oppression' come apart, because we can have the concept but not the category (i.e. everyone has considered the possibility of a 'biologically male woman' but simply rejected it as contradictory, so the category 'woman' doesn't change). That would involve ontological oppression in Dembroff's sense but not hermeneutical injustice.

Lawrence 2013). It's not clear whether transition satisfies that desire, but let's grant for the sake of argument that it does for at least some transwomen.

It is entirely unclear, however, what the best explanation of transwomen's sexual subordination is. Is there a social practice that targets the *feminine,* and (many) transwomen are feminine, so (many) transwomen are targeted by this social practice? Or is there a social practice that targets the *female,* and transwomen desire to be part of this social practice, and so adopt cues of femaleness in order to be? Only if it's the former do we get an argument for 'trans women are women'. If it's the latter, we have no reason to think differently about what a 'woman' is, only to note—for whatever it is worth—that the sexual subordination feminists are fighting to free female people from is desirable to some male people. That would actually be an argument *against* 'trans women are women', because accepting it would force us to say that some *women* desire sexual subordination and some don't, obscuring the fact that for some women (the females) it is imposed on the basis of sex and cannot be opted into or out of,[16] while for other women (transwomen) it is not.

If sexual subordination targets the *feminine* (in any sex), then feminine transwomen will be targeted, but we should also expect to see other feminine men (e.g. effeminate gay men) targeted, and masculine women not targeted. We do in fact see some targeting of feminine and effeminate men, but we do not see masculine women exempted from targeting. Thus a better explanation might be that *because of its association with female people, who are sexually subordinated,* femininity is being adopted in some non-female people who desire sexual subordination (e.g. autogynephilic transwomen).[17] It is impossible to know without doing detailed empirical research into the attitudes of sexual subordinators. So this argument for 'trans women are women' is inconclusive.

The violence argument. (The perlocutionary effects argument). This argument works by linking the *denial* of 'trans women are women' to specific physical harms. Katharine Jenkins makes this argument when she says '[f]ailure to respect the gender identifications of trans people is a serious harm and is conceptually linked to forms of transphobic oppression and even violence' (Jenkins 2016, p. 396). Jennifer Saul, writing in *The Conversation,* makes a version of this argument, when she says 'trans women are undoubtedly marginalized. Consider that 30% of trans female[18] teenagers attempt suicide; or that anti-discrimination laws that cover gender identity are rare; or that 72 percent of victims of anti-LGBTQ

---

[16] At least, cannot be opted into or out of without transitioning. (A female person who wishes to avoid it may transition to living as a man, and if he passes as male, may in fact escape sexually subordinating treatment).

[17] For detailed discussion of autogynephilic transwomen and feminism see (Joyce 2021, Chapter 2) and Lawford-Smith (2022, Chapter 5).

[18] Saul uses the sex term 'female' here as a gender term, tied specifically to gender identity. By 'trans female' she means what I mean by transwoman.

(or HIV-related) hate crimes were trans women. *An absolutely key component of this marginalization and discrimination is the denial of trans women's identity as women*' (Saul 2020, my emphasis).[19] Talia Mae Bettcher seems to be running a similar argument when she links 'transphobic violence' to the idea that transwomen are being deceptive when they present themselves as female because such a person is 'really a boy' or 'really a man' (Bettcher 2007, p. 48).

The most common form of this argument is to link the denial of transwomen's identity claims not to violence perpetrated by others, but to violence perpetrated by transwomen against *themselves*, in other words, to suicide, or suicide attempts. There is a much-circulated figure of 41% suicide attempts in the trans community, although this figure is inaccurate (Biggs 2015). Whether we're interested in self-inflicted or other-inflicted violence, the assumption seems to be that if only everyone accepted transwomen's identity claims, believing that they really were women, there would be substantially less violence. Avoidance of violence becomes a reason to accept, and proclaim, that 'trans women are women'.

There are a number of problems with this argument. The first is to do with the link between what we assert and what people think. It is an empirical question whether having increasing numbers of people assert that 'trans women are women' is really going to make people *believe* that transwomen are women, and *treat* transwomen as women. Making it socially unacceptable to say particular things, or socially mandating the saying of particular things, *can* contribute to changing attitudes and actions, but it can also just drive the same beliefs underground (the shift in psychology from old-fashioned to modern sexism and racism scales is trying to capture this, see e.g. Swim et al. 1995 and discussion in Barreto and Ellemers 2005). But in the case of gender identity, things are even more complicated, because even among progressives, there is disagreement about the best way to change the world. Accepting trans people's identity claims may not be the

---

[19] The suicide statistic Saul gives comes from a study reported in the journal *Pediatrics*, which asked 120,617 adolescents the question 'have you ever tried to kill yourself?' 202 (0.2%) of the participants were transgender, male to female (transwomen). 30% of those answered the suicide question affirmatively (Toomey et al. 2018). Michael Biggs has argued on the basis of their data that the biggest risk factor for suicide is actually sexual orientation (Biggs 2018); another group of researchers working on suicide ideation among young males found similarly that 'greater conformity to heterosexual norms was associated with reduced odds of reporting suicide ideation' (King 2020, p. 5). Thus it may be misleading to focus on the *trans* suicide attempt rate in particular, as though it is being trans / how trans people are treated that causes this. The hate crimes statistic Saul gives comes from a report by the National Coalition of Anti-Violence Programs (NCAVP), and refers specifically to 'hate violence homicides in 2013'. The NCAVP report states that 'the total homicides for 2013 remains among the highest ever recorded by the NCAVP' (NCAVP 2013, p. 8). The total number of hate violence homicides in that year was eighteen. 72% of those, which is thirteen people, were transwomen; 67%, which is twelve people, were transwomen of colour (p. 8). Elsewhere in the same report it is acknowledged that transwomen of colour are disproportionately represented in two notoriously violent industries, namely prostitution and the drug trade. The report states that '34% of transgender Latin@ respondents and 50% of transgender Black respondents had engaged in sex work or sold drugs at some point in their lives' (pp. 61–2). Nonetheless, the homicides are attributed to 'anti-LGBTQ and HIV-affected hate violence' (p. 8).

only way to avoid violence against them, and if it is not the only way, and working towards it conflicts with the social justice projects of other marginalized groups (female people; lesbian, gay, and bisexual people) then it is not the route we should take.

There seems to be an assumption in Saul's argument that it's the public conception of 'woman' that needs to change, to accommodate all transwomen, rather than the public conception of 'man'. But it's men who perpetrate violence against transwomen, and that violence is more likely tied to perceived violation of norms of masculinity (as in King et al. 2020) than to perceived violation of norms of femininity. The transwoman is assessed relative to the male standard, and found wanting because feminine; not assessed relative to the female standard, and found wanting because masculine. If it was the latter, we would expect to see a lot more physical violence against masculine women, but we do not. (On this way of understanding things, we get an explanation of why transwoman Aimee Stevens was fired from her job; if we thought she was being assessed relative to standards of femininity it would be utterly perplexing that she was fired for wanting to wear the women's uniform—see discussion at Hungerford 2020). Here's an alternative, which establishes that accepting trans people's identity claims is not the only way to avoid violence against them: work for acceptance that there's no 'right' way to be male, so that directing violence at gender non-conformists comes to be seen as inappropriate. Instead of insisting that 'trans women are women', insist that 'feminine men are men'.[20]

There are two advantages to this. First, it supports a broader message that is liberating for everyone: there's no right way to be male, and there's no right way to be female, so all the ways of expressing yourself are equally fine. This is good for all 'gender non-conforming' people, not just trans people. Second, it is compatible

---

[20] It has been suggested to me that this would not help, because in exactly the situations that involve violence, it is the fact of the transwoman being 'really a man' that causes the issue, e.g. in the 'trans panic' defence where a transwoman is assaulted upon being discovered to be male, and the defence given is that the assailant believed they were to have a sexual encounter with a female. The question here is which strategy is more likely to be successful: widespread uptake of the idea that being biologically male is a way to be a woman, or widespread uptake of the idea that being feminine (here presumably female-passing) is a way for a biologically male person to be. I suspect that neither are much likely to help with the sexual situation just described, for as long as biologically male women / female-passing men are in the minority. For then it will still be assumed that a female-appearing person is in fact female, and where this is highly relevant to a person's sexual orientation, frustrating that assumption without prior warning may be a trigger for violence. Given the importance of sex to sexual attraction, sexual orientation, and sexual consent, I think the best approach is transparency about biological sex. Because the transwoman *is in fact male*, I don't see it as a promising strategy to try to convince violent men either that 'man' is not the same thing as 'male' and while they don't want to have sex with a *man* it's quite fine to have sex with a *male*, or, that a man/male can occasionally be female-passing so every occasion of consent to a sexual encounter with an apparent-female is in fact to chance a sexual encounter with a male/man, *and that is perfectly fine*. So long as it's fine for men to be heterosexual, which I think it is, then it's fine for men to refuse sexual encounters with biologically male people. This is not to excuse violence done in any such situation, but is to point out that this situation is highly unlikely to be resolved by insisting that 'trans women are women'.

with the social justice projects of other marginalized groups, particularly lesbian, gay, and bisexual people, and women. 'Heteronormativity' is the norm that female people should be attracted to men only, and male people to women only. Discrimination happens in response to perceived violations of this norm. We cannot track this discrimination accurately while pretending heterosexual males are 'lesbians' because of their gender identities. Sexism/misogyny positions female people as inferior in the male/female sex hierarchy; discrimination depends on enforcing this norm (you are female therefore you are inferior) and on policing violations of this norm (you are female but you don't 'know your place'). We cannot track this negative sex-based treatment accurately while pretending feminine men are subject to it as well. In insisting that 'trans women are women', we force reforms to the self-understanding and social justice projects of both lesbian, gay, and bisexual people, and women, as groups. In asserting, instead, that 'feminine men are men', we don't.

In summary, short of evidence about the link between asserting that 'trans women are women' and reduced violence (including self-harm) against trans people, we have no reason to accept this as an argument for saying that transwomen are women. In light of alternatives that can be expected to do an equally good job in reducing violence *and* are more compatible with the social justice projects of other groups, we can reject the violence/perlocutionary effects argument.[21]

The libertarian self-determination argument. Michael Hauskeller writes 'as far as I am concerned, people should be free to be whatever they want to be, provided they do not harm other people in the process' (Hauskeller and Lawford-Smith 2022). He extends this thought to biologically male people who want to be addressed as women. The general idea is a familiar liberal one: people should be free to pursue their own conception of the good, in their own way, with the only constraint being that they do not cause harm to others in the process. If a male person's conception of the good involves living as a woman (whatever that

---

[21] Another version of the perlocutionary effects argument focuses on the harm to young girls in particular: unnecessary medicalization and surgeries for girls who think they're trans, but whose feelings about their gender may in fact be explained by something else, for example that they're lesbians, or autistic, or influenced by social contagion, or have undiagnosed medical issues. Radical and gender-critical feminists are particularly worried about these girls, and usually advocate for no transition before the age of consent as an answer to it. But an alternative would be to *speed up* the social acceptance of 'trans men are men' (and 'nonbinary people are neither men nor women') while simultaneously insisting that there's no right way to be trans (so that being a trans man or being nonbinary is perfectly compatible with having an unmodified female body). The sooner this becomes an identity *only*, the better from the perspective of unnecessary physical interventions which may turn out to have harmful long-term effects. Because gender identity ideology is symmetrical between men and women, this would be an indirect argument for saying that 'trans women are women'. We should say 'trans women are women' *because* we should say 'trans men are men'. Whether this argument succeeds depends on its likelihood of uptake, and the tradeoff in reduction of harm to young girls against the increase in harm to adult and child female people from losing the sex-based concept of 'woman'. I am sceptical about both.

means), then they should be free to do this, and it would be wrong for any of us to intervene and stop them. In the case of sex/gender, this freedom is particularly important, because it is tied to self-determination and self-expression.

Does this libertarian argument vindicate 'trans women are women'? That depends on how much others have to cooperate with your personal conception of the good, past merely not interfering with your pursuit of it, and on whether your personal conception of the good involves harm to others. Hauskeller goes on to say 'I appreciate that this can cause problems in certain contexts (for instance when it comes to the use of public bathrooms or changing rooms, or in sports where it raises issues of fairness in sex-segregated athletic competitions), but apart from that we should respect people's choices to live and present themselves any way they want' (Hauskeller and Lawford-Smith 2022). The problems that recognizing male people as women might cause in certain contexts—e.g. for accurate demographic information, crime statistics, women's sports, rape and domestic violence shelters, homeless shelters, changing rooms and bathrooms, women-only hiring lists, shortlists, and prizes—give us a basis for arguing that there *is* harm to others, specifically to female people.

But even supposing that there wasn't harm to others in this way, the question of cooperation remains. To what extent can our pursuit of the good make demands (short of harms) on other people? If a male person's good consists in living as a woman, and they are not harming anyone by doing that, I should not interfere to stop them. But almost no one who objects to the dogma 'trans women are women!' is trying to *stop a male person living as a woman*. Compare attitudes to drag: although there is a small minority of women who consider males in drag to be parodying womanhood in an offensive way, most women are fine with males in drag. Most gender-critical feminists would *actively encourage* males to experiment with more feminine forms of presentation, as a way of pushing back against masculine gender norms and so speeding their collapse. The issue is not the feminine presentation, it is the male person's claim that *they are a woman,* or that *they are female.* But at least in the case of the latter, the claim is simply false. If the former and the latter are synonymous, which most gender-critical feminists think they are, then both claims are false. Libertarian self-determination might permit a climate change denier to go around espousing silly conspiracy theories about the macadamia nut industry's clean energy grab, but they don't require that the friends and acquaintances of the conspiracy theorist *endorse* his claims. Similarly for transwomen's claims about being women, or being female.

For all the contexts where there can be shown to be harm in endorsing 'trans women are women', we have no argument for endorsing it; and for the remaining contexts, we have merely an argument for not interfering with how the male person wishes to live. We do not have an argument for accepting that 'trans women *are* women'.

The first-personal authority argument. Talia Mae Bettcher argues that whether one identifies as a woman or a man (or neither) is a fact that belongs in a category of things that only we can know about ourselves. We have 'first-personal authority' over things like our experience of pain and pleasure, our fleeting thoughts, our beliefs, fears, desires, and wishes. Bettcher does not defend this as an infallible source of *knowledge*, because she acknowledges that all sorts of things can get in the way: 'denial, self-deception, wishful thinking, and unconscious attitudes are common' (Bettcher 2009, p. 100). Rather, she defends first-personal authority as *ethical*, saying that a person takes responsibility for her mental states, including when they turn out to be 'inappropriate, false, or irrational' (p. 102). We think a person is wronged, morally, when someone violates her first-personal authority, e.g. by telling her that she is tired and wants to go home (attributing both a feeling and a desire, on which she is the ultimate authority) (p. 102). Bettcher thinks telling a transwoman 'you are really a man' is just like telling someone 'you are tired and want to go home now', because both disrespect the other's authority over those matters (p. 115).

Is *self-identifying as a woman* in the same category as pain, pleasure, desire, etc.? And if it is, does that vindicate 'trans women are women' as true? For Bettcher, gender is an important part of one's self-conception, and is 'existential'. She talks about a person identifying as a teacher, despite never having been employed or trained as a teacher, because 'one is an unactualized teacher who has never had the chance to be "who one really is"' (p. 111). In this same sense, who a male person 'really is' could be a woman. It's important that this claim is existential rather than metaphysical, because 'the latter involves a broad conception of men and women more generally and, consequently, risks running into conflict with the self-conception of others' (p. 111). This is a striking claim: one person's existential claim to be a woman has *no implications* for what a woman means in any general sense, and so does not threaten anyone else's different conception.

At this point, it becomes entirely unclear what Bettcher's argument gets us. We have learned that there is something 'existential' that most ordinary people using the word 'woman' don't mean by it. If we stick to that conception, *and* agree both that gender is gender identity and that 'woman' refers to this identity, then each individual is an authority on whether she is a woman. Therefore, 'trans women are women' is true (because trans women believe they're women). But feminists are not interested in the 'existential', they're interested in the metaphysical (and the political). So one person's understanding of 'woman' *does* have implications for another's self-conception. And it remains an open question whether gender is gender identity.[22] So this argument is unsuccessful.

---

[22] On this point see Chapter 2, and discussion in Stock (2021), Joyce (2021), and Gheaus (2022).

The aspirational argument. This argument is perhaps most explicit in B. R. George and R. A. Briggs' 'Science fiction double-feature: Trans liberation on Twin Earth' (George and Briggs, manuscript), which argues that the gender categories 'woman' and 'man' have a historical origin in being identified with sex, but can evolve through time such that their membership is 'liberalized', up to a point where the 'woman' category is a mix of male and female people, and the 'man' category similarly a mix of male and female people. This is a vision of a future in which 'membership in gender categories such as *woman* and *man* [is] fully voluntary' (George and Briggs, manuscript, p. 1;[23] see also Bach 2012). This vision of the future might underpin the claim that 'trans women are women'—it is not that they are, now, but that they should be. We say that something is the case, partly in order to bring it about.

There are two weaknesses to this argument. One is that we don't all share the same vision of what the good future looks like when it comes to gender. Aiming to retain the gender categories but make them voluntary is extraordinarily underambitious when compared to the radical feminist project of abolishing gender categories altogether.[24] Anyone who disagrees with the merely revisionist goal has no reason to assert that 'trans women are women'. Second, even if we did all share the same vision, it's not clear that the best way to bring it about is to go around speaking as though it were already the case. This is the methodology of linguistic activism (or conceptual engineering, or 'amelioration') which aims to intervene primarily on language and concepts rather than on actions and attitudes. A pioneer of this methodology in feminist theory was Mary Daly, in her books *Gyn/Ecology* (1978) and *Webster's First New Intergalactic Wickedary of the English Language* (1987). It can be successful in reclaiming slurs and terms of abuse, and in dissolving stereotypes, but it's not clear that it can do the work of actually intervening on bad social norms or conventions. As Kirun Sankaran puts it, 'changing pernicious conventions requires more than the epistemic remedy that contemporary critical social theorists prescribe. It also requires overcoming strategic impediments like high first-mover costs' (Sankaran 2020, p. 1442).

Thus the aspirational argument for 'trans women are women' fails too.

3.2 New arguments

While the arguments that have been given so far do not vindicate the claim that 'trans women are women', that doesn't mean there isn't an argument that could work. In this section I consider four further arguments, the first two drawing

---

[23] Page references refer to the 25th March 2019 version of the paper archived at <https://philpapers.org/rec/GEOSFD>, accessed 19th August 2020.

[24] See also discussion in Chapter 1.

from ideas first presented in the work of radical feminist philosopher Ti-Grace Atkinson. These are what I'm calling 'the Star of David argument', and 'the war argument'. The final two I'm calling 'the recognition respect argument', and 'the woman-izing argument'.

The Star of David argument. Atkinson was interested in the strategy and tactics of feminism as a political movement, and focused on the relations between feminists and men, and feminists and lesbians. She conceptualized males/men and females/women[25] as separate ranks ('oppressor' and 'oppressed'), with lesbians in the 'buffer zone' between the two, a kind of outlaw from the strict requirements of female socialization (which included being opposite-sex attracted) (Atkinson [1971] 1974).[26] At the time there was still a great deal of social stigma about same-sex attraction. This created a risk—that if outcast from the ranks of women, lesbians could be co-opted to men's ends in the battle of the sexes. Both this argument and the next come from Atkinson's concern with growing the ranks of the feminists ('pro-rebellion'). Atkinson wanted the buffer zone absorbed into the ranks of the feminists, and she suggested, toward this end, that 'all feminists began wearing buttons reading "I am a lesbian"' (Atkinson [1971] 1974, p. 155). She modelled this idea on what she describes as 'the tactic of the Danish king against the Germans during World War II' (although this is not historically accurate),[27] 'when the King rode out one morning wearing the Star of David, and most Danes followed suit, the effect was to frustrate the Nazi identification of Jews in that area' (p. 155). If all feminists identify themselves as lesbians, then the actual lesbians are more protected from harassment and abuse, and in return for this support they may be more inclined to join the ranks of the feminists, thus expanding the size of the 'pro-rebellion' group within the ranks of the oppressed.

Can the same argument be made for 'absorbing' transwomen as women? Here's how it would go: the parallel to non-lesbian feminists wearing 'I am a lesbian' badges is non-trans feminists wearing 'I am trans' badges. This makes it difficult for those men who would target transwomen to know which female-appearing people are trans and which are not. If done in significant numbers, it will make the targeting of transwomen impossible, and therefore end it, just as it would have confounded the German soldiers had the Danish legend been true. This protects transwomen, and shows solidarity likely to draw them in to the feminist movement.

Does this argument succeed? I think it does not. Firstly, feminists can pass as lesbians, and Danes as Jews, because many in fact are, and because there's no

---

[25] I'll use these slightly cumbersome combined terms in order to track Atkinson's actual meaning but avoid ambiguity given the usage in the rest of the essay (Atkinson herself used 'women' and 'men' and meant 'females' and 'males' by them).
[26] See in particular the strategy chart on p. 141 of her book.
[27] Mikkelson (2000) says the origin of this legend might be a Swedish newspaper cartoon depicting a similar discussion between the Danish king and the former Danish prime minister.

particular incompatibility between the way people in these social groups generally look. But that's not true for males/men and females/women. Most feminists are recognizably female, many if not most transwomen are recognizably male. Anyone wanting to target transwomen could simply target the visibly male among those wearing 'I am trans' badges. The 'protection' strategy fails, and in failing it does not offer solidarity and so cannot draw transwomen into the pro-rebellion group (the feminists). Secondly, feminists in the 1970s had a reason to want to bring lesbians in particular into the feminist rebellion, namely that they were female. Feminism was a movement by female people for female people, so bringing more female people in to the political project was an uncomplicated win. But it's not clear whether feminists today have any reason to want to bring transwomen into the feminist rebellion. To the extent that feminism is still a movement by and for female people, bringing male people into that project is not uncomplicated.[28]

The war argument. The war argument is fairly closely related to the Star of David argument, but comes from thinking about the relation between feminists and men, rather than feminists and lesbians.

Here's how it goes: like lesbians (at the time), transwomen (now) are similarly 'outlaws', except in this case from the ranks of the oppressor. They are the contemporary buffer zone. There is a risk—that if outcast from the ranks of *men*, they could be co-opted to *women's* ends in the battle of the sexes. And they are in fact outcast from the ranks of men. Feminists should take advantage of this, in order to grow the ranks of the feminist rebellion. Or more straightforwardly: feminism is war, and we need all the soldiers we can get.

Whether this argument is successful depends on whether Atkinson's conception of feminism—at least in that essay—as an issues-based political movement is correct.[29] If that is what it is, then, in a democracy, the more people who agree on the issues, the better. But if feminism is, or is also, something else, then it is less obvious that it should take anyone it can get for strategic/tactical reasons.

Deborah Cameron distinguishes three broad types of thing feminism might be: an idea, an intellectual framework, a collective political project (Cameron 2019, p. 2). If it is an idea, like 'women are morally equal to men', then we should take everyone we can get. If it is a collective political project, then it depends on the project. For the project to secure free, safe, and legal abortions, we should take everyone we can get; for the project of lesbian separatism, we should take only lesbians. If it is an intellectual framework, like using consciousness-raising in

---

[28] For those who think feminism is a movement by and for *feminine* people, or by and for *everyone*, this problem dissolves. Perhaps this explains why 'trans women are women' is true for liberal and intersectional feminists, and false for radical and gender-critical feminists.

[29] She talks about coalitions to advance particular rights or solutions to practical problems, like free housing, free food, free transportation (Atkinson [1971] 1974, p. 160), and eventual concentration on a single solution, like basic income (p. 169).

order to make progress on revealing the 'lived experience' of women's oppression, then it might also depend. If we want to reveal the shape of street harassment, then we won't want to take everyone we can get, we'll want to limit the group to those who have experienced street harassment. That is likely to include *some* transwomen: those who 'pass' as female will be subject to that harassment. If we want to reveal the shape of treatment by the medical system when it comes to pregnancy and birth, it won't make sense to take everyone we can get, we'll want to limit the group to those who have experienced pregnancy and birth. That means excluding all transwomen (and some women, too), and including some transmen.

Furthermore, even if tactically, feminism should take everyone it can get (for at least some of these projects), that doesn't mean *all feminists are women*. Atkinson also defends the idea of bringing *men* into the 'pro-rebellion' ranks, but it is not likely that she thinks this makes them oppressed, or makes them women. It is one thing to attract support for a political cause, and quite another to declare that all supporters are women now. Atkinson herself thought we had to get rid of the category 'woman', not merely expand its membership (Atkinson 1974, p. 149). So neither of these arguments end up vindicating 'trans women are women', even if they might vindicate 'trans women can be feminists'.

The recognition respect argument. Some talk as though recognizing a transgender person's gender identity *as* their sex/gender is a human right, a matter of respecting basic human dignity. The judge in the original tribunal for Maya Forstater's employment case in the UK, for example, decided that Forstater's understandings of sex and gender (which included that it is impossible to change sex) were 'incompatible with human dignity' and in 'conflict with the fundamental rights of others'.[30] The influential (although lacking official legal status) Yogyakarta Principles declare that when states require individuals to provide information on their sex or gender, it's necessary that 'such requirements respect all persons' right to self-determination of gender' (Principle 6, p. 18).[31] The fact that many trans people react so strongly to 'misgendering' may be taken as evidence that gender identity is psychologically of enormous importance to them.[32]

---

[30] <https://www.gov.uk/employment-tribunal-decisions/maya-forstater-v-cgd-europe-and-others-2200909-2019>; there has since been an appeal, which overturned this original judgement and sent the case back to a fresh tribunal. In 2022 she was found to have been discriminated against on the basis of her gender-critical beliefs. <https://www.doyleclayton.co.uk/resources/news/forstater-v-cgd-europe-ors-maya-forstater-succeeds-employment-tribunal/>

[31] <http://yogyakartaprinciples.org/>

[32] It was suggested to me that the transgender suicide attempt rate provides indirect evidence for this: 'misgendering' makes trans people feel hopeless and want to self-harm, and this shows that it is a form of 'misrecognition', that trans women *really are* women, and that the denial of this *really is causing* (self-) harm. One recent study on a clinical cohort of trans children found 41.8% suicidal ideation (thoughts about suicide) and 10.1% suicide attempts. It is hard to separate out causes of suicide ideation/attempts given 'affirmation-only' approaches to transgender care, which fail to separate out background issues like family conflict, parental mental illness, separation from important figures, sexual abuse, and bullying; and comorbid mental health conditions like anxiety, depression, behavioural disorders, and autism (Kozlowska et al. 2021). See also fn. 19.

Stephen Darwall uses 'recognition respect' to refer to 'giving appropriate consideration or recognition to', for example, 'the law, someone's feelings, and social institutions with their positions and roles' (Darwall 1977, p. 38). He also defines a narrower concept of *moral* recognition respect: 'some fact or feature is an appropriate object of respect if inappropriate consideration or weighing of that fact or feature would result in behaviour that is morally wrong' (p. 40). Most at issue from Darwall's list is *someone's feelings*: the feelings the trans person has *that* they are a particular sex/gender. If this is a moral matter, then failure to take these feelings into account would result in behaviour that is morally wrong.

This gives us the basic shape of an argument. Transwomen's feelings will be hurt[33] if we deny that they are women. To show recognition respect to a transwoman, we take this into account. If this is also a moral matter, then failing to take these feelings into account will result in behaviour that is morally wrong. Being about identities, which are important to many people, this *is* a moral matter. So denying that transwomen are women is a failure of recognition respect, and is morally wrong.

Does this establish that 'trans women are women', though? It seems to fall short, and establish merely that *we should take transwomen's feelings into account* when we talk about sex/gender, or debate policy or law relevant to sex/gender. These feelings matter, but they are not the only thing that matters. This means we can take them into account and still end up thinking that sex caste is important, that we need some words to refer to it, and that the best words are the ones that are already in widespread use. Recognition respect is not *deference*; trans people's feelings do not set a limit on what categories we can have and what policies we may put in place. So it is possible to deny 'trans women are women' e.g. because we think that's just not what 'woman' means, while still showing recognition respect to transwomen.[34]

The woman-izing argument. Finally, in a discussion of holding responsible, Philip Pettit distinguishes two forms of regulation, one based on deterrence, the other based on development. We can threaten agents with sanctions and punishments as a way of deterring them from doing bad things. But we can also do something aimed at moral development, as parents do with children. Even if a child is not yet fully fit to be held responsible for his actions, we may yet hold the child responsible *in order to* bring about the right kind of development. Pettit

---

[33] This might sound trivializing but is not meant to; I am simply framing the issue in Darwall's terms. 'Transwomen's feelings will be hurt' here is equivalent to something with more gravity, like 'transwomen's deeply-held sense of identity will be hurt'.

[34] A closely related argument is the 'moral equality' argument, which equates denying someone's self-determination of sex/gender with denying his moral equality. Denying that any humans are moral equals with the rest *is* morally bad. But men have traditionally been the ones taken as the standard for moral equality: women are equal *to* men (MacKinnon 1987). So it's hard to see how denying that a male is a woman is denying his moral equality. Moral equality is about being human, not about being a particular sex.

writes, 'by treating the children as if they were fit to be held responsible, the parents may help to induce in them the sort of self-awareness and self-regulation that such fitness requires'. He says 'although the word is not attractive, it has been usefully described as a process of "responsibilization"' (Pettit 2009, p. 95).

What does this have to do with whether transwomen are women? We might make basically the same type of argument. They may not be women *yet*, but by treating them as women, we may make them women. If we think it's a good thing for some males to become women, just as we think it's a good thing for people who are not yet fully fit to be held responsible to become fit to be held responsible, then we should treat those males as though they are women already. A similar analysis might be offered of Bishop Myriel's treatment of Jean Valjean in *Les Miserables* (1862): Valjean was a thief, but the Bishop treated him with dignity, and this was a transformative moment in his life story that made him *become* morally good.[35] There is an empirical question and a moral question in applying this idea to transwomen. Do we want some males to become women? That's the moral question. Does treating a male *as* a woman work to *make* them a woman? That's the empirical question.[36]

Let's take the empirical question first. Transgender[37] author Julia Serano talks in *Whipping Girl* about the shift, during her transition, in how people treated her. She says 'In public, strangers began standing much closer to me. Women seemed to let their guard down around me. Men, for no apparent reason, would smile at me. Everybody spoke to me differently, interacted with me in different ways' (Serano 2016, p. 218). She also comments on the negatives of being treated as a woman, having people comment on her weight, calling her a 'bitch' for standing up for herself, being condescended to, being sexually harassed (p. 223). This gives us some evidence that she is treated *differently* than before. The question is what that differential treatment causes. There is no real evidence about this. We do not have studies on whether transwomen are 'more like female people' across a range of social traits in which there are average sex differences, and on whether they are less like female people at the start of transition and more like female people later in transition. So it is impossible to answer the question of whether being treated as a woman makes one a woman. (Note that I have translated 'makes you a

---

[35] I owe this point to Miranda Fricker, who made it in a lecture at the Australian National University in 2018.
[36] I'm focusing on what social treatment does, but we could also ask this question from the other direction, about what the repeated *doing* of something does. Aristotle talked about the achievement of excellence coming through the repeated doing of a task; could 'woman'-ing be like that? Again, there would be a moral question and an empirical question. Is 'woman'-ing an accomplishment or achievement that can only be earned by doing? And is the current form of the 'doing' of it, by 'living as a woman', a way of accomplishing or achieving it?
[37] The word 'transsexual' is usually reserved for people who have had sex reassignment surgery, but Serano both uses it (the subtitle of her book being 'a transsexual woman on sexism and the scapegoating of femininity') *and* writes that she has not had sex reassignment surgery (Serano 2016, p. 221).

woman' into 'makes you like a female person', because there's no way to make sense of what 'makes you a woman' means otherwise).[38]

What about the moral question? There are some people who have exaggerated ideas about the innate goodness of women, or who fantasize about matriarchal utopias in which everyone (male and female) is a woman. On views like those, the more men who become women, the better. The objection to accepting some men as women, at least for all purposes, is that this compromises important feminist projects. Still, if treating men as women *makes them women,* then—eventually—at least some part of this concern will disappear. Then the problem at least reduces in size: perhaps there will be a compromise of some important feminist projects in the short term, but depending on just how short the short-term is, and just how many men are transitioning, maybe on balance we should go ahead. (The problem of creating an *ad hoc* class, and therefore disrupting the possibility of a political movement in its name, will remain). But the greater the numbers, and the longer the 'woman-izing' takes, the less likely it is to be true that on balance we should go ahead.

Without the relevant empirical evidence, it is impossible to declare this argument successful.

3.3 Conclusion

Although some have been more promising than others, ultimately none of these arguments for 'trans women are women' have turned out to be successful. Thus, *either* there is some extremely promising argument yet to be discovered, despite years of impassioned activism both inside and outside the academy; *or*, there is no such argument to be found, and 'trans women are women' is, after all, false.

References

Atkinson, Ti-Grace. 'Strategy and tactics: A presentation of political lesbianism' in *Amazon Odyssey* (New York: Links Books, [1971] 1974), pp. 135–89.

Bach, Theodore. 'Gender is a natural kind with a historical essence', *Ethics* 122/2 (2012), pp. 231–72.

---

[38] An alternative to thinking that treating a male person like a woman (whatever that means) makes them a woman is to think that using the word 'woman' for a male person changes the meaning of the word so that it eventually becomes true that they are a woman. This is different to the responsibilizing argument, because that was about causing people to have a moral trait by treating them as if they already had it, whereas this verbal version would be like changing what it meant to be 'responsible' to include not being responsible, by using the word 'responsible' for people who weren't (and not expecting them to change).

Balsamo, Michael, and Sisak, Michael. 'AP investigation: Women's prison fostered culture of abuse', *AP News*, 7th February 2022. Online at <https://apnews.com/article/coronavirus-pandemic-health-california-united-states-prisons-00a711766f5f3d2bd3fe6402af1e0ff8>

Barreto, Manuela, and Ellemers, Naomi. 'The perils of political correctness: Men's and women's responses to old-fashioned and modern sexist views', *Social Psychology Quarterly* 68/1 (2005), pp. 75–88.

Beauvoir, Simone de. 'The girl', in *The Second Sex* (1949), Volume II, Part 1, Chapter 2, pp. 352–93.

Bettcher, Talia Mae. 'Trans feminism: Recent philosophical developments', *Philosophical Studies* 12/11 (2017), pp. 1–11.

Bettcher, Talia Mae. 'Evil deceivers and make-believers: On transphobic violence and the politics of illusion', *Hypatia* 22/3 (2007), pp. 43–65.

Bettcher, Talia Mae. 'Trans identities and first-person authority', in Laurie Shrage (Ed.) *You've Changed: Sex Reassignment and Personal Identity* (Oxford: Oxford University Press, 2009).

Biggs, Michael. 'Attempted suicide by American LGBT adolescents', *4thWaveNow*, 23rd October 2018.

Biggs, Michael. 'The 41% trans suicide attempt rate: A tale of flawed data and lazy journalists', *4thWaveNow*, 3rd August 2015.

Brownmiller, Susan. *In Our Time: Memoir of a Revolution* (New York: Dial Press, 1990).

Cameron, Deborah. 'What is feminism?' in *Feminism: A Brief Introduction to the Ideas, Debates, & Politics of the Movement* (Chicago: University of Chicago Press, 2019), pp. 1–12.

Long Chu, Andrea. *Females* (New York: Verso Books, 2019).

Cox, Karen. 'Most women in prison are victims of domestic violence. That's nothing new', *Time*, 2nd October 2017. Online at <https://time.com/4960309/domestic-violence-women-prison-history/>

Criado-Perez, Caroline. *Invisible Women* (London: Chatto & Windus, 2019).

Daly, Mary. *Gyn/Ecology* (Boston: Beacon Press, 1978).

Daly, Mary. *Webster's First New Intergalactic Wickedary of the English Language* (Boston: Beacon Press, 1987).

Darwall, Stephen. 'Two Kinds of Respect', *Ethics* 88/1 (1977), pp. 36–49.

Dembroff, Robin. 'Real talk on the metaphysics of gender', in Bianka Takaoka and Kate Manne (Eds.) *Philosophical Topics*, Special Issue on 'Gendered oppression and its intersections', 46/2 (2018), pp. 21–50.

Feng, Lydia. 'Australian study finds risk of sexual assault and violence significantly higher for trans women of colour', *ABC News*, 26th June 2020.

Fricker, Miranda. *Epistemic Injustice* (Oxford: Oxford University Press, 2007).

George, B. R., and Briggs, R. A. 'Science fiction fouble feature: Trans liberation on Twin Earth', manuscript, as at 25th march 2019.

Gheaus, Anca. 'Feminism without "gender identity"', *Politics, Philosophy & Economics* (2022) [online first].

Haslanger, Sally. 'Why I don't believe in patriarchy: Comments on Kate Manne's *Down Girl*', *Philosophy and Phenomenological Research* 101/1 (2020), pp. 220–9.

Hauskeller, Michael, and Lawford-Smith, Holly. 'Gender', in Michael Hauskeller (Ed.) *The Things That Really Matter: Philosophical Conversations on the Cornerstones of Life* (London: UCL Press, 2022), Chapter 4.

Hungerford, Elizabeth. 'Sex and transgender status in American employment law— the Bostock case', *Woman's Place UK*, 2nd July 2020.

Jenkins, Katharine. 'Amelioration and inclusion: Gender identity and the concept of Woman*', *Ethics* 126 (2016), pp. 394–421.

Joyce, Helen. *Trans: When Ideology Meets Reality* (London: Oneworld, 2021).

Kay, Barbara. 'Barbara Kay: The complicated truth about transwomen in women's prisons', *National Post*, 21st June 2021. Online at <https://nationalpost.com/opinion/barbara-kay-the-complicated-truth-about-transwomen-in-womens-prisons>

King, Tania, Shields, Marissa, Sojo, Victor, Daraganova, Galina, Currier, Dianne, O'Neil, Adrienne, King, Kylie, and Milner, Allison. 'Expressions of masculinity and associations with suicidal ideation among young males' *BMC Psychiatry* 20/288 (2020), pp. 1–10.

Kozlowska, Kasia, McClure, Georgia, Chudleigh, Catherine, Maguire, Ann, Gessler, Danielle, Scher, Stephen, and Ambler, Geoffrey. 'Australian children and adolescents with gender dysphoria: Clinical presentations and challenges experienced by a multidisciplinary team and gender service', *Human Systems: Therapy, Culture and Attachments* (2021), pp. 1–26 [early view].

Lawford-Smith, Holly, and Phelan, Kate. 'The metaphysics of intersectionality revisited', *Journal of Political Philosophy* 30 (2022), pp. 166–87.

Lawford-Smith, Holly. *Gender-Critical Feminism* (Oxford: Oxford University Press, 2022).

Lawrence, Anne. *Men Trapped in Men's Bodies* (New York: Springer, 2013).

Lee White, Lauren. 'The California jail where women say guards and medics preyed on them', *The Guardian*, 2nd May 2019. Online at <https://www.theguardian.com/lifeandstyle/2019/may/02/california-prison-women-say-they-are-preyed-on-by-guards-and-staff>

MacKinnon, Catharine. 'Feminism, Marxism, method, and the state: An agenda for theory', *Signs* 7/3 (1982), pp. 515–44.

MacKinnon, Catharine. 'Difference and dominance', in *Feminism Unmodified* (Massachusetts: Harvard University Press, 1987), pp. 32–45.

Mallon, Ron. '"Race": Normative, not metaphysical or semantic', *Ethics* 116/3 (2006), pp. 525–51.

McKinnon, Rachel. 'The epistemology of propaganda', *Philosophy and Phenomenological Research* XCVI/2 (2018), pp. 483–9.

McKinnon, Rachel. 'I won a World Championship. Some people aren't happy', *The New York Times*, 5th December 2019.

Mikkelson, David. 'The King of Denmark Wore a Yellow Star', <https://www.snopes.com/fact-check/a-star-is-borne/>, 5th July 2000.

Mikkola, Mari. *The Wrong of Injustice: Dehumanization and Its Role in Feminist Philosophy* (Oxford: Oxford University Press, 2016).

Pettit, Philip. 'Responsibility incorporated', *Rechtsfilosofie & Rechtstheorie* 38/2 (2009), pp. 90–117.

Reilly, Wilfred. 'Are we in the midst of a transgender murder epidemic?' *Quillette* 7th December 2019.

Sankaran, Kirun. 'What's new in the new ideology critique?' *Philosophical Studies* 177/5 (2020), pp. 1441–62.

Saul, Jennifer. 'Why the words we use matter when describing anti-trans activists', *The Conversation* 6th March 2020.

Serano, Julia. *Whipping Girl* (Berkeley: Seal Press, [2007] 2016).

Stock, Kathleen. *Material Girls: Why Reality Matters for Feminism* (London: Fleet, 2021).

Stock, Kathleen. 'Blackface is evil—why isn't drag?' *Standpoint Magazine*, 23rd October 2019. Online at <https://standpointmag.co.uk/blackface-is-evil-why-isnt-drag/>

Stoljar, Natalie. 'Essence, identity, and the concept of woman', *Philosophical Topics* 23/2 (Fall 1995), pp. 261–93.

Swim, Janet, Aikin, Kathryn, Hall, Wayne, and Hunter, Barbara. 'Sexism and racism: Old-fashioned and modern prejudices', *Journal of Personality and Social Psychology* 68/2 (1995), pp. 199–214.

Toomey, Russell, Syvertsen, Amy, and Shramko, Maura. 'Transgender adolescent suicide behaviour', *Pediatrics* 142/4 (2018).

II
POLICY

4
Women-Only Spaces and the Right to Exclude

4.1 'Sex' in the law

In August 2019, a bill was passed in Victoria, Australia, making it possible for people to change their official record of sex in the birth register by making a statutory declaration that they believe their sex to be as nominated. From May 2020, any person observed male at birth was able to change their legal sex to 'female', and any person observed female at birth was able to change their legal sex to 'male'. Similar bills have been considered in other countries (most prominently the UK), and have already passed into law in other states of Australia (Tasmania) and in other countries (Ireland, Malta, Norway, Argentina, Portugal, and others).[1]

Such bills have implications for access to single-sex spaces, services, and provisions (see e.g. Gilligan 2019; Alves 2018; Patrick 2016; Murphy 2018). If any biologically male person can change their legal sex to female, what implications does this have for women's—in this chapter I'm using 'female' and 'woman' interchangeably—sports, women's scholarships, girls' schools, women's rape and domestic violence shelters, female prisons, and more? There are rising numbers of trans people, so this is no longer an issue of tiny numbers of people needing to be accommodated within existing legal and social categories (which it was in the 1960s when the conflicts between radical feminists and transwomen first gained some prominence; see Goldberg 2014).[2] Most transwomen go through a male puberty (which is relevant to women's sports) and increasing numbers are choosing not to have sex reassignment surgery (which is relevant to spaces involving full or partial nudity).[3]

---

[1] The earliest change was Argentina in 2012, followed by Ireland and Malta in 2015, Norway in 2016, and Portugal in 2018. So there hasn't been a lot of time, in most cases, to assess the social and legal implications of these changes (Greaves and Hudson 2018). For a survey of law relating to legal sex, see Grenfell and Hewitt 2012.

[2] For changes in both the numbers and the categories being identified into, see Fair Play For Women 2018; for discussion of the rise in young girls transitioning to live as boys—which has increased 4,400% in less than eight years—see Rayner 2018.

[3] The only transwomen who don't go through a male puberty are those who had childhood gender dysphoria and were taken to a gender clinic that prescribed puberty-blockers. This will be a relatively small proportion of transwomen simply because there is great variety in the age at which trans identification begins (or is admitted in a way that could lead to medical interventions). Some transwomen

It is common for media and political debate to present the stakeholders in the legal change as being trans groups only. But there are obviously (at least) two stakeholder groups: the biological males who wish to acquire the legal sex 'female', and those who are as a matter of biological fact female. Legal recognition of a new category, like 'nonbinary', is a different matter from legal recognition as a member of an already existing category.[4] The first need involve no one but the members of the new category while the second invariably involves those already in the category. It is a principle of liberal democracy that people have a say in matters that affect them. Changing the definition of legal sex in a way that affects access to single-sex services, spaces, and provisions will obviously affect women.

Some would respond to this by pointing to the way that transwomen are marginalized. But marginalization cannot function as a trump here, because women are also marginalized, which is one reason why women-only spaces, services, and provisions exist. It needs to be worked out what interests women-only spaces serve, and whether we have adequate reason to maintain them as women-only, *even given* facts about transwomen's marginalization. The central question of the chapter is: do women have the right to exclude transwomen from women-only spaces?[5] If they do, the conflation of sex and gender identity in law should be resisted.

---

transition as teenagers or young adults, and some later in life. In a recent article for *The Conversation*, psychologist Jae Puckett reports on a survey he and co-authors ran, which found that 'overall, trans women reported later ages of starting to live in their affirmed gender and receiving gender-affirming medical care relative to the other gender groups. Trans women were, on average, around 31 when living in their affirmed gender all of the time' (Puckett 2021; see also Puckett et al. 2022). A 2015 survey of 27,715 trans people in the United States, 33% of whose respondents were transwomen, reported that 12% of the transwomen had vaginoplasty or labiaplasty (James et al. 2016, pp. 45 and 102). That means 88% had not, putting transwomen without sex reassignment surgery in the great majority of transwomen.

[4] An alternative to either (allowing change of legal sex, or creating new legal categories in the vicinity of sex/gender), is to add 'gender identity' or 'gender expression' as a protected attribute to anti-discrimination law. Gender identity ideology includes the idea of universal gender identity, meaning that everyone has a gender identity. One way to explain what it means to be trans given this assumption is that non-trans people's gender identities are 'congruent' with their sex, while trans people's gender identities are 'incongruent'. (For criticism of the understanding of transness in terms of 'incongruence' see Vincent and Jane, forthcoming. For the reasons they give, a better term compatible with the assumption of universal gender identity would be 'typical' and 'atypical', which is purely descriptive). But it is difficult to make universal gender identity coherent. Gender identities are mental states, which not every woman has the capacity to have (e.g. women in vegetative states; see discussion in Barnes 2020). Many women expressly reject the idea that they have any identification with or affinity for womanhood or femininity, saying they simply are female. In these cases it is odd to simply insist that such people have 'woman' gender identities, just because they *don't have* 'man' or 'nonbinary' gender identities. The motivation for saying that everyone has a gender identity is clearly to normalise gender identity, like insisting that everyone has a sexual orientation. But when you present heterosexual people with a definition of heterosexuality (attraction to the opposite sex), they will agree that this describes them. Many women do not agree that they have 'woman' gender identities, or any gender identity at all. So while the motivation is understandable, it would be more coherent to simply say that *some people* (namely trans people) have gender identities; that having a gender identity at all is what makes you trans. However, I acknowledge that the ship may have sailed on this conceptual point.

[5] Another way to put this, which shifts the burden of proof, is 'do women have an obligation to include transwomen in women-only spaces?' On this framing, the presumption is with exclusion, and

In Section 4.2 I'll argue that biological sex matters politically, and should be protected legally—at least until such a time as there is no longer sex discrimination. In Section 4.3 I'll turn to the rationales for women-only spaces, arguing that there are eight independent rationales that together overdetermine the moral justification for maintaining particular spaces as women-only. I address a package of spaces, including prisons, changing rooms, fitting rooms, bathrooms, shelters, rape and domestic violence refuges, gyms, spas, sports, schools, accommodations, shortlists, prizes, quotas, political groups, clubs, events, festivals, and language. I do this instead of taking each space in turn, for two reasons. The first is that these spaces have something in common, namely, that they were established in response to women's marginalization in male-dominated societies; the second is that women themselves have demanded—and in many cases themselves established—these spaces, services, and provisions as a way to advance their own political interests. For example, as women entered the workforce and faced harassment from men in men's facilities, they pushed for women's bathrooms (Burlette-Carter 2018); women in the second-wave of feminism established, funded, and volunteered at women's refuges and shelters (Jeffreys 2018, pp. 57–60). In Section 4.4 I turn to the objection that I've obtained my conclusion through linguistic sleight of hand, and answer it by saying that choices about naming don't affect the underlying questions about the basis for inclusion or exclusion.

The arguments of this paper together make a strong case against self-identification as the basis for legal sex.[6] With self-identification, the category of legal sex conflates sex and gender identity, and this makes sex-based exclusion difficult (in many cases, illegal) where it should be simple and legal.[7]

---

we're asking about the moral reasons for inclusion. This framing would come with the added benefit of avoiding the language of rights, which is ambiguous between legal, political, and moral claims. But because there's such unreflective social support for the idea of 'inclusion' at the moment ('diversity and inclusion' is on the corporate agenda), I think that framing may make the discussion even more difficult.

[6] I don't mean this to refer narrowly to bills that change the requirements for either legal sex or gender recognition (see fn. 7). I also mean to refer to the wider conflation in some countries' law between the two distinct protected attributes of sex and gender identity (in some places 'gender reassignment', or 'transgender status'). The Victorian Equal Opportunity and Human Rights Commission, for example, can appear to believe that having a gender identity 'trumps' having a sex, so that in conflict cases (like a boy with a 'girl' gender identity wanting to go to a non-religious girls' school) gender identity wins (meaning, the boy should be admitted to the girls' school). It is entirely unclear why this should be the case given that there is no formal hierarchy of protected attributes, and given that no other protected attribute is taken to trump any other. (To illustrate how absurd this would be, imagine the Commission dispensing the advice that Jewish schools were permitted to exclude all non-Jewish students, except non-Jewish *black* students). If their reasoning is not that gender identity trumps sex, then it can only be that gender identity *changes* sex, i.e. a male person who identifies as a female *is thereby female*. That is a controversial understanding of sex.

[7] The precise details depend on the state/country. In Victoria, we went straight to changing legal sex. In the United Kingdom, there is a separate process for gender, the Gender Recognition Certificate (GRC). There is also explicit provision for sex-based exclusion in specific cases. Their move to

4.2 Sex matters politically, and should be protected legally

Around the world, women are subject to sex-specific forms of violence, including Female Genital Mutilation (FGM), female infanticide, child marriage, forced marriage, rape, domestic violence, intimate partner strangulation, 'accidental' killing during sex, prostitution, pornography, and forced surrogacy. Women are presented across the media as sexual objects for men's gratification. Women in poorer countries (and poorer parts of rich countries) experience period poverty. The 'default male' assumption in medicine and product design puts female people at greater mortality risk (Criado Perez 2019). Women are under-represented in politics, and in some employment areas, as well as at upper-levels in all employment areas. Women still don't have full reproductive rights in many countries, and are still subject to pregnancy and breastfeeding discrimination in the workplace and in access to public life. Women undertake a disproportionate share of unpaid labour, e.g. in childcare and the running of households.

In international law, the Convention on the Elimination of All Forms of Discrimination against Women (1979) (CEDAW) notes that despite various legal instruments existing to uphold the equality of men and women, 'discrimination against women continues to exist' (CEDAW, p. 1).[8] It is clear from the wording of the Convention that it means 'women' to be understood as synonymous with female sex; for example, 'Bearing in mind the great contribution of women to the welfare of the family and to the development of society, so far not fully recognized, *the social significance of maternity* and the role of both parents in the family and in the upbringing of children, and aware that *the role of women in procreation* should not be a basis for discrimination but that the upbringing of children requires a sharing of responsibility between men and women and society as a whole' (CEDAW, p. 2, my emphasis).

It defines discrimination against women as 'distinction, exclusion or restriction made *on the basis of sex*' which affects the 'enjoyment or exercise *by women*... of human rights and fundamental freedoms' (CEDAW, my emphasis). Article 5 talks about prejudices based on ideas about the inferiority or superiority of either of the sexes, and about stereotyped roles for men and women; Article 6 talks about measures to suppress the traffic of women and the exploitation of women through prostitution; Article 11 talks about prevention of discrimination against women in employment, particularly relating to pregnancy and maternity leave; and Article 12 talks about pregnancy and lactation.

---

self-identification changes eligibility for a GRC, not eligibility to count as legally female. Still, guidance suggests those with a GRC should be treated as the sex they identify with for most purposes.

[8] Some countries believe that CEDAW includes transwomen as women and so include data about transwomen in their reporting. New Zealand is one such country. I have been advised by an International Human Rights Law academic that New Zealand's approach is idiosyncratic.

In Australia specifically, women first got the right to vote in South Australia in 1895. The first women were elected to the House of Representatives and Senate in 1943. It wasn't until 1956 that the Marriage Bar (which prohibited women from continuing to work after marriage), was lifted for women in education. It wasn't until 1961 that women could acquire the contraceptive pill (and even then, only with a husband). Indigenous women didn't get the right to vote in Federal elections until 1962. The Marriage Bar for women working in the Commonwealth Public Service was only lifted in 1966. The first abortion rights came in 1966.

In 1972, Australian women were granted the right to equal pay. In 1974, the minimum wage was extended to female workers. In 1975, the first women's refuges received government funding. In 1975, women became able to file for no-fault divorce. Rape in marriage was outlawed in South Australia in 1976. In 1977 the Victorian Equal Opportunity Act outlawed discrimination on the grounds of gender or marital status. In 1979 women who had been employed for twelve months or more became entitled to fifty-two weeks of unpaid maternity leave. Sexual harassment was outlawed by an amendment to the Victorian Equal Opportunity Act in 1995. The first female Prime Minister was elected in 2010.[9]

All of this is fairly recent history. There are Australian women alive today who will have been forced to give up their jobs for marriage, who will have had unwanted pregnancies, who will have been paid less than a man for doing the same work, who will have been prevented from voting in elections that affected them, who had no legal recourse when forced into sex within their marriages. *Most* Australian women spent most of their lives without seeing a woman occupy the highest political office in the country. Older Australian women lived through a time when they were socially subordinated to men (as wives and homemakers lacking in social and political rights) and excluded from work, from political life, from public life, and from sport.

This sex-based marginalization has not been fully mitigated, and is not yet over. Australia has not achieved women's liberation. The same can be said of most, if not all, other countries. Some of the ways that we can mitigate women's historical exclusion and ongoing underrepresentation are by maintaining single-sex spaces, services, and provisions. For example, women are underrepresented in politics, and we can partly remedy this by having women-only shortlists; women have been historically excluded from sport in a way that has long-lasting effects, and we can remedy that by having women's sports, and pushing for them to be equally funded and publicized. Until such a time as sex doesn't make such a difference to how people's lives go, it should be protected legally. Women-only spaces, services, and provisions are part of this protection.

---

[9] All of the facts in this paragraph and the last come from the 'Gender Equality Milestones' page of the Victorian Women's Trust. Online at <https://www.vwt.org.au/gender-equality-timeline-australia/>, accessed 30th June 2019.

4.3 Moral rationales for women-only spaces

Using the terminology of 'women-only spaces' makes it seem like there's one specific kind of space that serves one specific purpose. But that couldn't be further from the truth. The term is used to refer to a diverse range of things, some of which aren't really 'spaces' at all in any strict sense.[10] When radical and gender-critical feminists talk about the importance of keeping women-only spaces *women-only*, they might be referring to any or all of:

- Prisons
- Changing rooms
- Fitting rooms
- Bathrooms
- Shelters
- Rape and domestic violence refuges
- Gyms
- Spas
- Sports
- Schools
- Accommodations
- Shortlists
- Prizes
- Quotas
- Political groups
- Clubs
- Events
- Festivals
- Language[11]

Sheila Jeffreys writes in *The Lesbian Revolution* about the various kinds of women-only spaces available to the women of the second-wave of feminism, and the role they played in their feminist organizing. These include feminist bookstores (Jeffreys 2018, pp. 39–41), women's squats (pp. 42–4), women's discos (pp. 47–8), women's and lesbian theatre (pp. 48–50), and feminist conferences (p. 50). But the

---

[10] Jane Clare Jones makes a conceptual distinction between physical spaces (e.g. toilets, changing rooms), virtual/social spaces (e.g. shortlists, participation in feminism), and conceptual spaces (e.g. the definition of 'woman'), which I find helpful (Jones 2019).

[11] I've included language as a conceptual space, for instance 'lesbian', 'female', 'woman', 'mother'. Women have an interest not only in sharing certain physical spaces with other women, but in having the capacity to label themselves together with other women (given that they share biological interests e.g. when it comes to healthcare, political interests, reproductive rights). If gender identity activists force a revision of the term 'lesbian' then female homosexuals lose this capacity, and the same point might be made about the other sex-specific terms.

moral justification for *having* these spaces seems to have been more or less taken as obvious by feminists.[12] My project here is to articulate those underlying justifications.

There are at least eight distinct moral rationales for women-only spaces, or so I suggest, and elaborate upon below. These are: i. safety; ii. privacy/dignity/comfort; iii. justice/fairness; iv. respite; v. likelihood of shared bodily experience; vi. intimate association; vii. self-determination; and viii. intent of the creators.[13] The first two are regularly suggested by radical and gender-critical feminists in public discussions over spaces like prisons, bathrooms, changing rooms, fitting rooms, bathrooms, and toilets. The others are less commonly invoked (although fairness looms large in the discussion about transwomen competing in women's sporting categories), but are no less important. I take each of these in turn.

4.3.1 Safety

Women have an interest in being safe, from physical assault and sexual violence. We know that the risk of physical assault and sexual violence is highest for women in their own homes, and from men they know; not from men in public spaces. The risk of the latter is not zero, however, and this is worth emphasizsing because of the way that fact is often used to dismiss women's concerns about safety in public spaces. One study of 849 female patients reporting to a sexual assault clinic over a 40-month period found that the perpetrator was known to the victim in 72% of cases, a stranger in 28% of cases (Jones et al. 2004, p. 454). Assaults by unknown perpetrators happened in the victim's home in 43% of the cases, outdoors in 23% of cases (p. 456). The risk also goes up as the egregiousness of the offence goes down: stranger rape is fairly rare, while voyeurism is less so. What risk should we accept? Given the harms that are at stake, and their long-lasting effects, it seems that we're justified in deploying a precautionary approach: exclude from women-only spaces involving physical vulnerability *all* males, unless and until there is evidence establishing that a particular subgroup of males are no more of a threat to women than other women are.

The safety rationale seems to justify female-only prisons—there have already been problems of sexual assault from housing transwomen in the female estate in the UK and the USA,[14] not to mention that the incentives for heterosexual males

---

[12] Jeffreys gives some justifications elsewhere, in a paper about women's toilets. See discussion in Chapter 6.
[13] There is more about the first three rationales in Chapter 5.
[14] On the well-known case of transgender prisoner Karen White in the UK see e.g. Parveen (2018) and *The Guardian* (2019a). For the reporting of a lawsuit alleging rape by a transgender inmate of a female inmate in an Illinois prison, see Masterson (2020).

to transition and gain access to women would be significant.[15] (Threats to safety posed by transwomen themselves should be separated from threats to safety posed by men because of loopholes created by trans-inclusive law and policy. Both are relevant). Data from the UK in 2018 showed that women were at higher risk of sexual assault in unisex changing rooms, with 90% of complaints about sexual assault, voyeurism, and harassment coming from unisex facilities (Hosie 2018). The extent to which these incidents are relevant depends on whether this same outcome is likely in only *partially* unisex rather than fully unisex changing rooms and bathrooms—including only transwomen rather than all males. There is no reason to think it isn't. There have been assaults in women's bathrooms (Corbishley 2019) and incidents in women's spas (Ngo 2021) involving transwomen. Even if the experience of childhood gender dysphoria can be expected to have some inhibiting effect on male socialization (the socialization of males into masculinity), not all transwomen experienced childhood gender dysphoria. Transwomen whose identifications as women have political motivations (Butler 1990; Stone 1987), social causes,[16] or are explained by salient comorbidities,[17] are on a par with any other biologically male person when it comes to the likely effects of male socialization. Statistically, the risk will be lower simply because it's *fewer* males using the spaces, but the difference between including transwomen and including all males is quantitative not qualitative.

In any spaces where women are vulnerable—so those involving full or partial nudity, or intimate physical contact, or sleeping—there is a precautionary safety rationale for exclusion. Of the spaces in our list, the safety rationale justifies retaining as women-only: prisons, changing rooms, fitting rooms, bathrooms, shelters, rape and domestic violence refuges, gyms, spas, sports, (boarding) schools, and accommodations (shelters, refuges, and boarding schools because they involve accommodations; gyms, spas, and sports because they involve toilets, showers, and locker rooms).

4.3.2 Privacy/dignity/comfort

Women have an interest in privacy, dignity, and comfort, which requires protection from voyeurism (a risk in mixed-sex spaces involving full or partial nudity) and the male gaze, and in some cases, the mere presence of male people

---

[15] See also Chapter 3, fn. 10.
[16] For discussion of social contagion around trans identification, see Littman (2018); Schrier (2020); Marchiano (2017).
[17] See e.g. discussion in Kozlowska et al. (2021), who mention as alternative explanations for a person's distress about their gender: anxiety, depression, behavioural disorders, and autism; as well as histories of family conflict, parental mental illness, separation from important figures, bullying, and maltreatment (emotional abuse, physical abuse, sexual abuse, or exposure to domestic violence).

(particularly important for sexual and domestic assault survivors and some religious women).[18]

Women don't want to be leered at, or sexually objectified, or filmed, or photographed, when they're naked or partly naked. Many women want to be served by people of the same sex in intimate situations, like for some medical examinations, or for airport body searches. Medical examinations made the news in 2017 when a woman in the UK went to the NHS for a smear test, and despite having requested a female doctor, was assigned to a transwoman nurse (Paterson 2017). A hospital in the UK in 2022 cancelled a woman's life-saving surgery because she requested female-only aftercare and the hospital employed a transwoman nurse. The hospital said 'we do not share your beliefs and are not able to adhere to your requests and we have therefore decided that we will not proceed with your surgery' (Hatchet 2022).

Some trauma survivors feel in danger around men, particularly in intimate situations, and more relaxed and comfortable around women only. This fear for safety and inability to relax around men can be coded as a comfort-based reason to justify having some female-only spaces, with shelters and refuges being of particular importance (see also discussion of respite below). In 2018 Kristi Hanna filed a Human Rights suit against the Jean Tweed Centre—a women's shelter in Toronto—after she was forced to share a room with a transwoman (Chart 2018).

Of the spaces in our list, the privacy/dignity/comfort rationale justifies retaining as women-only: prisons, changing rooms, fitting rooms, bathrooms, shelters, rape and domestic violence refuges, gyms, spas, sports (because of toilets, showers, and locker rooms), schools (for the same reasons as sports), and accommodations.[19]

4.3.3 Justice/fairness

Women also have an interest in justice and fairness, justice understood as the mitigation of historical exclusion, and fairness understood as fair terms of competition. One way to mitigate historical exclusion is to have categories that guarantee women's representation in male-dominated public arenas or employment areas, for example in politics (women-only political party shortlists, such as exist in the UK), or in STEM (women-only hiring shortlists), or in recognition of

---

[18] Privacy has recently become an issue in US high schools, with the question being whether girls have a right to 'visual privacy', i.e. not being seen naked by a person of the opposite sex. See discussion in Gerstmann (2019).

[19] In the case of both sports and schools, it would clearly be possible to provide for women's privacy, dignity, and comfort by providing sex-separated toilets, showers, and locker rooms. If this were the only rationale justifying women-only sports or schools, then that might seem the better solution. But I will argue that it's not the only rationale in either case.

overlooked accomplishments in the arts (women's fiction writing prizes). Justice may rationalize female-only schools, if evidence can be provided that these result in better educational outcomes for girls. It also rationalizes the language necessary for women to self-refer and act politically to advance their own interests, which is why the appropriation of the terms 'woman', 'female', and 'lesbian' by gender identity activists have been so fiercely contested by gender-critical feminists.

Fairness requires e.g. sporting categories in which women compete against each other, rather than against male people (give that the latter have a significant physical advantage).[20] Note that even if a case can be made for some male people competing on fair terms with women—e.g. a transwoman who took puberty-blockers so did not go through a male puberty, and so does not have a body that benefited from the historical effects of testosterone—that case will not extend to males who did go through a male puberty.

The justice/fairness rationale justifies keeping as women-only: sports, schools, shortlists, prizes, quotas, and language.

4.3.4 Respite

Women also have an interest in respite. By 'respite', I mean a break from male attitudes, expectations, and behaviours. Women and men are socialized very differently in most societies, and this leads to differences in the average behaviour of women and men, which colours their interactions.[21] Women can experience men as both imposing and exhausting. Men take up more physical space; in conversations they interrupt more, explain things to women that women know more about, and take up more time (my philosopher-readers will have firsthand experience of this from running philosophy tutorials); they may look at or speak to women in sexualized ways; they may make clear in their attitudes, comments, or behaviours that they have certain expectations about how women ought to present themselves, or speak, or act.

All of this can (obviously) be tiresome for women to deal with, and they will be forced to deal with it in mixed-sex spaces. Women-only spaces can provide an important respite from this. Many university campuses have women's rooms for roughly this reason. If transwomen will bring some or all of these male-typical

---

[20] Knox et al. (2019); Roberts et al. (2021); Harper et al. (2021); Hilton and Lundberg (2021). It might be possible to organize some sports such that there are categories providing fair competition that are not delineated by sex. That would mean taking seriously all the average physical differences between men and women that are relevant to sporting performance (bone size and density, myonuclei, testosterone, muscle mass, height, grip strength, speed, Q-angle...) and figuring out a way to separate people into leagues on the basis of these (see discussion in Knox et al. 2019).

[21] I leave open whether there are other explanations of difference in average behaviour that are either non-social or only partly social.

attitudes, expectations, and behaviours into these spaces, then that is a *prima facie* reason to exclude transwomen from those spaces (Finlayson et al. 2019 argue that transwomen are likely to have rejected their male socialization, and so would presumably think they will not bring such attitudes into women's spaces. They do not provide any argument for why that rejection is likely to have been comprehensive. But if they are right, that would defeat this *prima facie* reason). Note that this rationale does not depend on it being the case that a particular male person *would in fact* bring male-socialized behaviours into a space. It's enough that women have to manage this possibility when men are around. Women-only spaces provide respite not just from certain sorts of behaviours, but from having to make contingency plans about what to do in light of certain sorts of behaviours—from being on guard.

There's also a much more serious kind of respite, which applies to women who have experienced severe or sustained male violence (rape, assault, domestic violence, intimate partner strangulation, etc.). For some women, it's difficult or impossible to feel fully comfortable around male people, and women-only spaces provide an important place to escape such discomfort (in this respect, the 'respite' rationale partly overlaps the 'privacy/dignity/comfort' rationale, on the point of comfort).

This rationale justifies shelters and refuges (at the extremes; respite from male violence), and things like campus women's rooms, or women's political groups or clubs, events for women such as those during university orientation weeks or as part of corporate events, festivals, dance-parties, etc.

4.3.5 High likelihood of shared bodily experience

There is also an interest that women have in a high likelihood of shared bodily experience in particular spaces. Prisons, changing rooms, bathrooms, shelters, and refuges may all involve shared facilities where there is full or partial nudity. Women are embodied in a particular way, which they have in common with each other and which they don't have in common with men. In bathrooms in particular, women may deal with a range of embodied experiences ranging from annoying through embarrassing through distressing (for example, not having tampons when you need them; bleeding through underwear and clothing while menstruating and attempting to deal with the mess; going through a miscarriage). There's something comforting and reassuring about being in a space with other people who are very likely to understand those experiences, and have the resources to help when necessary (e.g. to give tampons, relate over mess, provide comfort for distress). Obviously *not all women* will be interested in providing support and *not all women* will need it, but for those who are and do, having spaces where there is a high likelihood of shared experience is enormously important. This rationalizes keeping as women-only prisons, changing rooms, bathrooms, shelters, and rape and domestic violence refuges.

4.3.6 Intimate association

This rationale is borrowed from the literature on the ethics of immigration. In the debate over what right states have to exclude would-be migrants, Christopher Wellman has argued in defence of the right to exclude by appealing first to the importance of self-determination, and second to the connection between self-determination and freedom of association (Wellman 2008). If one is free to associate then one is also free to disassociate; so from self-determination we get the right to exclude. Wellman's initial argument depended on an analogy with marriage. He argued that it wouldn't matter how important it was to a potential suitor that he be accepted as a partner, the person faced with the option of accepting him has an absolute right to refuse. And then he argued that this is true of the state:

> ...just as an individual has a right to determine who (if anyone) he or she would like to marry, a group of fellow-citizens has a right to determine whom (if anyone) it would like to invite into its political community. And just as an individual's freedom of association entitles one to remain single, a state's freedom of association entitles it to exclude all foreigners from its political community (Wellman 2008, pp. 110–11).

He thinks the same is true of religious self-determination: '[i]f I elect to explore my religious nature in community with others, I have no duty to do so with anyone in particular, and I have no right to force others to allow me to join them in worship' (p. 110).

Wellman considers an objection that would block the generalization from marriages and religious association to citizenship, namely that 'the intimacy of marriage makes freedom of association immeasurably more important in the marital context than in the political realm. After all, in the vast majority of cases, fellow citizens will never even meet one another' (p. 113). Perhaps we should respect freedom of association in groups where there are intimate attachments, but not otherwise. Wellman responds to this by granting that freedom of association is more important in intimate associations, but says that it doesn't follow that it's *un*important in other kinds of associations. It's also less important when it comes to religious association, but still important (p. 113).

We can either side with Wellman, and think that all kinds of associations—intimate, expressive, and political—have a right to exclude, or we can side with the objection he entertains, and think that there is a right to exclude only in intimate and expressive associations.[22] If we do the latter, groups of women would have an absolute right to exclude *only* if they counted as intimate or expressive associations. The question becomes, what kind of association do women have?

The groups of women who make up political groups, e.g. local radical feminist activist groups, might be intimate associations if the women in them are friends; or they might be expressive associations. The groups of women who attend women's marches, and other kinds of women's events and festivals, likely count as expressive associations. Groups of women will have common or at least loosely-aligned political goals, and will interact on a semi-regular basis. The groups of women who use women-only prisons, changing rooms, bathrooms, toilets, fitting rooms, shelters, refuges, gyms, saunas, spas, or sports, don't seem to be intimate associations—at least not in the technical sense that romantic relationships and friendships are; of course there's intimacy in the sense of close proximity and full or partial undress. So there's no quick path to an absolute right to exclude there.

Those groups don't seem to be expressive or political associations either, at least not in the sense that the state is a political association. There are no formal institutions coordinating these women into mutual benefit relationships. It's not clear that *women*, as a class, are any association at all. Rather, they are simply a group of people who have certain interests in common, interests which are served by their being grouped together politically. Women are physically vulnerable to men. Sex-separated prisons protect women from sexual violence by men. Sex-separated bathrooms, toilets, and fitting rooms protect women from sexual violence, voyeurism, and harassment by men, and provide a space where those they interact with are likely to empathize with certain body-related predicaments. Sex-separated shelters and refuges give women safe haven from the class of people, men, from which individuals have caused them harm in the past. And so on.

From thinking about types of association, then, we see that if it's only intimate associations that justify exclusion, then women have an absolute right to exclude only from political groups and clubs where they are likely to have friendships. If there's an absolute right to exclude from expressive associations too, then women have an absolute right to exclude from all political groups, women's marches, and other kinds of women's events and festivals. (I'll assume it's both, but readers who disagree should make the relevant adjustments to my conclusions.)

---

[22] An example of an intimate association, as just mentioned, is a marriage. The parties to an intimate association generally have regular face-to-face contact and relate in ways that are deeply personal to those involved. An example of an expressive association is a church. Members of the same church have something that is important to them in common, and generally interact on a semi-regular basis. Finally, an example of a political association is a state. It's not clear that members have anything in common (although they might), and the scale of the association is usually such as to prevent face-to-face interaction between all members. They may nonetheless be coordinated in some way, including into mutual benefit relationships (we all pay taxes, and we all receive state services).

4.3.7 Self-determination

Women's oppression involves a particular feature: what it means to be a woman has been disproportionately determined—at least historically—by men, and women are still trying to shake that off and decide for themselves what it means to be a woman. Women of the past were determined by men to be decorative objects, to be wives and homemakers, mothers, people who serviced men's needs (think of even the working women being expected to pour the tea). Women have a lot more liberation now, but the effects of being denied a vote, or forced to quit one's job once married, or unable to access an abortion when wanted, and so on, will have long-lasting effects, even if only through social impacts on other women.

Women are particularly badly off when it comes to self-determination as a social group, because they have been other-determined, so they do not even really have the 'self' required to get started in thinking about a form of collective-oriented self-determination. Here's second-wave feminist Kate Millett ([1971] 1977):

> Under patriarchy the female did not herself develop the symbols by which she is described. [...] The image of women as we know it is an image created by men and fashioned to suit their needs (p. 46).

> As the history of patriarchal culture and the representations of herself within all levels of its cultural media, past and present, have a devastating effect upon her self image, she is customarily deprived of any but the most trivial sources of dignity or self-respect (p. 55).

For this reason it's particularly important that women, without men—the 'other' who did all the previous determining—decide what it means to be a woman (if anything), what needs to change about the ways women and men relate to each other, and what feminism should look like going forward. This justifies women having some spaces to be together, e.g. for consciousness-raising about feminism, for talking about shared experiences, for building feminist movements.[23] Given that the *content* of this self-determination is likely to extend to an understanding of what it means to be a woman, a lesbian, a mother, etc., this rationale will also extend to language.

The justification just given was instrumental: it said, women need spaces of their own *in order to* self-determine. But it is also possible to rationalize the creation/maintenance of women-only spaces as an *act of* self-determination. Part of

---

[23] For the case against compelled association on grounds of freedom of thought and expression see Shiffrin (2005); for a consideration of whether women should be considered as a minority group—considering that there are legal protections in many countries protecting minority groups' right to exclude—see Hacker (1951).

what men determined women to be is 'accessible to men', so in creating space in which to be inaccessible, women are *exercising* self-determination. Marilyn Frye puts it like this: 'When women separate (withdraw, break out, regroup, transcend, shove aside, step outside, migrate, say no), we are simultaneously controlling access and defining. We are doubly insubordinate, since neither of these is permitted. And access and definition are fundamental ingredients in the alchemy of power, so we are doubly, and radically, insubordinate' (Frye 1978, p. 38).

Self-determination (and relatedly, freedom of association, and freedom of thought and expression) justifies exclusion directly in spaces where there is the chance to talk and raise consciousness, e.g. in political groups, feminist events, and women's festivals. But it might also justify some, or even the rest of, the spaces *indirectly* too. Self-determination justifies there being 'some' women-only spaces rather than none; it doesn't really matter which these are. But given that the 'some' we have already include those contested in the debate between gender-critical feminists and gender identity activists, we might well think that *those* are the spaces that matter. Unlike other dominated social groups, most women live in intimate relationships with members of the dominating social group (e.g. husbands, fathers, sons) (Beauvoir 1949). This means there are fewer opportunities for developing resistance. Once women have some spaces, whatever they are, they can make them their own, and can co-opt them for political purposes (consider e.g. feminist graffiti on the insides of bathroom stalls) (see also Scott 1992).

The direct version of the self-determination rationale justifies keeping as women-only political groups, clubs, events, festivals, and language. The indirect version justifies *all* of the spaces listed at the start of the chapter.

4.3.8 Intent of the creators

Finally, it's relevant that for at least some women-only spaces—in particular, women's shelters and refuges—women established these themselves. Women funded, volunteered at, and ran these spaces as services *by women for women*. Some of those women have passed on the running of such spaces to the next generation of women, but are still around to watch how their legacies are handled. The fact that other marginalized groups may benefit from access to such spaces does not give them an automatic right to be included; perhaps such groups should do the same work that women during the second wave of feminism did and establish such spaces for themselves.

This rationale applies most clearly to shelters, refuges, clubs, political groups, and events and festivals with a historical lineage. It may also apply in some cases to prizes, scholarships, fellowships, and other kinds of bequests.

I have given eight distinct rationales for a package of women-only spaces, services, and provisions. These rationales are not mutually exclusive. For example, discussion around transwomen's inclusion in women's bathrooms tends to centre around the question of whether the former pose a threat of (sexual) violence to women and therefore compromise women's safety. If safety was the *exclusive* rationale for women-only bathrooms, and it was shown that there is no such threat, then there would seem to be no further justification for women-only bathrooms. But although they get less airtime, other rationales apply to bathrooms too, like privacy/dignity/comfort, respite, and (less obviously) self-determination (which, as discussed above, justifies there being *some* women-only spaces, where it's contingent rather than necessary that bathrooms are among these).[24]

These rationales together overdetermine the moral justification of women's retaining this package of spaces.[25] If including some males in those spaces were not undermining of those rationales, then there would be a reason to *at least start asking* how the relevant interests between the two groups trade off against each other. But including transwomen in women-only spaces is undermining of *all* these rationales. It will be especially so for transwomen who are transitioned in name and pronouns only, or who are recently transitioned, as they cannot have experienced the social treatment as a woman that may take the edge off their male socialization. If any male person willing to declare themselves a woman can become legally a woman (or is already legally a woman in virtue of the way gender identity is protected), and so cannot be excluded from women-only spaces, then: *safety* is undermined (at least to the degree it would be by allowing the same numbers of non-trans men); *privacy/dignity/comfort* is compromised because some women will feel uncomfortable (e.g. trauma survivors in refuges); *justice/fairness* is undermined because women are forced to compete with male-bodied people who have a physical advantage in sports, and because measures implemented to include more women in areas where they are underrepresented are used instead to include even more male people; *likelihood of shared bodily experience* is undermined because the likelihood is affected (the higher the numbers of transwomen using the space, the lower the likelihood); *intimate association* and *expressive association* are compromised because women are compelled to associate with people they may not be interested in associating with; *self-determination* is compromised because the 'other' who has been part of the story of women's being 'other-determined' is given a say in what it means to be a woman; and *intent of the creators* is undermined because the spaces women fought for, *by women for women*, are being given to male people.

---

[24] For a more extensive discussion of bathrooms, see Chapter 6.

[25] For a discussion of rationales for feminist separatism, which justify *some or other* women-only spaces (not necessarily the ones we have and which are under discussion in this chapter) see Phelan and Lawford-Smith (manuscript).

In some cases, there's even a direct contradiction, rather than just an 'undermining'. For example, if 'lesbian' means female homosexual, then it doesn't mean male heterosexual; so including transwomen in lesbian speed-dating events, or other types of events aimed at creating intimate association between lesbians is directly antithetical to what it means to be a lesbian. This issue received public attention when producers of the UK show *First Dates* sent a lesbian on a date with a transwoman (*The Guardian* 2019b). In Australia, lesbian groups have ended up in court, accused of discriminating against males with gender identities by refusing them tickets to lesbian-only (i.e. female same-sex attracted only) dances[26] and lesbian-only festivals.[27]

4.4 Women-only spaces: sex or gender identity?

It is easy enough to anticipate at least one objection from gender identity activists, which would go something like this.

Objection. You've been asking whether *women* have the right to exclude *transwomen* from women-only spaces. But your stipulation that you'll use 'woman' interchangeably with 'female', and your (related) choice to use 'transwoman' (no space) instead of 'trans woman' (space), begs the question. If you'd instead called them 'trans women', and even better if you'd referred to other women as 'non-trans women', it would be clear that you were actually talking about two groups of women, and whether one has the right to exclude the other. And that's actually the right way to pose the question, because *trans women are women!* So your question is: do *non-trans women* have the right to exclude *trans women* from women-only spaces?

This does reframe the question, and in doing so invites the reply that one group of women should not have the right to exclude another group of women from spaces that belong to both of them. Just as straight women wouldn't have the right to exclude lesbian women, or middle-class women wouldn't have the right to exclude working-class women, neither would non-trans women have the right to exclude trans women. Women-only spaces are for women, so no woman should be excluded. (Notice that if you accept 'trans women are women' then you get to position transwomen as subordinate to non-trans women, in virtue of being trans; whereas if you reject 'trans women are women' you get to position

---

[26] O'Keefe v Sappho's Party Inc [2009] SAEOT 50 (24 April 2009). The case was dismissed, but only on the grounds that the dance was judged to be a private rather than a public event. The minority opinion concluded that there was in fact discrimination. The details are online at <http://www8.austlii.edu.au/cgi-bin/viewdoc/au/cases/sa/SAEOT/2009/50.html>

[27] *Al Jazeera* reports that the Victorian Civil and Administrative Appeals Tribunal had granted an exemption to 'Lesfest', a lesbian women's festival, to have only 'female-born lesbians' attend or work at the festival, but the exemption was overturned after a complaint from a transsexual lobby group (Al Jazeera 2003).

transwomen as dominant relative to non-trans women, in virtue of being male. This surely accounts for quite a bit of the disagreement between trans rights activists and gender-critical feminists, because it sends people who agree on the relevance of marginalized-status hierarchies in two different directions.)

The problem with this objection is that it too begs the question. Even if there's some conception of gender (e.g. gender as identity) such that transwomen and women share a gender, and even if it would be best all-things-considered to use the terms 'female' and 'women' to refer to that gender category rather than to sex class, it remains true that some of the people in that class are *male* while others are *female* (in the original biological sense), and that sex differences matter morally and politically, at least at the moment. At best, this objection simply establishes that there's a sex class that might have an entitlement to women-only spaces, and there's a gender (as identity) category that might have an entitlement to women-only spaces, and the composition of these groups is different. Then we'd have to go through and figure out, for each of the women-only spaces in question, whether their justification is on the basis of sex, or gender identity. (Note that this also means dropping the package approach to spaces in favour of a piecemeal approach).

For all the spaces whose justification is safety, privacy/dignity/comfort, fairness, and likelihood of shared experience, the justification is sex class. Women face a risk of violence from male people. There is no evidence that this risk is from male people *except for those with 'woman' gender identities*. Until such a time as there is such evidence, there is no reason for women to make exceptions for that sub-group. (Consider also that it's likely that other sub-groups are exceptions, such as gay males, but that we don't think this means they should have access to women-only spaces). Women are subject to sexual objectification and harassment by male people. Male people—at least, those male people who have gone through male puberty—have a physical advantage over women when it comes to sport. Male people do not have an embodiment in common with female people, and so lack shared embodied experience. So for all these spaces, it is sex class membership, not gender (identity) category membership, that rationalizes inclusion and justifies exclusion.

What about respite, and self-determination? These give a little more latitude for inclusion. *Respite* is premised on a break from male-socialized attitudes, expectations, and behaviours. Again, there's nothing about a male's having a 'woman' gender identity that guarantees that these traits won't be brought into women-only spaces. But consider a transwoman who had severe childhood gender dysphoria which led to the rejection of any male-socialized behaviours over which they had conscious control; transitioned early rather than late in life; and passes as female and has therefore been *treated as* a woman for a significant period of time. It is considerably less likely that such a person would bring male-socialized traits into women's spaces.[28] Similarly, *self-determination* is premised on women being able to decide for themselves what and how they want to be. The whole point is to be able to do this free of males, who have historically played a massive and invasive role in deciding what and how women will be. So where transwomen bring male attitudes, expectations, and behaviours into women-only spaces rationalized by self-determination, they will be particularly damaging. Again, some transwomen can be expected to do this to a greater degree than others. But it remains a problem that they are not a member of the constituency of those who have been other-determined in the way that female people have, so even if they won't make a negative difference to women's self-determination, it still seems to matter that they are given any say at all.

It's not clear that it's really possible to throw off *all* male socialization. At least, doing so would take a lot of work, and it's not clear that transwomen have done that work (or how we could know if they had). So it's not clear that it's justifiable to include any males in such spaces. Unfortunately, the policy on exclusion or inclusion is unlikely to be able to track the nuance of which transwomen are actually likely to bring male-socialized behaviours into women-only spaces. Policies will have to be transwomen-inclusive or transwomen-exclusive. So we have to make a more sophisticated tradeoff. If we were to include *all* transwomen in spaces rationalized by self-determination, how likely is it that women's freedom of thought and expression in self-creating (self-determining *as* women) would be seriously compromised? If we were to exclude *all* transwomen from those spaces, how likely is it that we'd be perpetrating the harms of exclusion (even if these are only harms to the transwoman's feelings, or the small harm of a frustrated desire) against people who would not have compromised the spaces? Because gendered socialization is pervasive and all-encompassing, I think there's a serious risk of compromise to women's self-determination, and so a strong reason to exclude all transwomen from these spaces.

Thus, even if we make a sex/gender (identity) distinction and grant that transwomen might share a gender (identity) with (at least some) women,[29] this doesn't settle in advance that they cannot be excluded from women-only spaces. This question is not settled merely by choices about naming. Almost all women-only spaces are most clearly justified on the basis of sex, not gender identity; so almost all women-only spaces are such that women may exclude transwomen from them. Spaces for respite, like women's rooms on university campuses, may be the only exception to this general rule, at least if it is possible to make a more nuanced distinction between the types of transwomen who are less likely to bring male

---

[28] However, it may be relevant whether or not the transwoman passes as female, because if not, then the benefits of respite that come from simply not having to think about managing male expectations and behaviours may not be generated for the women in the space.

[29] The 'at least some' caveat relates to the assumption of universal gender identity. See discussion in fn. 4.

socialized behaviours into the space (e.g. those who had childhood gender dysphoria) and those who are more likely (e.g. those who did not have childhood gender dysphoria).[30]

In conclusion, changing the definition of legal sex in a way that affects access to single-sex services, spaces, and provisions will obviously affect women. Women have a moral right to exclude all males, including transwomen, from those spaces. Changes to the legal definition of sex would remove that right, so changes to the legal definition of sex should be resisted or rolled back.

References

Al Jazeera. 'Lesbian fete ordered to admit "men"', *Al Jazeera*, 1st October 2003. Online at <https://www.aljezeera.com/news/2003/10/1/lesbian-fete-ordered-to-admit-men>

Alves, Vera. 'Transgender woman accuses Wellington women-only gym of discrimination', *New Zealand Herald*, 29th May 2018.

Barnes, Elizabeth. 'Gender and gender terms', *Nous* 54 (2020), pp. 704–30.

Butler, Judith. *Gender Trouble* (Abingdon: Routledge, 1990).

Burlette Carter, W. 'Sexism in the 'bathroom febates': How bathrooms really became separated by sex', *Yale Law and Policy Review* 37 (2018), pp. 227–97.

de Beauvoir, Simone. *The Second Sex*. Constance Borde and Sheila Malovany-Chevallier (Translators) (Vintage Arrow, [1949] 2011).

Chart, Natasha. 'What's current: Canadian woman files human rights suit against female recovery shelter after being forced to share a room with a man', *Feminist Current*, 3rd August 2018.

Corbishley, Sam. 'Transgender woman, 18, sexually assaulted girl, 10, in Morrisons toilet', *The Metro*, 16th March 2019.

Criado Perez, Caroline. *Invisible Women*. (Australia: Chatto & Windus, 2019).

Fair Play For Women. 'Young vs. Old: the generational divide in the transgender community', <https://fairplayforwomen.com>, 18th July 2018.

Finlayson, Lorna, Jenkins, Katharine, & Worsdale, Rosie. '"I'm not transphobic, but…": A feminist case against the feminist case against trans inclusivity', *Verso*, 17th October 2019.

Frye, Marilyn. 'Some reflections on separatism and power', *Sinister Wisdom* 6 (1978), pp. 30–9.

Gerstmann, Evan. 'Do students have a right not to be seen naked by someone of (anatomically speaking) the other sex?' *Forbes*, 9th April 2019.

---

[30] I am not endorsing the claim that childhood gender dysphoria makes this difference, only allowing that it might.

Gilligan, Andrew. '"Europe's first jail in a jail" for trans women', *The Times*, March 22nd 2019.

Goldberg, Michelle. 'The Trans Women Who Say That Trans Women Aren't Women', *Slate,* 9th December 2015.

Greaves, Amy. and Hudson, David. 'These are the countries that already allow trans people to self-identify', *Gay Star News*, 16th October 2018.

Grenfell, Laura, and Hewitt, Anne. 'Gender regulation: Restrictive, facilitative or transformative laws?' *Sydney Law Review* 34 (2012), pp. 761–83).

Hacker, Helen Mayer. 'Women as a minority group', *Social Forces* 30/1 (1951), pp. 60–9.

Harper, Joanna, O'Donnell, Emma, Khorashad, Behzad Sorouri, McDermott, Hilary, and Witcomb, Gemma. 'How does hormone transition in transgender women change body composition, muscle strength and haemoglobin? Systematic review with a focus on the implications for sport participation', *British Journal of Sports Medicine* 55 (2021), pp. 865–72.

Hatchet, Jean. 'Over my dead body', *The Critic*, 22nd October 2022. Online at <https://thecritic.co.uk/over-my-dead-body/>

Hilton, Emma, and Lundberg, Tommy. 'Transgender women in the female category of sport: Perspectives on testosterone suppression and performance advantage', *Sports Medicine* 51 (2021), pp. 199–214.

Hosie, Rachel. 'Unisex changing rooms put women at danger of sexual assault, data reveals', *The Independent*, 2nd September 2018.

James, S. E, Herman, J. L, Rankin, S. Keisling, M, Mottet, L, and Anafi, M. *The Report of the 2015 U.S. Transgender Survey* (Washington DC: National Center for Transgender Equality, 2016).

Jeffreys, Sheila. *The Lesbian Revolution* (Abingdon: Routledge, 2018).

Jones, Jane Clare. 'The sovereign imaginary and patriarchal masculinity, or, why feminists are not Nazis', *Presentation at the University of Reading, Public Event 'What Is A Woman?'*, 14th May 2019.

Jones, Jeffrey, Wynn, Barbara, Kroeze, Boyd, Dunnuck, Chris, and Rossman, Linda. 'Comparison of sexual assaults by strangers versus known assailants in a community-based population', *American Journal of Emergency Medicine* 22/6 (2004), pp. 454–9.

Knox, Taryn, Anderson, Lynley, and Alison, Heather. 'Transwomen in elite sport: scientific and ethical considerations', *Journal of Medical Ethics* 45 (2019), pp. 395–403.

Kozlowska, Kasia, McClure, Georgia, Chudleigh, Catherine, Gessler, Danielle, Scher, Stephen, and Ambler, Geoffrey. 'Australian children and adolescents with gender dysphoria: Clinical presentations and challenges experienced by a multidisciplinary team and gender service', *Human Systems: Therapy, Culture and Attachments* (2021), pp. 1–26 [early view].

Littman, Lisa. 'Parent reports of adolescents and young adults perceived to show signs of a rapid onset gender dysphoria', *PLoS ONE* 13/8 (2018), pp. 1–44.

Marchiano, Lisa. 'Outbreak: On transgender teens and psychic epidemics', *Psychological Perspectives* 60/3 (2017), pp. 345–66.

Masterson, Matt. 'Lawsuit: Female prisoner says she was raped by transgender inmate', *WTTW News*, 19th February 2020.

Millett, Kate. *Sexual Politics* (UK: Virago Press [1971] 1977).

Murphy, Meghan. 'Trans activism is excusing and advocating violence against women, and it's time to speak up', *Feminist Current*, May 1st 2018.

Ngo, Andy. 'Wi Spa suspect still at large—has history of indecent exposure and masturbation', *New York Post*, 17th September 2021. Online at <https://nypost.com/2021/09/17/wi-spa-suspect-still-at-large-has-history-of-indecent-exposure-and-masturbation/>

Parveen, Nazia. 'Transgender prisoner who sexually assaulted inmates jailed for life', *The Guardian*, 12th October 2018.

Paterson, Stewart. 'NHS is forced to apologise after a woman having a smear test specifically requested a female only to be met by a pre-op transgender medic 'with stubble and a beard', *Daily Mail*, 31st December 2017.

Patrick A. Odysseus. 'Transgender Australians can choose any bathroom they want, but not everyone is happy about it', *The Washington Post*, 18th June 2016.

Phelan, Kate, and Lawford-Smith, Holly. 'Feminist separatism revisited', manuscript, as at 24th October 2022.

Puckett, Jae. 'Trans youth are coming out and living in their gender much earlier than older generations', *The Conversation*, 27th April 2021. Online at <https://theconversation.com/trans-youth-are-coming-out-and-living-in-their-gender-much-earlier-than-older-generations-156829>

Puckett, J, Tornello, S, Mustanski, B, and Newcomb, M. 'Gender variations, generational effects, and mental health of transgender people in relation to timing and status of gender identity milestones', *Psychology of Sexual Orientation and Gender Diversity* 9/2 (2022), pp. 165–78.

Rayner, Gordon. 'Minister orders inquiry into 4,000 per cent rise in children wanting to change sex', *The Telegraph*, 16th September 2018.

Roberts, Timothy, Smalley, Joshua, & Ahrendt, Dale. 'Effect of gender affirming hormones on athletic performance in transwomen and transmen: implications for sporting organizations and legislators', *British Journal of Sports Medicine* 55 (2021), pp. 577–83.

Schrier, Abigail. *Irreversible Damage* (Washington: Regnery Publishing, 2020).

Scott, James. *Domination and the Arts of Resistance: Hidden Transcripts* (New Haven, Yale University Press, 1992).

Shiffrin, Seanna. 'What is really wrong with compelled association?' in *Northwestern University Law Review* 99/2 (2005), pp. 839–88.

Stone, Sandy. 'The empire strikes back: A posttranssexual manifesto' (1987).

The Guardian. 'First UK transgender prison unit to open', *The Guardian*, 3rd March 2019a.

The Guardian. 'Blind date: "I'd like to see her glasses fog up again", *The Guardian*, 23rd November 2019*b*.

Vincent, Nicole, and Jane, Emma. 'Interrogating incongruence: Conceptual and normative problems with the ICD-11's and DSM-5's diagnostic categories for transgender people', *Australian Philosophical Review*, forthcoming.

Wellman, Christopher. 'Immigration and freedom of association', *Ethics* 119 (2008), pp. 109–41.

5

Sex Self-Identification and Costly Signals of Assurance

5.1 Introduction

In 2018, the UK Government held a public consultation over proposed changes to the Gender Recognition Act (2004) which would allow 'self-identification' for sex, by way of a simple, single-step, statutory declaration.[1] New Zealand was poised to implement a similar change into law, via the Births, Deaths, Marriages and Relationships Registration Bill, when it was announced in February 2019 that the Bill would be deferred because of procedural issues in the select committee process.[2] In 2021, the bill re-emerged and was passed (Tinetti 2021*b*). In April 2019, the state of Tasmania in Australia passed law allowing both self-identification for sex, and for sex to be left off birth certificates entirely (Humphries and Coulter 2019), and in August 2019, the state of Victoria in Australia passed law allowing sex self-identification (Koob 2019). Similar changes had already been introduced in Argentina, Canada, Ireland, Malta, Denmark, Norway, Sweden, Portugal, and three US states (New York, California, and Nevada) (Greaves and Hudson 2018; Stock 2019).

Allowing 'self-identification' for sex creates a radical departure between the biological concept of sex and the legal concept of sex. The biological concept creates two categories of people, female and male, the former who produce large immobile gametes (or have gone some way down the developmental pathway toward doing so), the latter who produce small mobile gametes (same caveat).[3] The legal concept creates two very different categories of people, people who identify as women and have made a statutory declaration to that effect (who may be either male or female according to the biological concept), and people who identify as men and have made a statutory declaration to that effect (same caveat). The legal concept also sets a social precedent which interferes with the biological

---

[1] <GOV.UK> (2018).
[2] <Beehive.govt.nz> (2019). A press release in June 2021 confirmed it would be moving forward, this time with a public consultation (Tinetti 2021*a*; see also commentary at Speak Up For Women 2021).
[3] There are other plausible ways to understand biological sex, but I think this is the best. See also (Joyce 2021, Chapter 3, esp. pp. 64–5); and alternative understandings of sex in (Stock 2021, Chapter 2).

concept, by legitimizing the idea that sex should be a matter of self-identification, not biology.

The biological concept still matters, however. There are significant bodily differences between male and female people that matter (whether in work, in sport, for safety, or otherwise); there is historical injustice against female people that has not yet been fully mitigated; and there is ongoing social, economic, and political injustice and/or inequality, which differs in content and magnitude depending on the country. By acknowledging and accommodating sex differences, we can ensure genuine equality of opportunity for female people, and resolve sex-based injustices. We cannot do this if we are unable to even *refer* to female people as a class, because the only concept we are left with refers to a mixed-sex category based on a subjective identity claim. There should be a legal concept of sex coextensive with the biological concept (whether or not there are also *further* legal categories, for example 'transgender' and 'nonbinary'). That is a reason to reject sex self-identification *tout court*. Indeed, it is a reason to reject the possibility of a change of legal sex *tout court*, except in cases where intersex people have had their sex incorrectly assigned and wish to correct it.

Still, given that many countries already allow change of legal sex, at a minimum on the basis of having had what is sometimes misleadingly called 'sex reassignment surgery' (alternatively 'gender affirmation surgery'), it would be rather pointless to stubbornly maintain *we should have never allowed the concept of legal sex to depart from the concept of biological sex*. Whether or not that's true, there's a more pressing question about how much we should want to liberalize the category of legal sex. There are a range of options on the table in different countries, and we can ask about the appropriateness of each. The popular discussion so far has been dominated by the interests of transwomen to the exclusion of any acknowledgement or discussion of possible tensions or conflicts with women's interests. Needless to say, transwomen are not the only stakeholders in the category of legal sex; and female people, as a set of stakeholders, are a *much* larger group. I'll approach this question from the perspective of protecting the interests female people have in single-sex spaces. In this chapter, like the last one, I'll use 'female' and 'woman' interchangeably.

5.2 Costly signals

I borrow from the philosophy of biology the concept of a costly signal. A 'signal' here is something that conveys information to others, whether a visible feature of an individual (e.g. a peacock's tail), a physical action (e.g. a spider plucking the thread of a web) or a verbal communication (e.g. a baby bird chirping when it's hungry). Signalling comes with what Ben Fraser calls *the problem of reliability*, which 'arises when we ask why signal senders do not mislead signal receivers, given the often strong incentive to do so' (Fraser 2012, p. 264). He asks:

> ...in cases where signalling dishonestly seems at least possible, [...] there is a real puzzle concerning the persistence of some signalling systems. Under such conditions, shouldn't signalling systems swiftly descend into a cacophony of dishonest proclamations, and eventually fall silent entirely? If everybody lies, nobody will listen, and if nobody listens, nobody will bother lying (Fraser 2012, p. 265).

A popular suggestion has been that signals are reliable when they are *costly*. Costliness has often been understood in terms of the organism's history. Some signals are only possible in light of a particular history, for example, a peacock can only display an impressive tail when it has been of high enough physical quality to avoid starvation or predation while being encumbered by it (Fraser 2012, p. 265). But costliness might also mean taking on risk, e.g. risk of predation in the course of developing the signal, or risk of injury in the course of sending the signal.

Fraser argues against both Maynard Smith and Harper (2003), and Searcy and Nowicki (2005), that something should count as a costly signal even when it only comes with a risk of punishment (rather than that it in fact incurred costs to send). That is to say, a further explanation of the reliability of certain signals is that if they were discovered to be deceptive, those with an interest in preserving the reliability of the signalling system would be motivated to punish the signaller. This makes the signal costly even when, oddly, the cost of sending the signal itself might be cheap or even free.

Much of the discussion between biologists about this idea concerns non-human animals. But some have asked similar questions about the reliability of signals between humans (e.g. Frank 1988). One of Frank's principles is that for something to function as a reliable signal it must be difficult or costly to fake. For example, there are some human facial muscles that operate reflexively when we experience particular emotions, and which only a small number of people can control. A micro-expression involving one of these muscles can therefore be assumed to be reliable. Clearly, signals can be more and less reliable, more and less hard to fake.

When thinking about reliable signals in the context of liberalizing legal sex categories, there are a number of important questions to keep in mind. First, who is the signal operating between? (Who is the signaller, and who is the receiver?) Second, what information must the signal provide? (For example, is it a signal of *sincerity* about identifying as a woman, a signal of *no risk of male violence,* or *no sexist attitudes*, or *no misogynistic policing behaviour*, or something else entirely that is needed?) Third, how reliable does the signal need to be? Is it enough if the signal makes it fairly likely that the information conveyed is correct, or should it provide *near certainty* that it's correct? Is the law an appropriate vehicle for securing the signals that would reassure women that their interests in women-only spaces will not be undermined by the inclusion of at least some males?

I'll address these questions as the paper goes on, framing them in terms of what it takes to provide women with assurance that select rationales for women-only spaces are not being undermined. I'll focus on three rationales in particular: (i) safety, (ii) privacy/dignity/comfort, and (iii) respite.[4] In Section 5.5 I'll accept Fraser's argument that threat of punishment can underwrite a signal's reliability, and use that to discuss policy options that might serve to give women the assurance they need. But before that, in Section 5.4, I'll follow the earlier discussion between biologists and ask about the costly signals that come from an animal's—here a human's—appearance or evidence of their developmental history.

5.3 Providing women with assurance

It is entirely uncontroversial that male violence against women and girls is a serious global problem. This violence takes different forms in different countries.

For example, in Bangladesh some women who reject men's sexual or romantic advances have acid thrown in their faces, the effect of which is to destroy those women's appearances and therefore their access to marriage, work, and education (Spencer 2018). UK retailers recently banned the sale of acids to people under 18 in order to reduce the prevalence of acid attacks in the UK (Press Association 2018).

Child marriage, and therefore in many cases sustained child abuse/rape, is widespread in parts of the world. In West and Central Africa, 14% of women aged 20–24 had been married by the age of 15 years, and 41% had been married by the age of 18 years. Across the least developed countries, it's 12% of women aged 20–24 married by the age of 15 years, and 40% of those women married by the age of 18 years (Unicef 2020).

One in 4 women in the United States have experienced severe intimate partner physical violence, 1 in 10 women have been raped by an intimate partner, and 1 in 7 women have been stalked by an intimate partner to the point of being fearful of themselves or someone close to them being harmed or killed (National Coalition Against Domestic Violence 2020). In 2017 alone, 139 women in the UK were killed by men, 105 of whom knew their killer, 30 of whom were killed by strangers (Perraudin 2018).[5]

---

[4] For those who have not read Chapter 4, I think there are eight distinct moral rationales for women-only spaces, which are: 1. safety, 2. privacy/dignity/comfort, 3. justice/fairness, 4. respite, 5. likelihood of shared bodily experience, 6. intimate association, 7. self-determination, and 8. intent of the creators.

[5] 21 of the 30 killed by strangers were killed in male-perpetrated terrorist attacks.

The effect of male violence on women is visible throughout their socialization as girls. To give some examples, girls might be taught not to get into cars with strange men; to yell out 'this person is not my Dad!' if they are picked up by a strange man in a public place; that '*It's O.K. to say No!*' to inappropriate contact from male people in their lives;[6] that they should be careful their drinks aren't spiked when they go out; that they watch out for each other around predatory men; that they should be careful in how they express discomfort with men's behaviour, for fear of being physically harmed in retaliation; that they should avoid walking alone at night, or carry some kind of weapon if they do; and so on, and so on. All of this conditioning limits women's access to public space and public life, which is the explanation of such movements as 'Reclaim The Night' where women go out together at night to reclaim public space that is ordinarily denied to them because of concerns about safety (MacKay 2015).

Perhaps some of this social conditioning is unnecessary; the risks overstated. After all, as discussed in Chapter 4, women are more likely to be assaulted by someone they know than someone they don't know (although the rare cases of stranger assault that make the news are usually extraordinarily vicious). But their prevalence is not the point here. The point is that *women are taught, from an early age, to be fearful of men, to be cautious around men, and to be careful in how they express themselves around men* (the latter is particularly important when those men have social or institutional power over them).

It is also uncontroversial that women and girls are subject to severe and persistent sexual objectification. There is a widespread cultural focus on a woman's appearance, and when women are represented in film, television, and advertising they tend to be sexualized. It is a common assumption that much of a woman's or girl's value resides in her attractiveness to men. This pressure causes large numbers of women to internalize self-loathing, and is likely a contributor to high rates of eating disorders, body dysmorphia, and self-harming among teenage girls (see e.g. Widdows 2018; Cameron 2019).

Although women and girls tend to internalize these misogynistic beauty standards, and are far from immune to imposing them on each other, they still have an interest in not having men and boys impose them. The difference is that even while some women act to further entrench misogynistic beauty standards, they are still the victims of them; the same is not true of male people.[7] It is hard to avoid this in mixed-sex spaces, but it is possible to provide women and girls with

---

[6] This was the title of a child safety book designed for parents and children to read together, published in 1985 (Lennet and Crane 1985).

[7] With the exception of transwomen who fully pass as female. These people will be victims of objectification in the sense that, believing them to be female, people impose the expectations upon them that they impose upon female people.

privacy, dignity, and comfort in single-sex spaces (freedom from the male gaze, freedom from being sexually objectified by males, freedom from scrutiny).[8]

Women-only spaces provide safety and respite from these kinds of concerns, by ensuring that no such threats are present. That the threats are not present means a woman is *safe*; that the threats are not present means a woman doesn't have to waste cognitive energy *worrying about the threats*. All women have an interest in the possibility of such respite, but women who are survivors of male violence have a particularly strong interest in this. Almost all public spaces are mixed-sex, and so place an emotional and cognitive burden on women to manage male responses in them. Women-only spaces allow women to avoid those burdens, without having to avoid public life entirely.

Because of their history of oppression and exclusion, and because of their interest in safety and respite, women have a very strong interest in retaining women-only spaces. Any law proposing to undermine this interest—as sex self-identification does by transforming single-sex spaces into mixed-sex spaces—would need to provide women with sufficient *assurance* that the goods those spaces were designed to secure (here focusing on safety, privacy/dignity/comfort, and respite) will still be secured.

There are two ways that such assurance can be provided: i) by each individual, or ii) by a law.[9] In the next two sections I take up each of these possibilities, asking what kinds of signals reliably assure women that they remain safe from the threat of male violence; retain their privacy, dignity, and comfort, especially from male sexual objectification; and provide respite from both the incidence of the former threats and from thinking or worrying about the former threats.

I argue that there is no such signal, and that because women cannot be provided with the assurance they need, there is no justification for law allowing male people into female-only spaces. The upshot is that law is worse when it lets more male people in, and better when it lets fewer male people in. So sex self-identification is the worst possible law from the point of view of women's interests, and the law requiring sex-reassignment surgery for a change of legal sex is the best possible law from the point of view of women's interests, holding fixed that the ship has sailed on *no* change of legal sex.

---

[8] Note that this is *not* a point about freedom from sexual *interest* or *attention*. Some women are attracted to women. It is a point about male attitudes, including seeing women as objects, and feeling sexual entitlement to women's bodies, especially in porn-saturated cultures. Women-only spaces secure against the latter.

[9] A sufficiently strong convention or social norm might do the same job, but I'll focus on law here.

5.4 Individual signals

In this section I'll discuss four individual signals that might provide assurance to women: physical cues for sex class membership; presentational cues for femininity; speech acts; and self-inclusion.

Here's an obvious signal that conveys relevant information: physical cues for sex class membership. We know that the bulk of sexual and other physical violence, including rape, murder, and terrorism, is inflicted by men.[10] That is not to say that *all men are violent*, it's to say that *most violent people are men*. And importantly, we don't know *which* men are the violent ones and which are not. So a way for women to keep themselves safe is to simply not be around men, in specific contexts. Bracketing trans people for a moment, it is usually possible to tell a person's sex by looking at them. Women have on average different body shapes and different facial features. Even so-called 'gender non-conforming' women, i.e. women who have short hair or wear pants, are usually reliably identified as being female (although lesbian friends have told me that mis-sexing happens more than you might expect).

If the information we want is simply whether a person is male or female, then we already have a pretty reliable source of that information (although imperfect, because we will classify some people incorrectly, and we will find some people difficult to classify). But there's a problem: this information tends to be confounded in the case of some (although not all, and perhaps not most)[11] trans and some nonbinary people. Some trans people have had so-called 'sex-reassignment' surgery so that some of their primary sex characteristics appear as those of the opposite sex; and some take cross-sex hormones so that their secondary sex characteristics align with those of the opposite sex. For example, a female nonbinary person might have a double mastectomy and so lack one prominent secondary sex characteristic that female people usually have; a male trans person might take estrogen and progesterone to develop breasts, and so come to have one prominent secondary sex characteristic that male people usually lack.

This creates two problems. One is that it makes the population-wide physical signal unreliable. A person who has the physical cues that suggest membership in the female sex class is likely to be female, but might be male (they might be a transwoman who has had 'sex-reassignment' surgery or is taking cross-sex

---

[10] As with 'female' and 'woman', I'm using 'male' and 'man' interchangeably in this chapter. The extension of both is sex, not gender identity category. I'll use 'male' alone when referring specifically to transwomen.

[11] Danielle Muscato and Alex Drummond are two high-profile transwomen who do not take *any* steps to confound their male physical appearance. It is relatively unusual to take *no* steps, but relatively common to take minimal steps that are not confounding.

hormones).[12] Another is that *treating* physical cues for sex class membership as a signal that conveys important information risks further entrenching injustice, both against trans people, by suggesting that they are being *deceptive* (see discussion in Bettcher 2007), and by suggesting that it is important to 'pass', which is especially unfair on late-transitioning males (see discussion in Wynn 2018); and against non-trans individuals, by stigmatizing conditions that affect their secondary sex characteristics, for example, polycystic ovary syndrome, androgen excess, or hypertrichosis producing facial hair sufficient to full beards in females.

Surely we should want people to be (i) okay with the bodies they have, however they are, and (ii) able to change their bodies if they feel extremely strongly that they are not okay with them, however they are. So physical cues for sex class membership are not a reliable signal of assurance for women in women-only spaces, and are not a good candidate for *working for* reliability because this risks serious harm to people who are already marginalized and stigmatized. Merely appearing to be male or female is not a reliable signal.

What about presentational cues for femininity, instead? This makes it the case that the signal can be sent by people who are obviously male, through their choices about presentation. For example, a male person might wear clothing that is frequently worn by women and only infrequently worn by men, such as a dress or a skirt. Or he might wear makeup, or jewellery, or style his hair in a way that is common in women and uncommon in men (for example he might wear it long and curl it).[13]

What information does this signal convey, and how reliable is the signal? The information is somewhat ambiguous. It could signal simple gender nonconformity; it could signal that the person understands themselves to be nonbinary or a transwoman; it could signal that the person has a sexual kink or fetish that is satisfied with feminine dress or accessories.[14] The person might sincerely believe themselves to be a woman and/or female, and be using a culturally understood language to convey that to others (Wynn 2019); but they might equally have a poor or distorted understanding of what womanhood is and be awkwardly

---

[12] They might also be an intersex person who is male but whose body appears female, but such intersex people are not the focus of this chapter (or indeed this book), primarily for the reason that my concern with male sex is as a heuristic for the type of socialization one has experienced, and most intersex people have been intersex since birth and so socialized as whatever sex they were assumed to be. An exception is the Guevedoces in the Dominican Republic, who are observed female at birth but then develop male genitals around the age of puberty, but this takes someone socialized female into the male category, not the other way around (BBC 2015).

[13] Obviously, some men wear makeup and some men wear dresses. I don't mean to endorse here the idea that either of these things is exclusive to women, only that they are *typically* not things men wear, and so may be useful signals for that reason.

[14] See discussion in (Bailey 2003); (Stock 2021, Chapter 7); (Joyce 2021, Chapter 2); and (Lawford-Smith 2022, Chapter 5).

reflecting that understanding back to the world.[15] In all such cases, it is likely that the signaller will be at risk of sanction for non-conformity with the expectations placed on male people. In patriarchal societies male departures from masculinity are policed more severely than female departures from femininity (just consider how much more liberated female presentation is than male presentation in most societies). The fact that the male person is willing to bear this risk suggests that they feel strongly, whether that is against gender conformity, about their identity as trans or nonbinary, or about their sexual interests. But strength of feeling about any one of those three things provides no assurance to women. A male person can be 'against masculinity' in presentation while being ignorant as to the extent of their male-socialized behaviour; they can identify passionately as neither sex while still exhibiting traits typical of males; and their sexual interest in femininity indicates nothing about whether they are likely to inflict violence, objectification, or discomforting behaviour onto women. There is both ambiguity in what the signal communicates, and a mismatch between the information it might communicate and the information women need to receive. Presentational cues for femininity, therefore, are not a reliable signal.

Speech acts are a further kind of signal which communicates information between parties. For example, an obviously male person might assert 'I am a woman', or even 'I am female' or 'I am a lesbian' (I see this on social media regularly; I don't know how often it happens in face to face interactions). The problem with this signal is that, again, it's not clear what information it conveys. We learn that unless the person is joking around, or engaged in counter-protest,[16] they probably believe that they are a woman, or are female, or are a lesbian. But why should this *belief* of theirs provide any assurance to women about how they are likely to behave in a female-only space? In the latter two cases, it seems to provide exactly the opposite: when confronted with people who believe what we take to be an obvious falsehood we are usually *less* trusting of them, not more trusting.[17] Furthermore, talk is cheap: especially in the case that a male person has taken on no other costs (such as acquiring physical cues of sex class membership, or presentational cues of femininity), the signal neither conveys the information women need nor does so reliably. Even if it sent relevant information, its reliability would be undermined by its costlessness.

---

[15] I develop this idea further in Lawford-Smith and Hauskeller (2022), drawing on Lawford-Smith (2020).

[16] #ManFriday was a counter-protest set up by a group of women's rights activists in the UK, where they would engage in what they called 'random acts of manliness'. One such act was to visit the Highgate Men's Pond on Hampstead Heath, wearing hand-knitted beards, and gain access by claiming to identify as men. <https://manfridayuk.org/2018/07/28/why-do-the-ponds-matter/>

[17] A male person's believing themselves to be a woman is not obviously false in the way that their believing themselves to be female, or a lesbian, is. I think both 'woman' and 'female' have different intensions but the same extension, which means they refer to the same people. But there is reasonable disagreement about what 'woman' means.

Finally, what about acts of self-inclusion in spaces that are reserved for women? For example, if a visibly male person uses a female bathroom, particularly when there is a male bathroom right beside it, this can act to communicate the information that they take this space to be appropriately used by them.

Some institutions go so far as to actively encourage such self-inclusion. Two universities in the UK (Bristol and Oxford), and a music hall in Portland, have been reported on social media as displaying posters in their bathrooms that say, for example: 'If you're in a public bathroom and you think a stranger's gender does not match the sign on the door, follow these steps: 1. Don't worry about it, they know better than you' (Bristol);[18] 'Do you feel like someone is using the "wrong" bathroom? Please don't: stare at them, challenge them, insult them; do not purposely make them uncomfortable. Instead please: respect their privacy; respect their identity; carry on with your day; protect them from harm. They are using the facilities they feel safe in. Please do not take that right away from them. Everyone has every right to be here: in this school, in this university, in this world' (Oxford);[19] 'If you're using this restroom and you think a person's gender doesn't match the sign on the door, follow these steps: 1. Don't worry about it, they know better than you' (Portland).[20]

Male self-inclusion in female-only spaces is also low cost. In general, male people pose a physical threat to female people, not the other way round, so the male does not take on cost by risking retaliation from females (because such retaliation is unlikely). A female person is less likely to challenge a male one, especially if he is physically intimidating in either his height or build, and even if she does, the male is unlikely to be physically harmed as a result. The people who might be motivated to harm this male if they knew about his self-inclusion—for example the male intimates of those women in the bathroom at the same time as him, who might feel protective of those women—will tend not to know he is in there, precisely because they are outside of that space. So the male does not take on cost by risking retaliation by other men, either. Thus male people *impose* costs when they use the female bathroom (or other female-only spaces), rather than *take on* costs, where the latter would be a way to underwrite the reliability of their signals.

Furthermore, and as above, it's just not clear what this action communicates. It might communicate the male person's feeling that the term 'woman' or 'female' (whatever is on the sign) applies to them; or feeling safer in the women's bathroom (perhaps because of a fear of harassment or violence by men in the male bathroom); or preferring to be among women; or a desire to test whether they

---

[18] Archived at <https://ifunny.co/picture/if-you-re-in-a-public-bathroom-and-you-think-415zl6wu3>
[19] Archived at <https://ifunny.co/picture/do-you-feel-like-someone-is-using-the-wrong-bathroom-VA35lR898>
[20] Tweeted by Kristy Smith @speedskater89 6.24 p.m. 26th August 2019. Online at <https://twitter.com/speedskater89/status/1165872653833404416>

'pass' as a woman, by checking whether they are challenged in a woman's space; or a desire for female cultural experience (having heard, perhaps, that women share confidences in bathrooms); or having a sexual interest in women or women's products (sexualized male behaviour on record in female spaces includes assault, exhibitionism, voyeurism, spycam use, and sexual fetishes for women's used sanitary products). Women cannot be expected to assume that any male including himself in a female bathroom has only the more innocuous of these intentions, and so poses no threat to her safety; and furthermore, that any male *with* one of those more innocuous intentions is unlikely to pose a threat to her interest in privacy/dignity/comfort, or respite.

None of these individual signals send women the information that they would need in order to be assured that their interest in having women-only spaces will not be undermined. And even if they did, the latter two, at least, are not costly enough to be reliable. In the next section I'll move on to laws that can regulate use of (many/most) women-only spaces, making misuse 'costly' with the threat of legal or social sanction.

5.5 Legal requirements

In this section I'll discuss legal requirements that might provide assurance to women instead, following real laws that are in place or have been proposed in various countries. These do not make the use of women's spaces costly in the same way as the individual signals, where a male person takes on pain, or financial expense, or social discrimination, etc., but rather count as costly in the way Fraser (2012) had in mind, incurring a *risk* of punishment (here legal, or social—the latter as a result of social support *for* the law).

The laws I'll consider are that a male is free to use women-only spaces if he: has had so-called 'sex-reassignment' surgery; has lived as a woman for two years; or has completed a statutory declaration of his self-identified sex (or 'gender', depending on the country). Assurance through law works differently to assurance through individual signals. When we're thinking about individual signals, we're thinking about what any given female person can know about any given male person when female-only spaces are challenged by them. When we're thinking about law, we're thinking about rules whose violation comes with a threat of punishment, and which have an influence on social norms and conventions. The law is not perfect in providing assurance, because people can always choose to break it. But the higher the costs of doing so, and the stronger the norms it influences, the less likely this will be.

There's a question about which form of official documentation of sex to consider as sufficient to change of legal sex. In Australia at least, the birth certificate is the best candidate, because while either a birth certificate or a passport is required for other official purposes like starting a new job, enrolling in university, or getting married, a birth certificate is required in order to get a passport. So the birth certificate is the 'foundation document' that underwrites all the others.

Sex-reassignment surgery. In the states of New South Wales and Queensland in Australia, sex-reassignment surgery is a requirement for change of legal sex. The problem with 'sex-reassignment' surgery as a signal is that while it reliably communicates *sincerity*—coming at considerable physical and financial cost—sincerity about *feeling like a woman/female* still does not provide female people with assurance that there will be no threat to their safety, privacy/dignity/comfort, or respite. Having severe enough dysphoria for surgical transition to be a serious option means that the person is likely to have suffered a lot; but there are many male people in the world who have suffered a lot, and who still pose a threat to women and women's interests. (If that was false, we should expect to see no violence against women and girls from men of colour, working class men, disabled men, etc., and yet we do). The rejoinder may be that only transwomen *identify with* women as part of their suffering (see discussion in Stock 2021, Chapter 6), but it is far from clear that what is identified with is deep (to the point of creating an understanding of *women's* interests in women-only space) rather than superficial (identification with presentation, e.g. being dolled up, or with apparent function, e.g. penetration by men, are clearly insufficient).[21]

Women don't need to know whether someone *feels like a woman* (whatever that means to them), they need to know whether a person *is female*, or *has been socialized as female*, or at the very least, *has done the work required to get rid of sexist beliefs and the impulse to interact with women as gender norms permit men to*. The problem should be clear: sex-reassignment surgery, despite its name, does not change sex[22] and cannot change sex-based socialization. Surgery alone is no guide to who has and who hasn't done the work against male socialization.

---

[21] For identifications of the latter two kinds, see the testimonies presented in Lawrence (2013) and Chu (2019).

[22] As explained in the note on language at the start of this book, I'm understanding sex as the production, all going well, of either large immobile gametes (ova: female) or small mobile gametes (sperm: male). Sex-reassignment surgery does not create a capacity to produce the opposite sex's gametes, so sex-reassignment surgery does not change sex. This is not the only way to understand sex, however. Alex Byrne gives a slightly different version of the gamete account: 'females are the ones who have advanced some distance down the developmental pathway that results in the production of large gametes', 'males are the ones who have advanced some distance down the developmental pathway that results in the production of small gametes' (Byrne 2018). This has the advantage of referring to foetal development, rather than requiring the filling in of an 'all going well' clause (for criticism of which see Mason, forthcoming). But similarly, because sex-reassignment surgery can't change one's developmental history, this account does not countenance change of sex. Stock discusses three potential understandings of sex, one of which is based on chromosomes, specifically, the presence or lack of a Y chromosome. 'A human male is a human with a Y chromosome. A human female is a human without a Y chromosome' (Stock 2021, p. 47). This account of sex, like the next one, has the disadvantage that

Furthermore, having 'sex-reassignment' surgery as a requirement for legal change of sex works to incentivize surgical transition. Severely dysphoric trans people desperately want to live as the opposite sex, so whatever the gatekeeping requirement on doing so, they are likely to attempt to meet it. We must, therefore, set gatekeeping requirements with this in mind. We shouldn't want people to feel that they have to have surgery on their perfectly healthy bodies in order to gain access to living as they want to live. 'Sex-reassignment' surgery can look initially like an appealing requirement for change of legal sex when focusing on the interests of women, because it ensures that only those who are very serious about transitioning can change their legal sex. But it's too much to ask of trans people, who should be able to have that surgery if they want it, but not because they can't get other things they want without it; and requiring it doesn't do anything useful for women—doesn't provide them the information they need.

Two years living as a woman and diagnosis of gender dysphoria. In the UK, the Gender Recognition Act (GRA) 2004 requires a person wishing to change their gender[23] to provide: two medical reports, one providing evidence that they have gender dysphoria and detailing treatment; documentation proving they have 'lived in their acquired gender' for at least two years; a statutory declaration of intention to live in the acquired gender until death; and for married people, evidence of the consent of a spouse (or the end of their marriage).[24] In 2018, a consultation was held considering reform to this process, potentially to make change of gender a matter of a single-step statutory declaration. I'll take the requirement of living in the acquired gender for at least two years and having a diagnosis of

---

(unlike the first two just discussed) it is specific to humans. Sex-reassignment surgery can't change chromosomes, so the chromosome-based understanding of sex doesn't vindicate change of sex either. (Indeed, as may be becoming obvious, given that what sex-reassignment surgery changes is genitals, only an understanding of sex based on genitals is likely to give the answer that sex-reassignment surgery changes sex. I know of no one defending a genitals-based theory of sex, although perhaps the folk theory is something close to that). A final way to understand sex is as a property cluster, where to be a sex is to have a sufficient number of the properties in the cluster, rather than to have any single necessary property. If we take the properties in the cluster to be the four primary sex characteristics (external genitalia, internal genitalia, gonads, and chromosomes), and we put sufficiency at 50% of the properties, then sex-reassignment surgery still does not change sex. A normal male would have all four properties, and a 'sex-reassigned' male would have two out of four properties (Lawford-Smith 2019). Also, I think Derek Parfit's origin view of the person, which makes your origin in a specific sperm and egg combination an essential property of you, also makes your sex an essential property. That is an independent reason to deny the possibility of change of sex, because a person cannot change their essential properties (Lawford-Smith, manuscript).

[23] The GRA consultation document distinguishes sex, gender, and gender identity, understanding sex as '[a]ssigned by medical practitioners at birth based on physical characteristics. Sex can be either male or female' (p. 9); gender as '[o]ften expressed in terms of masculinity and femininity, gender refers to socially constructed characteristics, and is often assumed from the sex people are registered as at birth'; and gender identity as '[a] person's internal sense of their own gender. This does not have to be man or woman. It could be, for example, non-binary' (p. 7). The consultation document is online at <https://assets.publishing.service.gov.uk/government/uploads/system/uploads/attachment_data/file/721725/GRA-Consultation-document.pdf>

[24] <http://www.legislation.gov.uk/ukpga/2004/7>

dysphoria as the second possible legal requirement (I'll address single-step statutory declaration as the third option). Note that the 'two years' part of this is arbitrarily specific. What matters is that it's some significant length of time. Enough, perhaps, to establish a commitment.

Right off the bat, there's a serious question to be asked about what it means for a person to live in their acquired gender. Say a male person decides they are a woman and want to live as a woman. How does a woman live? It seems that they can live as a *particular* woman lives (by imitating her), or as a *composite* of women live (by patching together some elements of how women who they're aware of live), or as a *stereotype* of a woman lives (by applying certain ideas they have about what women are like to how they live). But will they be recognized as having lived as a woman if the particular woman they imitate is radical feminist Kate, who has short hair, always goes about in shorts or trousers, and doesn't remove her body hair? If they will, it's not clear why *they* live as a woman while other men don't. If they won't, there's a worry that what the requirement amounts to is presentation that might reasonably be perceived as mocking, appropriating, or reifying stereotypes about, women or womanhood.

It makes sense that because certain ways of presenting are typically not available to men (e.g. wearing skirts or dresses, or any clothing items made of particular fabrics (like silk, satin, or lace), wearing makeup, wearing decorative jewellery, having long hair that is styled or has a fashion cut like a fringe or layers, a male person who wants to present in these ways might feel that they are not a man. They might reason that only women present in this way, so they must be a woman. That doesn't mean they are committed to the thought that all women present in this way, or all women ought to present in this way. So a more charitable reading of what it means for a male person to live as a woman is to say that they live in ways that are typically not available to men, and typically available to women. (Note that if we had a third sex/gender category recognized in law, then such males could feel they are not men without that entailing their feeling that they are women). Gender non-conforming men may also meet this requirement, but remember that the policy option is conjunctive: living as a woman for at least two years *and* having a diagnosis of gender dysphoria. Living as a woman for two years, understood as living in ways not typically available to men for two years, is moderately costly. No one would do it on a whim, or on the off-chance of being able to get some good spycam footage from the women's changing room. So that makes it fairly reliable, as a signal of commitment/sincerity. But does this reliable signal of sincerity give women the information they need? It would appear not. There is nothing about sustained atypical gender presentation that guarantees the relevant male will not compromise women's interests in women-only spaces.

What about a diagnosis of dysphoria? Assuming that sympathetic doctors don't simply start handing these diagnoses out to anyone who asks for them, and that trans people without dysphoria don't simply learn what they need to say in order to get such a diagnosis (both of which have happened in the past; see discussion in Joyce 2021), this is a legal option that carves a neat separation between people who cannot be asked to bear the costs of contributing to women's liberation, and people who can. For people with severe dysphoria, their experience involves a great deal of psychological/emotional suffering, and transition is one of the ways to ease that suffering. Even if transition doesn't involve full inclusion as a member of the opposite sex, because for some purposes we prefer to provide third spaces than to disrupt female-only spaces, it involves inclusion for most purposes. It is over-demanding to ask such people to live as feminine men, rather than asserting that they are women/female. But this request is not over-demanding when it comes to male people who have a trans identity without gender dysphoria.[25]

A policy requirement of a diagnosis of gender dysphoria protects the vulnerable, without being over-inclusive and protecting those whose interests could be met in an alternative way. This is a good outcome. Indeed, given the positives of this outcome compared to the worries with the 'living as a woman' requirement, why not drop the latter? One reason not to is that the latter is evidence of the former. That is to say, a male person with severe gender dysphoria, as defined in the DSM-5,[26] is highly unlikely to be happy to present as male while merely insisting that they are female/a woman. Their dysphoria is likely to motivate them to take steps to appear as female, or at least to communicate that they wish to be treated socially as a woman. So the requirement of living as a woman goes hand in hand with the requirement to have a diagnosis of dysphoria, by providing further evidence of the latter (which is useful in cases where we think the latter might be easily gamed).

---

[25] A complication likely to raise objections from radical and gender-critical feminists is that a diagnosis of gender dysphoria (at any age) does not separate out what some clinicians have taken to be two quite different categories of transwomen, those with childhood gender dysphoria who tend to have a same-sex sexual orientation, and those with later-onset gender dysphoria (as teenagers or adults, sometimes quite late in life) who tend to have an opposite-sex sexual orientation or a novel sexual orientation known as 'autogynephilia' (see also fn. 11 in Chapter 9). Another legal option, then, would be a diagnosis of *childhood* gender dysphoria in particular. I suspect this is as close as it would be possible to get to a compromise acceptable to radical and gender-critical feminists; it is significantly more reliable than, for example, having had sex-reassignment surgery, which remains the 'gatekeeping' requirement on a change of legal sex in some states of Australia.

[26] Gender dysphoria in adolescents and adults in the DSM-5 is defined as 'a marked incongruence between one's experienced/expressed gender and assigned gender' of at least six months in duration, manifesting in at least two of the following six conditions: incongruence between experienced/expressed gender and primary and/or secondary sex characteristics; strong desire to be rid of one's primary and/or secondary sex characteristics because of that incongruence (or, if a young person, to not go through the puberty that would produce them); a strong desire for the primary and/or secondary sex characteristics of the oppose sex (they say 'other gender'); strong desire to be another gender; strong desire to be treated as the other gender; strong conviction that one has 'the typical feelings and reactions of the other [or another] gender' (DSM-5, p. 453). There also has to be 'clinically significant distress or impairment in social, occupational, or other important areas of functioning' (p. 453).

The problem, however, and as we have seen several times over already, is that even a reliable diagnosis of gender dysphoria is no guarantee to women that there will not be any threat to their interests in having women-only spaces. It provides *highly reliable* information, but not the information that women need. Knowing that a male person has a certain set of beliefs or feelings about their gender identity, and that they are extremely strongly held, is not the same as knowing that a male person is low- or zero-risk when it comes to women's safety, privacy/dignity/comfort, or respite. We have no reason to think that the *content* of gender dysphoric beliefs or feelings is the same as the *content* of female experience or female beliefs and feelings after female socialization. It is perfectly possible that a male person has experienced dysphoria and taken steps to present as feminine in order to alleviate that dysphoria, and yet has still adopted some of the attitudes, beliefs, and behaviours of a male person socialized under patriarchy, for example in his attitudes of entitlement to women's bodies. Some gender identity activists will argue that childhood gender dysphoria leads a boy to reject gender socialization (see e.g. Finlayson et al. 2019), but they can only reject what they recognize as such, and gender conditioning is extremely pervasive.[27] A diagnosis of gender dysphoria and living as a woman for a period is not a costly signal *of assurance that women's interests in women-only spaces won't be undermined*, even if it is a costly signal of sincere belief.

Statutory declaration of self-identified sex. Finally, the third option. In New Zealand, sex self-identification recognized through a single-step statutory declaration was passed into law via the Births, Deaths, Marriages and Relationships Registration Act 2021. The Act is specifically about a change to the process for birth certificates; New Zealand already allowed a change of sex on driver's licences and passports with minimal hassle. The Act allows eligible adults, 16- or 17-year-olds with the consent of a guardian, and guardians on behalf of children, to change their (the child's) registered sex. Applicants can choose between 'male, female, or any other sex or gender specified in regulations' (p. 25). They must make a statutory declaration stating that they (or the child) identify 'as a person of the nominated sex' and understand the consequences of the application (p. 25). In the case of a guardian applying for a child, they must also include a letter of support from 'a suitably qualified third party' confirming that the child understands the consequences of the application (pp. 25–6). A birth certificate issued after the 'registration of nominated sex' (as the Act calls it) 'must...contain the information that it would have contained if...the person's nominated sex had always been their registered sex' (p. 26). There is a nominal fee associated with making the application.

---

[27] If it weren't we shouldn't expect to see such striking average differences between men and women. (The alternative explanation of those differences is, of course, biology—but that is hardly helpful to the gender identity activists' cause). See also discussion in Chapter 2.

I will take forward single-step statutory declaration (colloquially 'sex self-ID') as the third possible policy proposal. The problem with this proposal, from women's point of view, is that it is virtually costless. The application fee itself is likely to be cheap in financial terms: in New Zealand it is $55 to register the nominated sex (and in related costs, it is $33-$35 for a new birth certificate, and $170 for a change of name).[28] The only other cost is the minor administrative hassle of filling out the forms. A male person can declare 'female' as their nominated sex on a whim, or for a joke, or to get cheaper car insurance (*NZ Herald* 2018), or because they want to collect the prize money in women's sports,[29] or for any other reason they like. Being legally female, they can access legal protections on the basis of sex, such as being housed in the female prison estate if they are sent to prison; or being able to take a place on a female-only shortlist for a job, or in a political party; to win a female-only prize, or scholarship. Where 'sex-reassignment' surgery came at very high cost to the male person, and living as a woman for two years came at moderate cost, single-step statutory declaration comes at extremely low cost.

That means that even only as a sign of sincerity or commitment, having completed a statutory declaration of self-identified sex is not a reliable signal. It's plagued by the same problems as every other signal we've discussed so far, namely that *what* it signals doesn't correspond to anything that women have an interest in knowing. Being the kind of male who would register his nominated sex as 'female' *might* mean being the kind of male who poses a risk to women, and might mean not being that kind of male. It just has very little to do with it either way. Unlike some of the other individual and policy-based signals, which at least tell us that the signaller is not someone at the extremes of toxic masculinity (because such a male would not be willing to undergo sex-reassignment surgery, or present in a feminine way), this signal doesn't even tell us that, because a male could nominate their sex as female simply because they find it funny to do so, or want to intimidate women they have a problem with by showing up in spaces that those women value and from which the male would ordinarily be excluded.

As before, we're not looking merely for signals of sincerity or commitment, we're looking for signals of a lack of male socialization that might make a male person a threat to the specific interests that are protected by female-only spaces. Single-step statutory declaration of sex is a particularly bad policy option, because it undermines assurance. Women have reason to be wary of men, in relation to the three interests I've been concerned with women-only spaces protecting. Sex self-ID entrenches as law, and therefore influences as a norm, the idea that legal sex—and therefore, entitlement to single-sex services—cannot be generally

---

[28] <https://www.dia.govt.nz/bdmreview>
[29] There is $150,000 USD at stake for the winner of the women's category of the Boston Marathon (Owens and Gartsbeyn 2019).

assumed on the basis of appearance, that a fully male-appearing person could nonetheless be legally female.[30] This means women's case for challenging male-appearing people in their spaces is substantially weakened, which leaves them more vulnerable. We shouldn't accept this greater vulnerability simply because it makes things a little easier for those who desire sex self-ID. Single-step statutory declaration for change of sex should be rejected outright. It is an unreliable signal, and it does not provide women with the information they need. It is the worst of the three legal options.

5.6 Conclusion

There are a range of individual signals that male people can send while using female-only spaces. They can appear to belong to the female sex class, or to have some of the characteristics associated with belonging to it. They can present themselves in a feminine way. They can assert that they are female, or a woman. And they can simply use the spaces. None of these signals provide women with assurance that their safety, privacy/dignity/comfort, or interest in respite, will be maintained. Mere assertion of femaleness/womanhood, and mere self-inclusion in women's spaces, are too costless to reliably signal anything.

Moving to legal requirements, 'sex-reassignment' surgery is undesirable, because it is extremely costly to transwomen without providing women with the assurance that is needed. Sex self-ID is undesirable, because it is costless and doesn't provide the assurance that is needed. A diagnosis of gender dysphoria and living for a period of time as the sex one wishes to acquire is moderately costly and somewhat informative, even though it still fails to guarantee that women's interests in women-only spaces won't be undermined.

If we have to have one of the three, the legal requirement that the UK currently has—two years 'living as a woman' and a diagnosis of gender dysphoria—is the one to be preferred. But retaining women-only spaces *as women-only,* while providing third / gender-neutral spaces for transwomen, would be even better.

---

[30] Note that this will be true of both a trans man who has not registered a legal change of sex, *and* a transwoman or male nonbinary person who presents as male and has registered a legal change of sex. If an apparently-male person was known to be a trans man, women would have the assurance they need that the person would not pose any threat to the interests protected by women-only spaces, the problem is that in many public spaces we are interacting with strangers, and so won't normally have that information. This does suggest that norms for inclusion may be able to operate differently in spaces where people are known to each other, like workplaces, however.

References

Bailey, J. Michael. *The Man Who Would Be Queen: The Science of Gender-Bending and Transsexualism* (Washington: Joseph Henry Press, 2003).

BBC. 'The extraordinary case of the Guevedoces', 20th September 2015. Online at <https://www.bbc.com/news/magazine-34290981>

Beehive.govt.nz. 'Births, Deaths, Marriages and Relationships Registration Bill to be deferred', 25th February 2019. Online at <https://www.beehive.govt.nz/release/births-deaths-marriages-and-relationships-registration-bill-be-deferred>

Bettcher, Talia Mae. 'Evil deceivers and make-believers: On transphobic violence and the politics of illusion', *Hypatia* 22/3 (2007), pp. 43–65.

Byrne, Alex. 'Is sex binary?' *ACR Digital*, 2nd November 2018. Online at <https://medium.com/arc-digital/is-sex-binary-16bec97d161e>

Cameron, Deborah. *Feminism: A Brief Introduction to the Ideas, Debates, and Politics of the Movement* (Chicago: University of Chicago Press, 2019).

Chu, Andrea Long. *Females* (London, Verso, 2019).

Finlayson, Lorna, Jenkins, Katharine, and Worsdale, Rosie. '"I'm not transphobic, but…": A feminist case against the feminist case against trans inclusivity', *Verso*, 17th October 2019.

Frank, Robert. *Passions Within Reason: The Strategic Role of The Emotions* (W. W. Norton & Co.: New York, 1988).

Fraser, Ben. 'Costly signalling theories: beyond the handicap principle', *Biology & Philosophy* 27 (2012), pp. 263–78.

GOV.UK. 'Consultation outcome: Reform of the Gender Recognition Act 2004', 3rd July 2018. Online at <https://www.gov.uk/government/consultations/reform-of-the-gender-recognition-act-2004>

Greaves, Amy, and Hudson, David. 'These are the countries that already allow trans people to self-identify', *Gay Star News*, 16th October 2018.

Hauskeller, Michael., & Lawford-Smith, Holly. 'Gender', in Michael Hauskeller (Ed.) *Fundamental Things: Philosophical Conversations* (London: UCL Press, 2022).

Humphries, Alexandra, and Coulter, Ellen. 'Tasmania makes gender optional on birth certificates after Liberal crosses floor', *ABC News*, 10th April 2019. Online at <https://www.abc.net.au/news/2019-04-10/birth-certificate-gender-laws-pass-in-tasmania/10989170>

Joyce, Helen. *Trans: When Ideology Meets Reality* (London: Oneworld, 2021).

Koob, Simone Fox. '"Momentous night": Victorian birth certificate reform passed', *The Age*, 28th August 2019. Online at <https://www.theage.com.au/national/victoria/momentous-night-victorian-birth-certificate-reform-passed-20190828-p52leu.html>

Lawford-Smith, Holly. 'No conflict, they said', in Petra Bueskens (Ed.) *Heterodox Feminism* (Winchester: Zero Books, manuscript as at 3rd March 2022).

Lawford-Smith, Holly. *Gender-Critical Feminism* (Oxford: Oxford University Press, 2022).

Lawford-Smith, Holly. 'Trans men are men (but transwomen are not women)', 12th May 2020. Online at <https://hollylawford-smith.org/trans-men-are-men-but-transwomen-are-not-women/>

Lawford-Smith, Holly. 'Is it possible to change sex?' *The Article*, 19th February 2019. Online at <https://www.thearticle.com/is-it-possible-to-change-sex/>

Lawrence, Anne. *Men Trapped In Men's Bodies: Narratives of Autogynephilic Transsexualism* (New York: Springer 2013).

Lenett, Robin, and Crane, Bob. *It's O.K. to Say No!: A Parent/Child Manual for the Protection of Children* (New York: Tor Books, 1985).

Mackay, Finn. *Radical Feminism: Feminist Activism in Movement* (London: Palgrave MacMillan, 2015).

Mason, Rebecca. 'Women are not adult human females', *Australasian Journal of Philosophy*, forthcoming.

Maynard-Smith, John, and Harper, David. *Animal Signals* (Oxford: Oxford University Press, 2003).

National Coalition Against Domestic Violence. *National Statistics* (2020). Online at <https://ncadv.org/statistics>

NZ Herald. "Getting screwed over': Man changes gender on ID to get cheaper car insurance', 30th July 2018. Online at <https://www.nzherald.co.nz/business/getting-screwed-over-man-changes-gender-on-id-to-get-cheaper-car-insurance/TCCYBYKJAB44TWPGMSPHWCX3JU/>

Owens, Isabel, and Gartsbeyn, Mark. 'How much prize money do you get for winning the Boston Marathon?', 15th April 2019. Online at <https://www.boston.com/sports/boston-marathon/2019/03/18/2019-boston-marathon-winners-prize-money/>

Perraudin, Frances. 'Femicide in UK: 76% of women killed by men in 2017 knew their killer', *The Guardian*, 18th December 2018. Online at <https://www.theguardian.com/uk-news/2018/dec/18/femicide-in-uk-76-of-women-killed-by-men-in-2017-knew-their-killer>

Press Association. 'UK retailers to ban sale of acid products to under-18s', *The Guardian*, 7th January 2018. Online at <https://www.theguardian.com/world/2018/jan/07/uk-retailers-to-restrict-sale-of-acid-products-to-under-18s-b-and-q-wickes-tesco-attacks>

Searcy, William, and Nowicki, Stephen. *The Evolution of Animal Communication* (New Jersey: Princeton University Press, 2005).

Speak Up For Women. 'Let's talk about sex self-identification', 15th May 2021. Online at <https://speakupforwomen.nz/lets-talk-about-self-id-2021/>

Spencer, Danielle. 'When acid attacks become a weapon of patriarchy', *The Guardian*, 11th January 2018. Online at <https://www.theguardian.com/world/2018/jan/11/when-acid-attacks-become-a-weapon-of-patriarchy>

Stock, Kathleen. 'Ignoring differences between men and women is the wrong way to address gender dysphoria', *Quillette*, 11th April 2019.

Stock, Kathleen. *Material Girls: Why Reality Matters For Feminism* (London: Fleet, 2021).

Tinetti, Jan. 'Progress towards simpler process for changing sex on birth certificates', 13th June 2021*a*. Online at <https://www.beehive.govt.nz/release/progress-towards-simpler-process-changing-sex-birth-certificates>

Tinetti, Jan. 'Self-identification a new milestone in New Zealand's history', 9th December 2021*b*. Online at <http://www.beehive.govt.nz/release/self-identification-new-milestone-new-zealand%E2%80%99s-history>

Unicef. 'Child marriage', April 2020. Online at <https://data.unicef.org/topic/child-protection/child-marriage/>

Widdows, Heather. *Perfect Me* (Princeton: Princeton University Press, 2018).

Wynn, Natalie (as ContraPoints). 'The aesthetic', *YouTube*, 19th September 2018.

Wynn, Natalie (as ContraPoints). 'Gender critical', *YouTube*, 30th March 2019.

6

The Never-Ending Dispute over Public Bathrooms

In the public imagination, the words 'women-only space' mean one thing: bathrooms. In 2021, I started a website noconflicttheysaid.org as a personal project to collect anonymous testimonies from women about disruptions to their use of women-only spaces as a result of legal and social changes to accommodate gender identities. As a result, reporter Karl Quinn for *The Age* wrote in a piece profiling a 'nonbinary' female person about their bathroom usage:

> Who gets to use which bathroom became a matter of public debate last Tuesday with the launch of a website by a University of Melbourne academic to which women are encouraged to anonymously post tales about how their use of 'women-only spaces has been impacted' by the incursion of trans women (those assigned male at birth but who identify as female, whether they have medically transitioned or not) into such places (Quinn 2021).

Women-only spaces encompass many more types of spaces than just bathrooms. There's a sense in which bathrooms are the least of our worries. I'm reluctant to feed the narrative that 'women-only space' means 'bathrooms' by discussing bathrooms in detail here. But there are two good reasons to talk about them that pull against that reluctance. The first is that, given that people already make this association, bathrooms deserve a careful conversation. The second is that bathrooms are likely the women-only space where transwomen have the best case for inclusion. This means we're being maximally charitable to those in favour of transwomen's inclusion in women-only spaces by addressing this space, rather than one more obviously favourable to exclusion.[1] Considering the best case also makes possible an additional argument: if we can show that even in that case exclusion would be permissible, that would provide some *a fortiori* justification for exclusion from the rest of the spaces.

Many feminists who support transwomen's inclusion in women-only spaces simply insist that there is no conflict of interest, *because* transwomen are women.

---

[1] Women's prisons, women's sports, and women's peer support groups (in particular trauma recovery groups, drug and alcohol recovery groups, and lesbian groups) are three examples of spaces where exclusion of transwomen is more intuitive.

Stella Perrett satirized this situation with a cartoon showing a salivating crocodile eyeing up alarmed newts in a pond, a speech bubble above the newts reading 'But—you can't come in here! This is our safe space!', the reply below the crocodile reading 'Don't worry your pretty little heads! I'm transitioning as a newt!'[2] The cartoon was printed in *The Morning Star*, but then removed after activists organized a petition against the newspaper. Activists objected on the grounds that it represented transwomen as predators. But from a gender-critical perspective—the perspective from which Perrett was working,[3] the crocodile represents not transwomen in particular but *men* in general. The imperfection in the parallel is not that a transwoman is depicted as a crocodile, but that in depicting a transwoman as a crocodile Perrett suggested that *all men are predators* (all crocodiles would be a threat to any newts), rather than that *some men are predators, but we don't know which*, and so the blanket exclusion of all men is justified in order for women to keep themselves safe.

Are there any other animals such that most of them are perfectly delightful, but a minority of them are rapists, paedophiles, child abusers, terrorists, murderers, torturers, kidnappers, traffickers, and more?[4] Probably not, so there's no perfect animal metaphor for the situation we're in.[5] Perhaps there are some nice crocodiles, such that we'd want to get a #notallcrocodiles going on Twitter. Still, gender identity activists and the feminists who support them don't generally frame their objections to transwomen's exclusion from women-only spaces as objections to *men's* exclusion from women-only spaces. They don't generally argue against women-only spaces and say that all spaces should be mixed sex. They don't generally think that *any* male who wants in should be permitted to come in. They want there to be women-only spaces, they just want transwomen to be included in them.[6] For these people, transwomen are not like other males. By insisting that 'trans women are women' they can simultaneously push for men's exclusion *and* transwomen's inclusion, seeing no contradiction.[7]

---

[2] The cartoon is archived at <https://wildwomanwritingclub.wordpress.com/2020/02/27/on-the-no-true-trans-newt-cartoon/>

[3] There's a useful discussion between Perrett and Meghan Murphy of *Feminist Current* here: <https://www.feministcurrent.com/2020/05/20/podcast-stella-perrett-on-why-free-speech-and-satire-should-matter-to-feminists/>

[4] One good example of a non-human creature with a bad reputation based on a minority of its members is the mosquito, about which can be said 'mosquitos carry malaria' even though it is only the female *Anopheles* mosquito that spreads it. I have this example from Greg Restall, who uses it to explain generics. See also <https://www.health.nsw.gov.au/Infectious/factsheets/Pages/malaria.aspx>

[5] A reviewer suggested that another example here might be dogs: most are lovely, but some are dangerous, and we generally teach small children to take certain precautions like to not touch strangers' dogs, to not touch dogs while they're eating, etc.

[6] One exception here might be those who campaign for gender-neutral bathrooms to replace sex-separated bathrooms across an entire workplace or public space, e.g. university student 'stalls for all' campaigns.

[7] On arguments for 'trans women are women', see Chapter 3.

For radical and gender-critical feminists, this move is baffling. No evidence is offered to support the claim that transwomen are not like other males. It is as though our opponents are tenderly stroking the crocodile's head, and earnestly insisting that trans newts are newts. Even if it were true that #notallcrocodiles, you could understand why the newts wouldn't want to take the risk. But perhaps this is the crux of the issue: if 'not all males' (in its more popular form, 'not all men') is a massive understatement, because *most* males are just fine and only a minority are not, then the chance of any particular male being a predator is low, and if a particular male had a compelling reason to be in a women-only space, perhaps we might think that reason outweighed the small chance of their posing a risk to women. According to our opponents, we can suppose, transwomen have this compelling reason (even though our opponents wouldn't put things this way publicly).[8]

In Chapter 4 I took the whole package of women-only spaces together, and asked about rationales for those spaces. I also took the perspective of women alone, asking what interests they have in women-only spaces. I think as feminists we have the right to do this, to defend women's interests, and to leave it to the policymakers, and sometimes the people (through democratic mechanisms), to work out the trade-offs between competing groups' interests. I argued that women have the right to exclude males, *all males regardless of gender identity*, from women-only spaces. But I said there that an alternative approach to the question of inclusion in women-only spaces would be to go space-by-space, thinking about the specific rationale(s) for that space alone, and to ask about all stakeholder groups, and do the work that the policymaker would have to do.[9] That is what I will try to do in this essay, focusing on the particular women-only space of women's bathrooms.

---

[8] In my (Lawford-Smith 2019) I explore the idea that our opponents cannot explain publicly what they actually think, especially where they agree with us, because that would undermine their goals. I suggested that our opponents believe that the social acceptance of transwomen as women would reduce transwomen's suicide risk, and that's why they insist so vehemently that transwomen *are* women (rather than saying what they really mean, which is that we should all *act as though* transwomen are women). Mary Leng discusses a similar phenomenon, of our opponents agreeing with us that sex exists and being in some contexts important, but refusing to say so because they deem it 'hateful', and so denouncing us, for that reason, for saying it. She later named this general move the 'Reverse Voltaire': 'I agree completely with what you say, but I'll fight to the death to prevent you from saying it' (Leng 2020). Kathleen Stock also discusses this move in Stock (2021).

[9] I should note that this is (unfortunately) an idealized claim—policymakers around the world have been making changes to laws that affect women without consulting with women, in the name of protecting gender identity. For example, in Australia, the definitions of 'man' and 'woman' were removed from the Federal Sex Discrimination Act in 2013 without any public consultation, nor even any media coverage. In 2019, Tasmania and Victoria (states of Australia) introduced self-identification for legal sex without a public consultation and without adequate consultation with women's groups.

6.1 Why are bathrooms sex-segregated?

A good place to start in thinking about whether we want to change the sex-segregated nature of public bathrooms, whether to go fully mixed-sex or to simply move to a partially mixed-sex model (to accommodate gender identities), is *why* we segregate bathrooms by sex in the first place. That is a historical question rather than a normative question: why did we start doing it? Once we know that, we can ask whether those reasons still support doing it today.

Note that the background facts generally include there not being public provisions for women at all, rather than spaces being welcoming of women but mixed sex. History did not diverge from one set of mixed spaces into two sets of single-sex spaces, but rather evolved from one set of single-sex spaces—spaces for men—into two sets of single-sex spaces, one for men and one for women. Here are some of the historical explanations on offer:

- Moralism about privacy/modesty[10]
- Feminist campaigns for women's bathrooms[11]
- Upper-class gentility and elitism[12]
- Protection of women's safety and privacy interests[13]
- Prototypical anti-sexual harassment interventions[14]

Moralism about privacy/modesty. Sheila Jeffreys writes that 'there is disagreement in scholarship on toilets as to whether the creation of separate toilets for women at this time was the result of a feminist campaign for women's rights, or the result of a moralistic determination to segregate women's bodies from men's view' (Jeffreys 2014, p. 46). A proponent of the latter view is Terry Kogan, who claims that the practice of sex separation in bathrooms only emerged in the late nineteenth century in the United States, as the Industrial Revolution pulled women out of the home and into the factories; and only emerged in the Victorian period in England (Carter 2018, pp. 238 and 268; see also Kogan 2010). The view seems to be that there were social anxieties about women leaving the private sphere and entering public space, violating an ideology of separate spheres for men and women, and thus bringing along concerns about how privacy and modesty would be protected in a mixed public sphere (Jeffreys 2014, p. 46). Authorities worried that men and women using the same toilets was 'indecent' (Carter 2018, p. 238).

For this explanation to be correct, it would have to be the case that bathrooms were not sex-separated prior to the late nineteenth century, or that only male

---

[10] This explanation is discussed in both Jeffreys (2014) and Carter (2018).
[11] This explanation is discussed in Jeffreys (2014).
[12] This explanation is discussed in Carter (2018).
[13] This explanation is discussed in Carter (2018).
[14] This explanation is discussed in Carter (2018).

bathrooms existed, and this was the best explanation of why female bathrooms were added when they were. But W. Burlette Carter argues that this is false, giving a number of examples of sex separation that preceded both the Victorian period and the Industrial Revolution. One comes from a letter to a New York newspaper in 1786, describing a convention for when men and women could use a hot spring for bathing (women in the early morning, signalled by an apron on a pole; men in the late morning, signalled by a hat on the pole) (Carter 2018, p. 269). This was a public space using prototypical versions of signs for 'women' and 'men'. As Carter says, this 'tells us that, around the time of America's founding, people deemed it natural to separate themselves by sex when performing intimate activities like bathing' (p. 269). She gives the further examples of commercial/public bathhouses from the late 1700s offering sex-separated bathing areas (pp. 270–6); ships offering sex-separated bathrooms at either end of the ship (p. 277); schools offering sex-separated bathrooms for pupils (p. 277); sex-separation in prisons being normal in Europe and America (pp. 277–8); and sex-separated public toilets in parks (p. 278). Thus we can reject the claim that bathrooms came to be sex-separated only due to Victorian moralism.

Feminist campaigns for women's bathrooms. Without public toilet provisions, women were subject to a 'urinary leash', a term which refers to a metaphorical leash tying women to their homes, where bathrooms are (i.e. women could only go as far from their homes, and for as long, as determined by the period of time between their needs to urinate).[15] Academics interviewed for a BBC News article on the urinary leash in 2017 commented on Victorian ideas about it being 'improper' for women to use public facilities, where 'the lack of public facilities for women was intentional as a way of controlling their movements and keeping them out of public spaces'; and explained the lengths women had to go to in order to 'extend' the leash, including to drink less water, to hold urine in for long periods, and to simply reduce time spent in public space (Mitra 2017). Jeffreys writes:

> '...women's toilets were created out of a recognition that they were essential to women's equality. Women's subordination on the grounds of their sex has, historically, been organized through the relegation of women to the private sphere and their exclusion from public space...The absence of adequate toilets for women has impeded their entry into the public world. The idea that women have a right to toilets of their own was won fairly recently in the West, and is still being campaigned for in many parts of the world...In the nineteenth century in the UK, for instance, there were no toilets for women in the workplace or in public spaces. This meant that women were at a severe disadvantage, and their

---

[15] Note that some working-class women will have had no choice but to be working outside the home regardless of this problem in toilet provision.

ability to be in the workforce or to use the city and its shopping facilities, which were developing apace in the late nineteenth century, was compromised' (Jeffreys 2014, p. 46).

There is solid historical evidence in favour of the feminist campaigning explanation. Jeffreys reports on work by architectural historian Barbara Penner, who has traced the history of the Ladies Sanitary Association's campaigns from the 1850s onwards, and the Union of Women's Liberal and Radical Association's campaigns from the late 1800s onwards, to create women's toilets in British cities (Jeffreys 2014, p. 46; citing Penner 2001). Men opposed these changes. Jeffreys writes that 'The campaign for toilets was about what would now be understood as the human right of women to existence and movement in public space' (Jeffreys 2014, p. 46). Activists in India still campaign for sex-separated toilets 'on the grounds that women and girls…cannot access work, education or public space on terms of equality whilst there are no women's toilets' (Jeffreys 2014, p. 47).

This explanation can be true without being *exclusive*. It might be that, as Carter argued, people simply find it natural to separate themselves by sex for some purposes (like public bathing), and this explains the sex-separation of some existing public provisions, while the fact that women had been excluded from other domains meant that feminist campaigning was needed to have further provisions for women introduced.

The existing disagreement over which of these first two explanations is correct helps to shed light on why there are tensions between feminists when it comes to women-only spaces. Feminists who see sex-separated spaces as men *relegating* women to a separate space—sex-*segregation* would be a more appropriate term—are more likely to class this together with the long history of men's attempts to relegate women to the separate domain of the domestic, e.g. to keep women in roles as wives, mothers, and caregivers. Seeing these things as similar, such feminists will want to resist being partitioned off from men. Feminists who see sex-separated spaces as hard-won gains over a public space designed *by* men *for* men, on the other hand, are likely to not want to give up these spaces.

Upper-class gentility and elitism. This explanation of the sex-separation of bathrooms is offered by Sheila Cavanagh (Carter 2018, p. 237). Cavanagh connects sex-separated public toilets with a specific event: a ball held at a restaurant in Paris in 1739. She saw this as 'intended to accentuate sexual difference and project its difference onto public space…[and] meant to indicate class standing and genteel respectability' (Cavanagh 2010, p. 28; quoted in Carter 2018, p. 255). In Cavanagh's view, separating the sexes was something the upper-classes did as a signal of class differentiation, not something inherently 'about' the sexes themselves. But Carter traces a line back to the documentary evidence we have about the ball to argue that the innovation at the ball may rather have been placing chamber pots into small separate rooms, not sex-separating the bathrooms.

She also provides evidence of sex-separated bathrooms that predated the Paris ball (Carter 2018, pp. 254–63), and argues that a better explanation of the significance of the bathrooms at the ball was that religious 'authorities were attempting to extend bathroom sex-separation norms into the masquerades and other frivolities' (p. 264). The masquerades were a place of 'raucous drinking and wild sexual behaviour', and may have been seen as a safe space for sexual minorities (there is historical evidence of an attendees' cross-dressing); so the point may rather have been that '*even the masquerades,* which were to be about fun and frolic, were subject to certain limits. The treatment of bathrooms in this case was a message that there could be absolutely *no* deviations from a binary, heterosexual norm' (p. 266; her emphasis).

Protection of women's safety and privacy interests. Carter argues that contra both the moralism about privacy/modesty and the upper-class gentility and elitism explanations, in fact 'the practice [of bathroom sex-separation] dates back to ancient times, [and]...was rooted...in protecting women and children from harassment and violence, including sexual assault' (Carter 2018, p. 238). The Paris ball, featuring heavily in Cavanagh's explanation of sex-segregation as a signal of class status, is documented as having military personnel posted 'at all the doors and each staircase' leading to the bathrooms, suggesting 'that organizers had concerns for everyone's safety...where the bathrooms were located' (p. 258).

Spaces that weren't sex-segregated were generally spaces where 'the safety of women...was not a serious concern', for example where the women involved were poor or dispossessed (p. 278). This included some prisons. Carter writes that 'the story of bathrooms cannot be told without including the story of women's struggles with rape and sexual harassment and their fight for safety within intimate spaces' (p. 254; on the history of rape and sexual harassment see pp. 250–4). And she criticizes the alternative stories (two of which are provided above: moralism and elitism) for erasing or ignoring women's history (pp. 289–90).

Prototypical anti-sexual harassment interventions. Finally, and consistent with the last explanation that sex-segregation has been primarily a matter of women's safety and privacy, Carter suggests that bathroom sex-separation laws were among early labour protection laws, aimed at protecting women from workplace sexual harassment (p. 279). Women entering workplaces previously employing only men were faced with a single set of spaces they would have been forced to share. A report of factory inspections in New York in 1886 recommended sex-separated bathrooms with separate entrances, and female overseers for female workers, in order to put a stop to sexual harassment in the factories, and noted that women had no recourse against their employers or co-workers in the event that they were assaulted (p. 281). Laws were introduced to make stairs in women's work areas opaque (so men couldn't look up their skirts) and to prohibit 'obscene markings' in their bathrooms, both of which indicate ongoing sexualized harassment or bullying (p. 285). There are examples of these early laws in both the UK and the US (pp. 281–7).

If moralism and elitism were credible explanations of why we came to have sex-separated bathrooms, they would be undermining—at least so long as we couldn't offer superseding reasons for maintaining them. But neither was credible. The other three explanations are supportive. Still, we should ask whether the reasons that supported the establishment of sex-separated bathrooms on each of these explanations still hold. Clearly, women still have an interest in their safety and privacy interests being protected, and in policy interventions which protect them from sexual harassment. Women also still have an interest in being in the public sphere. These are all reasons to make sure there are adequate, safe, public bathroom facilities. But that alone does not settle the question of whether women's bathrooms can continue to satisfy those reasons compatible with becoming partly mixed-sex.

6.2 What interests do women have in female-only bathrooms?

Jeffreys, writing against the inclusion of (in her terminology) 'men who transgender' in women's toilets, writes:

> Women-only spaces are either set aside on the grounds that women need the safety and security of places where men are not present, or on the grounds that women as a subordinate group need to be able to meet and organize without members of the ruling group in attendance and until recently, equal opportunity laws have sought to accommodate this understanding by saying that in some situations women may indeed exclude men from services and events. In charters of rights and legislation on equality, women are regularly afforded exemptions from the need to not discriminate on the grounds that as a vulnerable group, albeit a majority one, they may need to meet in women only groups and require spaces such as women only toilets (Jeffreys 2014, pp. 42 and 44, references omitted).

There are three justifications for the existence of women-only space offered here: safety/security, political resistance, and vulnerability. The first is straightforward. On safety, Jeffreys cites Mary Anne Case, who writes 'perusal of sources ranging from newspapers to law report indicates that robbery, assault, molestation, rape, and even murder are not infrequently perpetrated by men who have followed or lain wait for women and girls in the toilet' (Case 2010, p. 220; cited in Jeffreys

2014, p. 48).[16] Young girls visiting mixed-sex toilets in India have been kidnapped and raped (Jeffreys 2014, p. 47; citing Sugden 2013).[17] On security, Jeffreys mentions voyeuristic pornography using hidden cameras, as well as men's desires for exhibitionism/indecent exposure to women (Jeffreys 2014, pp. 48–9). By political resistance Jeffreys seems to mean something like, that the oppressed cannot organize political resistance against their oppressors with their oppressors in the room, or worse, one might think, being given a say in the decision-making about how that resistance is to be accomplished. The last, vulnerability, is not as well filled out. It may overlap with the safety justification, although the reference to the potential need for women-only groups suggests Jeffreys might have something broader in mind, like the consciousness-raising that can help marginalized peoples eventually become politically mobilized.

Do Jeffreys' justifications all really apply to toilets? Safety/security certainly does, but political resistance and vulnerability (understood as being about consciousness-raising) probably do not, given that this doesn't happen in the bathroom in particular.

In Chapter 4 I put forward eight independent rationales for women's sex-separated spaces (the bundle of spaces considered there, not just bathrooms). They were:

- Safety
- Privacy/dignity/comfort
- Justice/fairness
- Respite
- Shared bodily experience
- Intimate association
- Self-determination
- Intent of the creators

The first overlaps one of Jeffreys' justifications. Of the rest, several are irrelevant to bathrooms in particular: justice/fairness, intimate association, self-determination, and intent of the creators. For all of these it would be possible to make a case for how they do in fact apply (e.g. feminist campaigners fought for sex-separated bathrooms for women in public space, as we saw above, and so in that sense there is an intent of the creators to consider; there is a kind of 'culture' to women's

---

[16] Case's solution is fully mixed-sex toilets, so that the 'good men' can defend women from the 'bad men'.
[17] Jeffreys cites an article by Joanna Sugden in the *Wall Street Journal* called 'Why women go to the toilet in groups', from 2013. The link to the article is now broken and there is no record of it on the WSJ's blog. Sugden herself tweeted on 19th November 2013: 'In India, many women go to the bathroom in groups out of fear rather than companionship', <https://twitter.com/jhsugden/status/402684110591647744>

public bathroom usage, and so in that sense bathrooms may contribute to intimate association between women more broadly)—but I won't rely on any such case. So we're left with:

- Safety
- Privacy/dignity/comfort
- Respite
- Shared bodily experience[18]

To this list we can add, specific to bathrooms:

- Different needs (sex/body-based)
- Older women/intergenerational gender politics
- Respect for women's boundaries
- Democratic preferences (procedural justice)

Women have different bathroom-related needs to men, including needing to deal with menstruation, being more likely to have small children with them who need assistance, and being more likely to want to check or refresh hair and makeup in bathroom mirrors. Alone, this is only a reason to ensure adequate bathroom provisions for women (whether mixed-sex or not); together with other rationales like privacy and dignity, and shared bodily experience, it gives additional support to keeping women's bathrooms sex-separated.

Older women who have lived through much more explicitly sexist times may be especially reluctant to suddenly have men in intimate spaces like bathrooms. There are intergenerational politics to be considered here. The younger generation feel differently about sex and gender, seeing sex as less important and gender (as identity) as more important, but that doesn't give them the right to *force* the older generation to relate to each other in the ways that they (the younger) prefer. If younger men have really changed so much that sex-separation for that generation is unnecessary (which I personally doubt very much, hearing what

---

[18] In his book *Psychology in the Bathroom*, Nick Haslam notes the support and solidarity shown between women in public bathrooms through graffiti, saying that research into this graffiti—or 'latrinalia' – has shown 'Women's tends to be more confessional, more friendly, more likely to express solidarity with other women, more socially acceptable and more romance-related'; that it 'more often involves replies to existing items than men's'; and that 'Women tend to engage in more exchanges in which advice is sought and given, and inputs are generally helpful and sisterly' (Haslam 2012, p. 124). Elizabeth McClintock, writing for *Psychology Today*, reports asking colleagues at a conference about their use of the bathrooms, whose signs had been papered over as 'unisex'. She wrote that 'Men expressed far greater discomfort', in part because of 'differences in gendered restroom cultures', namely that 'women are more relaxed and chatty in public restrooms and make less effort to avoid eye contact or adjacent stalls' (McClintock 2015; on the last claim referencing Moore and and Breeze 2012). These differences in how men and women use bathrooms might amount to cultural losses if we move away from sex-segregation.

some teachers and parents say about the sexual harassment of teenage girls by teenage boys in schools, and what girls themselves have documented in one recent project)[19] then that is well and good, but it doesn't entail that *older men* have changed, and therefore that sex-separation is unnecessary across all generations. Imagine being in a workplace in which your persistent sexual harasser now claims to be a woman, and so is supported by management and your other colleagues in sharing your bathroom. That quite literally removes the last safe space in the workplace.

Respect for women's boundaries is a somewhat abstract consideration, which relates to bathrooms as much as any other women-only space. Following Marilyn Frye (1983) we can note that in a male-dominated society, the assertion of boundaries is an affront to men: women are not supposed to *have* boundaries, and certainly do not have the privilege to 'exclude' men from anything. As she put it, 'It is always the privilege of the master to enter the slave's hut. The slave who decides to exclude the master from her hut is declaring herself not a slave' (Frye 1983, p. 104). Historically, men resisted the *establishment* of women's public bathrooms, as part of their increasing entry into public space. But they have not otherwise been interested in those spaces. Now, however, some progressive men have taken an interest in women's bathrooms (and indeed the full suite of women-only spaces), in the role of acting as allies to transwomen. A YouGov (UK) survey from 2020 showed public support for transwomen's access to women's toilets, although the extent of that support dropped when it was made clear the transwomen hadn't had sex-reassignment surgery (which, as we saw in Chapter 5, most haven't) (Smith 2020). To those who support transwomen's inclusion, the insistence of radical and gender-critical feminists that they should be excluded is seen as an affront. Feminists should have anticipated this. Women's boundaries are respected for precisely as long as men have no interest in what is being cordoned off from them. As soon as they have an interest, we cannot expect women's boundaries to be respected. This is one further explanation of the otherwise inexplicable insistence in the public debate over women-only spaces that inclusion would be good for transwomen and bad for no one. Women are *no one*.[20]

Finally, there are democratic preferences to consider. There is substantial disagreement about transwomen's inclusion in women-only spaces in countries that have allowed a public debate on this issue (such as the UK, which held a public consultation on changes to the Gender Recognition Act in 2018). When people are polled, serious disagreement about who should use which spaces is revealed (Smith 2020). When there is reasonable disagreement on an issue of serious

---

[19] Sydney woman Chanel Contos started a petition for sexual consent education in schools, asking for both signatures and testimonies from those who had been assaulted as students. There were more than 6,000 testimonies as of May 24th 2021. See <https://www.teachusconsent.com/>

[20] See also my essay 'No conflict of interests, they said', to appear in Petra Bueskens (Ed.), *Heterodox Feminism* (in preparation).

consequence, liberal states ought to defer to fair procedures, rather than simply impose a substantive conception of the good on everyone.[21] The UK did the right thing in this respect to have a public consultation; the Australian states of Tasmania and Victoria did the wrong thing. (New Zealand did something closer to the Australian states: a consultation that was poorly advertised, open only for a very brief period of time, and coincided with a stringent lockdown). It is not unreasonable to suppose that a public consultation would have revealed similar opposition in Australia to replacing sex with gender-identity as emerged in the UK and New Zealand, with grassroots movements of women rising up to defend sex-based rights.[22] Whether that movement would have ultimately been successful in Australia, there is a serious disrespect of citizens in the fact that it was not allowed to happen.[23]

These are all interests that are served by women having sex-separated bathrooms. But as I mentioned at the end of Section 6.1, there is a difference between having *perfectly* sex-separated bathrooms (only female people using one, only male people using the other), and having *imperfectly* sex-separated bathrooms. Changing the social rules around inclusion in women-only spaces, moving from sex to gender identity as the basis of inclusion, does make those spaces mixed sex, but it is not as though it makes the ratio 1:1 male/female as it would if *all* bathrooms were made unisex. If all bathrooms were made unisex, we (as a society) would lose all of the goods for women secured by sex-separated bathrooms, even if we gained other goods in exchange. Strictly speaking, we do give up 'sex-separation' when we shift from sex to gender identity. But what we end up with is still spaces used disproportionately by one sex. Most males will still use the men's bathroom, and most females will still use the women's bathroom. It's just that a few males will use the women's, and a few females will use the men's. It's only transwomen that women are being asked (or in some places, being made, by law)

---

[21] When there is *unreasonable disagreement,* this is not the case. Sue Kedgley talks in her book *Fifty Years a Feminist* about holding public consultations all around New Zealand to hear from women about women's issues, which were attended by large numbers of conservative women opposing changes that would advance women's rights. The government simply chose to end the consultation, presumably judging that conservative opposition was *unreasonable*—expanded rights for women didn't take anything away from women who wanted to remain housewives, it simply gave opportunities to women who didn't want to do that (Kedgley 2021).

[22] Key to those movements were the organized groups, in New Zealand Speak Up For Women and Save Women's Sports Australasia, in the UK Fair Play for Women, Woman's Place UK, Standing for Women, For Women Scotland, MurrayBlackburnMackenzie, and chapters of ReSisters throughout the country.

[23] The likely response will be that the law should sometimes lead, and not only follow. It may help to remember that in introducing equal marriage, Australia held an extravagantly expensive postal ballot (playing a similar role to a referendum), rather than 'leading' the public by changing the law and hoping for social attitudes to follow, and this was only a matter of allowing gay people to marry their partners, not changing the whole meaning of sex and impacting countless other issues in law and social life by doing so. There is no easy explanation for why self-identification for sex should be a 'law should lead' issue but gay marriage a 'law should follow' issue.

to include in women's bathrooms. This is relevant to considering the extent to which the interests at stake are negatively affected.

I'll say more about this in Section 6.5, when we get to talking about the trade-offs between different stakeholders. But for now it's worth noting two points.

The first is psychological: it may be a cause of anxiety in women that (some) males are *allowed* to use women's bathrooms, even when it is rare for any individual woman to actually encounter a male in a public bathroom. This point is often dismissed in the public debate. One reason for this seems to be that in any conflict of interests between a woman and a transwoman, it is assumed that the woman is the 'oppressor' and the transwoman is the 'oppressed', so that the woman's feeling anxious about the transwoman is on a moral par with a white person feeling anxious about the presence of a black person as racial segregation was ending. But sex-separation is not ending: pretty much all sides agree that males are responsible for the bulk of the sexual and other physical violence, and that women have good reason to worry about this and take precautions against becoming a victim of it. They're just not supposed to feel anxious when a particular subgroup of males claim 'not me, though!', in virtue of their identification with women/womanhood.

The second is that relative numbers—the difference between women's bathrooms being fully mixed-sex (unisex) versus being nominally sex-separated but inclusive of gender identities—might not be so important, if *one male* is enough to cause a serious setback to the interests advanced by sex-separated bathrooms. For example, some women have post-traumatic stress disorder as a result of being violently assaulted by males. If such a woman encounters a male in a relatively deserted public bathroom, this may be triggering for her. Knowing that this could happen and keep happening may cause her to start self-excluding from women's public bathrooms, which effectively puts her back on the 'urinary leash' women were subject to before public bathrooms were ever introduced. So we should be wary of women's interests in sex-separated bathrooms being dismissed with the claim that we're not talking about *many* males using those spaces.

6.3 What interests do transwomen have in being included in women's bathrooms?

Like many of the feminist philosophers who are open about their views on this topic, Jennifer Saul thinks that 'trans women are women and should therefore be allowed to use women's toilets' (Saul 2012, p. 204).[24] We might want to know *why*

---

[24] Esa Diaz-Leon seems to have a similar view, given that she has to suppose a 'trans-misogynist community' to be the context where a discussion of 'whether Charla [a transwoman who has not had genital surgery] should be allowed to use women's restrooms' takes place (Diaz-Leon 2016, p. 249).

she insists that transwomen are women, given that this makes the question of their inclusion semantic (because they are women) rather than a matter that needs to be settled by working through the relevant issues. Sometimes, Saul simply reports this as a 'feeling':[25] 'Many others, like me, feel that it is important to count trans women as women' (Saul 2012, p. 200); 'I feel quite strongly that we should recognize the preferred categorizations of trans women (and trans men)' (Saul 2012, p. 201); 'It matters a great deal to me to find out how trans women want to use and to define "woman"' (Saul 2012, p. 213).[26]

But at other points, she offers something of a justification, including that 'it is generally very important to trans women that they be considered women' (Saul 2012, p. 200); that 'most if not all trans women face enormous obstacles due to this self-identification, obstacles that include discrimination, ostracization, and violence' (Saul 2012, p. 200); and that biological views of womanhood 'exclude trans women from places where they want to be and things that they want to do' (Saul 2012, p. 204). She specifically mentions in this connection their use of women's restrooms. In summary form:

- Personal importance
- Avoidance of discrimination, ostracization, and violence
- Inclusive (/not exclusionary)

The first justification is straightforward: if it is important to transwomen that they be considered women, and to consider someone to be a woman is to endorse their use of spaces intended for women, then it will be important to allow transwomen to use the women's bathroom. The only question we need to ask here is

---

She characterizes a 'trans-misogynist community' as a community 'where most people believe that trans women should not be treated as women in legal and practical matters: for instance, members of that community believe that trans women should not be allowed to use women's restrooms, and so on' (Diaz-Leon 2016, p. 247). It may strike the reader as puzzling that the term 'misogyny'—usually used to characterize men's attitudes about women or men's treatment of women—is here being used to describe mostly women's political beliefs about males' use of social spaces. (The gender-critical movement, a vocal dissident as to this use of spaces, has mostly women members). But for people who define transwomen as women in advance, 'misogyny' can be extended to some males without difficulty, on the grounds that those males are women too. Diaz-Leon is assuming that disagreement with the idea that transwomen should be treated as women in legal and practical matters must be a form of 'misogyny', because it's treating some *women*, on her understanding, badly.

[25] Saul worries at multiple points about 'doing justice to' transwomen's claims of womanhood (Saul 2012, pp. 210–12). It's not clear whether this is a 'feeling' *that* we should do justice to such claims, or a hat tip to a justification, namely that the self-identifications of people outside a category into a category have a particular significance or importance that underwrites others' taking them seriously. One can imagine, for example, giving such a justification in terms of radical self-determination.

[26] Interestingly, Saul says explicitly 'I consider their views [trans women's] more important than, for example, those of right-wing Christians. And I would be very lacking in self-knowledge indeed if I did not acknowledge that political considerations inform this preference' (Saul 2012, p. 213). There is a background political view about whose views/values matter politically here, and this is driving Saul's deference in the matter of what 'woman' means. It is unclear where (non-trans) women fit in this hierarchy.

whether there's anything equally important to, or more important than what is important to transwomen, for example, what is important to women. Questions of inclusion are not settled simply by noting what is important to one set of stakeholders.

The second and third justifications are a little more complicated. Because transwomen identify as women, they face discrimination, ostracization, and violence. How could that *fact*, supposing that it is one, support the use of women's bathrooms? One answer could be, that men's bathrooms are a site of discrimination, ostracization, and/or violence, and women's bathrooms are the safest available option in avoiding those things. Another answer could be, that discrimination, ostracization, and violence are the result of a lack of acceptance of transwomen's claims *that they are women*, and so accepting that transwomen are women, and therefore that they belong in any space intended for women, including women's bathrooms, is a partial remedy to that lack of acceptance and therefore violence. It is a kind of pushback against others' lack of acceptance, or a way of avoiding making a contribution to the negative outcomes that transwomen face.

Saul's final justification was that biological views of womanhood stop transwomen from being in places they want to be. Suppose the women's bathroom is one such place. The idea seems to be that we want to exclude transwomen *only* because we have the wrong view of womanhood. If we didn't, we wouldn't. So, we should get the right view of womanhood, and welcome transwomen into women's bathrooms. This would be a fair point if the only purpose of a biological view of womanhood was to exclude transwomen, and there were no countervailing reasons to justify excluding transwomen from places they wanted to be and things they wanted to do. But to think this, you'd have to think either that there is no conflict of interests between transwomen's interests and women's interests, or that even if there is, transwomen's interests trump those of women.

Perhaps the biological view of womanhood is false, or spaces for biological women (only) serve no plausible interest that women have; or perhaps the biological view of womanhood is true, and spaces for biological women do serve a plausible interest that women have, but those things ultimately do not matter, because in any conflict of interests between transwomen and women, transwomen win. There is room for disagreement about whether the biological view of womanhood is true or false. I think it is true, Saul thinks it is false.[27] But it is far from obvious that spaces for biological women don't serve a plausible interest that those women have in being without (any/all) males, or that transwomen should

---

[27] To me, it makes much more sense to say that a woman is any female person, regardless of what she is like; than to say that a woman is a person *like this*, regardless of her sex. (*Like this* can be filled in in various ways: occupies this social position; plays this social role; fulfils this function; has this identity). For an excellent discussion of the mistake feminists have made in conceiving of 'woman' as a social role rather than a class of material persons, see Stock (manuscript).

win in any conflict of interests. Saul herself provides no justification for either of those claims.

6.4 Are there other interests to consider?

In Sections 6.2 and 6.3 I considered the two main groups of stakeholders to this issue: women, and transwomen. But there are other stakeholders, too, and in reaching a decision about policy, we must consider all of them. There are (non-trans) men, there are (non-trans) gender non-conforming people who are routinely mis-sexed and have difficulty in public bathrooms, there are children (particularly with regard to safeguarding), there are town and city councils, responsible for public bathroom provisions, and there are companies and corporations, responsible for bathroom provisions in workplaces and other privately-owned spaces that are visited by the general public.

Men. At least according to some research, men feel fear in men's bathrooms, whether they are trans or not. Emerging from an interview-based sociological study of the use and perception of public toilets, Sarah Moore and Simon Breeze report 'men's sense of fear concerning the threat of violence in these civic spaces and the relative absence of such feelings amongst the female participants' (Moore and Breeze 2012, p. 1172). They write (perhaps a little hyperbolically) 'For women...public toilets are a place of communality. For men, in contrast, they are nightmarish spaces' (p. 1178). They think men's fear is about 'being watched', and 'being made the object of sexual desire' (p. 1173).

It is likely that women do not feel this fear precisely because public toilets are sex-separated: the fear relates to men. But if there is a way to redesign public bathrooms so that men's fears—of other men—are alleviated, that will count in favour of the redesign. This helps to show that the solution to keeping transwomen safe in public bathrooms is not to simply have them use the women's bathrooms. Transwomen are not the only males who feel themselves to be unsafe in men's bathrooms, and there's no coherent way to have *all* the men who feel unsafe using men's bathrooms use women's bathrooms instead, at least not without utterly collapsing sex-separation. (Instead of 'men's' and 'women's' we'd either end up with 'self-aware violent men's' and 'everyone else's'; or we'd end up with two sets of unisex bathrooms that *everyone* feels unsafe in, because everyone is afraid of the men, including the men themselves).

Gender non-conforming people (who are not trans). The character of Jess in *Stone Butch Blues*—who had started off as a butch lesbian, transitioned to live as a man, and then detransitioned back to a kind of awkward in-between space (thinking of herself as a woman but generally perceived by others as a man)—says in a conversation with a new friend: 'When I was growing up, I believed I was gonna do something really important with my life, like explore the universe or cure diseases. I never thought I'd spend so much of my life fighting over which bathroom I could use' (Feinberg 1993, p. 278). It's important to take into account how exhausting and stressful it is for women perceived some or all of the time to be men to go through life having to worry about public bathrooms. Being questioned by women when using women's bathrooms, even being yelled at or having security called on you, is deeply unpleasant (see also Watson 2016). Radical and gender-critical feminists like myself, keen to reassert the importance of single-sex spaces to women, need to be careful that the policy proposals they support are not inadvertently hurting some women.

Children. There is an issue of safeguarding when it comes to bathrooms, which may be used by children and adolescents independently of their parents (e.g. at swimming pools). However small their number is, there are some males who are paedophiles, some males who are voyeurs, and some males who are exhibitionists, and any such males may have an interest in including themselves into women's bathrooms in order to access female children and adolescents as targets. Again, to avoid being misrepresented—as is all too common on this issue—I am not talking about males who identify as women in particular. I'm talking about males in general: all/any males, regardless of gender identity. We're all fairly good at saying who's male and who's female just by looking; but none of us can say just by looking what someone's gender identity is. A male may identify as a woman and yet do absolutely nothing to *express* that identity to the world. No woman or child coming into contact with such a male can know, just by looking, whether he is a non-trans male or a transwoman (or has some other gender identity, like 'nonbinary'). Thus making access to bathrooms a matter of gender identity removes the ability of women and children to keep themselves away from males, who *might* be predatory.[28] For fear of 'misgendering', women and children are asked to take it on trust that any male person including themselves in the women's bathroom in fact has a 'woman' gender identity.[29] To put that more starkly:

---

[28] A likely objection is that *women* may be predatory in all of these same ways too. That is true, but the numbers are much, much lower. The differences between the sexes in violent crime, and sexually motivated crime, are striking, and sufficient to justify sex-separation on precautionary and probabilistic grounds. For example, data on incarcerated Australians in 2021 show that about ten times more men than women were in for homicide and related offences, about fourteen times more men than women were in for acts intended to cause injury, and about sixty-two times more men than women were in for sexual assault and related offences. Sexual assault was a 98.4% male-perpetrated crime, and thirteen out of sixteen categories of serious crime are more than 90% male-perpetrated (Australian Bureau of Statistics 2021; Lawford-Smith, forthcoming). Nothing can make people perfectly safe, but sex-separation in some domains is a good way to keep women fairly safe.

[29] And further, that having a 'woman' gender identity makes that male person 'safe' in a way that wouldn't be true had he not that identity. For example, the Michigan Technological University had posters up in 2019 saying 'Do you feel like someone is using the wrong bathroom? Don't: Stare at them, Challenge them, Insult them, Purposely make them feel uncomfortable. Do: Respect their privacy, Respect their identity, Carry on with your day. Transgender and non-binary students. You have every right to be here: In this facility, In this community, In this University, In the this World'

because the protected attribute of 'gender identity' has no content apart from a mental state, a female child or adolescent (or indeed, a woman) faced with a male who *could be* a transwoman (in virtue of gender identity) or could be a sexual predator is asked to simply believe that they're the former. This completely undermines safeguarding for children and adolescents who use the women's bathroom.

Councils and companies. Finally, there are financial costs to consider. Some existing buildings have heritage status, and so cannot easily be renovated to change bathroom provisions. Many men's bathrooms have urinals in them, which would create a legal risk of indecent exposure if left in place while being relabelled as 'gender neutral' or 'unisex'. For new builds, some kinds of bathrooms are more expensive than others: fully enclosed rooms with floor-to-ceiling doors and their own washbasins, versus large rooms with multiple cubicles, versus rows of urinals. Such financial and legal costs also create opportunity costs—things that councils and companies could be doing with funding instead of bathroom renovations.

It's not clear whether councils and companies should be properly considered stakeholders. Their interests are purely financial, different in kind to the interests of the other stakeholder groups. We might want to say that we decide on bathroom policy by considering all the values at stake for different groups, and then we simply require that policy (at least for new builds) *regardless of the price*, so long as the price is not unreasonable. I'll assume that the price difference between different bathroom options for new builds is not so great as to be a decisive consideration in making the tradeoffs between the other stakeholders.

6.5 How do these competing interests trade off against each other?

There are a limited number of ways to build bathrooms, and a limited number of ways to think of inclusion in the bathrooms we already have. The status quo in public spaces is to have two sets of bathrooms: women's, and men's. These have traditionally been understood to segregate on the basis of sex. But in practice, transsexual and transgender people have long since been using the bathrooms of the sex they identify with. What has changed over time is the trans population itself, both in size, and in moving from 'binary' trans (conformity to norms of appearance for the opposite sex, which functions as a 'signal' of trans status in those who do not pass as the opposite sex) to 'nonbinary' trans, meaning that there is less importance placed on conforming to particular norms of

---

(Reneau 2019). Because we cannot detect other people's 'identities', this effectively means the MTU is asking women students not to challenge *any* male in the women's bathrooms (see also Chapter 5, Section 5.4).

appearance.[30] This has increased the conflict of interests, as more identifiably male people use women's bathrooms.

If we take existing spaces as they are, the options are a) strict sex-separation, b) non-strict sex-separation (the status quo), c) gatekeeper separation (i.e. social rules like 'if you pass, you pass'); co-opting existing alternative bathrooms (i.e. disabled bathrooms as third spaces for transwomen). None of these are particularly appealing. Strict sex-separation creates problems for passing transsexual and transgender people. Non-strict sex-separation creates problems for women. Gatekeeper separation allows challenge on the basis of appearance which will have negative impacts on gender non-conforming people who are actually using the bathrooms that correspond to their sex. Co-opting existing alternative bathrooms is bad for people with disabilities, who already have minimal provisions. The first three options are bad for nonbinary people, who don't want to be reminded of their biological sex every time they use a public bathroom. If we relabel, or renovate, or build new bathrooms, the options are:

- Two sets of sex-separated bathrooms, and a 'third space' bathroom for nonbinary, transsexual, and transgender people, and anyone else who wants to use them.
- Unisex fully-enclosed rooms with floor-to-ceiling walls and doors, and a washbasin.
- One set of unisex rooms with multiple cubicles (neither walls nor doors floor-to-ceiling) and communal washbasins.
- Two sets of unisex rooms as just described, but where one set also has some urinals, and the other set also has some sanitary bins.
- Four sets of bathrooms—male, female, nonbinary and transgender, and disabled.

(This last option could also be reduced to three sets, as it already is in some bathrooms, by adding a cubicle with provisions for people with disabilities into each sex-separated bathroom, rather than having these as additional spaces.)

Unfortunately, we can't simply give everyone what they want: some women want no males using women's bathrooms, and some males want to use women's bathrooms. So we have to trade off. There are a number of different ways to trade these interests off against each other, according to abstract principles. We might accord each group's interests equal weight, and then look only at the quality of the interests affected, and how many people are in each group having those interests affected. In principle, this would mean bigger groups with less serious interests could win out over smaller groups with more serious interests. This is just to throw everything into a utility calculus and see what emerges. Alternatively, we

---

[30] For a discussion of the signalling effects of clothing and other presentational choices, see Chapter 5.

might give some groups' interests greater weight. We might think children's interests, for example, matter a lot, and have greater weight than adults' interests. We might take a 'prioritarian' approach and make a prior judgement about which groups are the worst off in society, and then weight their interests most heavily against others.

I suspect each group could make a case for priority. To avoid attempting to referee such a competition I will simply take the first approach. This is already something of a novelty in the public discussion, which tends to focus on the interests of trans and nonbinary people and simply advocate the policy which advances their interests: people should be able to use the bathroom they prefer, and we should create new spaces for nonbinary people. This chapter is a reminder that trans people are not the only stakeholder in the bathroom debate, and that some of the other groups with distinctive interests (women, children, and gender nonconforming people who are not trans) are also marginalized. It is not remotely reasonable that bathroom policy be decided by simply considering the interests of one stakeholder group.

There is no avoiding taking a stand on the value of certain interests. I will assume that safety and privacy matter more than inclusion and validation of identity. Women and children have a safety interest in not having men use their bathrooms. Men feel fear about using men's bathrooms. It is not clear whether transwomen's safety interest in not using men's bathrooms *is* that fear, or is something more—I'll simply grant for the sake of argument that it's more. But there are more women and more children than there are transwomen. It is not clear whether transwomen are more at risk of violence from men in men's bathrooms than women and children are at risk of violence from men in women's bathrooms, because there is little empirical evidence on this point (beyond anecdotal reports of specific incidents). Transwomen are not at risk of violation of privacy in men's bathrooms, while women and children are at risk of violation of privacy from men in women's bathrooms. Men are uncomfortable using shared (unisex) bathrooms (McClintock 2015). Women object to unisex spaces that they are dirtier than single-sex spaces (e.g. urine on the toilet seats). There are cultural losses involved in shifting away from sex-separated spaces, especially for gay men.[31] How does the utility calculus turn out?

For new builds, the best option is unisex fully-enclosed rooms with floor-to-ceiling walls and doors, and a washbasin. For safety reasons, these should not be located in a deserted part of the building. This will involve a small cost for women who prefer not to use the same bathrooms as men because they are less hygienic in their use of such space, but it does pretty well on every other measure, giving everyone safety and privacy, and avoiding throwing the sexes together in

---

[31] See discussion in Jeffreys (2014) and Haslam (2012, Chapter 7).

awkward or embarrassing encounters in rooms with shared cubicles, or at communal washbasins. If we avoid labelling bathrooms as for a particular sex, we sidestep all issues about who may appropriately use them. Anyone may.

For existing buildings, the best option in buildings with multiple bathrooms (e.g. bathrooms on each level) is to leave some sex-separated, and repurpose some as third-gender/gender-neutral. That protects safety and privacy for women while ensuring that there are spaces that trans and nonbinary people can use without feeling uncomfortable. It involves a small cost for trans people who prefer to use the bathrooms of the opposite sex, who are asked not to, in the interests of a solution that works for everyone. Having some bathrooms that are sex-separated and some that are not gives everyone something of what they want, taking all stakeholders interests' seriously rather than prioritizing some over others.

Finally, the hard question: what about in buildings with only one set of sex-separated bathrooms, so that there is no option for co-opting some existing spaces and making them 'third spaces'? In my view, 'if you pass you pass' does more harm to gender non-conforming people who are not trans than it does good to women, or anyone else who wants to use strictly sex-separated bathrooms.[32] In such cases, there's a straight up conflict of interests between women and transwomen, and a difficulty for nonbinary people in which space to use. A potential solution in this case would be to relabel the men's bathroom as gender-neutral/unisex, and leave the women's bathroom sex-separated. Men's discomfort is the price of women's safety and privacy in this non-ideal situation. This puts some pressure on men, who are not at additional safety risk, to get used to having men and women with a diverse range of gender expressions in their bathrooms. In the short-term, however, it creates a risk to trans people of facing discriminatory comments or even violence from intolerant men. But the alternative—to create a risk to women and girls of voyeurism, exhibitionism, and assault; and to cause women anxiety and a heightened need for vigilance by leaving men's bathrooms to men, and opening up women's bathrooms to everyone else—is worse. (There are many more women than transwomen; it is worse because there is more disutility). If it can be demonstrated, with empirical evidence, that the latter risk (to women and girls) is lower than the former risk (to transwomen), that would tip the scales in the direction of non-strict sex-separation (the status quo).

---

[32] There's also the problem that trans people may believe they pass when they do not.

6.6 Conclusion

Women and transwomen are two marginalized groups, and there is still a lot of work to do before either has achieved social equality. The solution to conflicts of interests between them is not to declare one the 'winner' and ignore the other group, but to find a way to accommodate both of their interests, as far as that is possible. It is aggravating to gender-critical feminists that when the conflict of interests is pointed out, activists for transwomen don't back down and look for a compromise, but simply get louder. Trans rights shouldn't come at the expense of women's rights, and especially at the expense of women's safety. We can apply this thought to bathrooms in particular. The best solution for new builds, taking everyone's interests into account, is enclosed single-stall spaces not located in a deserted area of a building. The best solution for existing buildings with multiple bathroom areas is to retain some bathrooms as sex-separated and repurpose others as gender-neutral. Unacceptable are unisex bathrooms with cubicles (whether a single set, or two sets, one with urinals and the other with sanitary bins). Also unacceptable is the idea that any man who chooses to use the existing women's bathrooms may not be challenged. This advice effectively gaslights women by telling them that they can have safety and privacy only on a man's terms: if he decides he wants to be included then his interests trump, no matter who he is. And that is no safety or privacy at all.

References

Australian Bureau of Statistics (ABS*b*). 'Prisoner characteristics, Australia (Tables 1 to 13)', *Prisoners in Australia, 2021*, Table_1. Online at <https://www.abs.gov.au/statistics/people/crime-and-justice/prisoners-australia/latest-release#data-download>

Carter, W. Burlette. 'Sexism in the "Bathroom Debates": How bathrooms really became separated by sex', *Yale Law & Policy Review* 37 (2018), pp. 227–97.

Case, Mary Anne. 'Why not abolish laws of urinary segregation?' in Harvey Molotch and Laura Noren (Eds.) *Toilet: Public Restrooms and the Politics of Sharing* (New York: New York University Press, 2010), pp. 211–25.

Cavanagh, Sheila. *Queering Bathrooms: Gender, Sexuality and the Hygenic Imagination* (Toronto: University of Toronto Press, 2010).

Diaz-Leon, Esa. '*Woman* as a politically significant term: A solution to the puzzle', *Hypatia* 31/2 (2016), pp. 245–58.

Feinberg, Leslie. *Stone Butch Blues* (Michigan: Firebrand Books, 1993).

Frye, Marilyn. *The Politics of Reality* (New York: Crossing Press; 1983).

Haslam, Nick. *Psychology in the Bathroom* (Hampshire: Palgrave Macmillan, 2012).

Jeffreys, Sheila. 'The politics of the toilet: A feminist response to the campaign to "degender" a women's space', *Women's Studies International Forum* 45 (2014), pp. 42–51.

Kedgley, Sue. *Fifty Years a Feminist* (Wellington: Massey University Press, 2021).

Kogan, Terry. 'Sex separation: The cure-all for Victorian social anxiety', in Harvey Molotch and Laura Noren (Eds.) *Toilet: Public Restrooms and the Politics of Sharing* (New York: New York University Press, 2010), pp. 145–66.

Lawford-Smith, Holly. 'How the trans-rights movement is turning philosophers into activists', *Quillette*, 20th September 2019. Online at <https://quillette.com/2019/09/20/how-the-trans-rights-movement-is-turning-academic-philosophers-into-sloganeering-activists/>

Lawford-Smith, Holly. 'Female offenders', in Jesper Ryberg (Ed.) *Oxford Handbook of Punishment Theory and Philosophy* (Part 5, 'Punishment and special offenders') (New York: Oxford University Press, forthcoming).

Leng, Mary. 'Harry Potter and the Reverse Voltaire', *Medium*, 13th July 2020. Online at https://medium.com/@mary.leng/harry-potter-and-the-reverse-voltaire-4c7f3a07241

McClintock, Elizabeth. 'Why some welcome unisex bathrooms, and some steer clear', *Psychology Today*, 17th September 2015.

Mitra, Rotwika. '100 Women: How the "urinary leash" keeps women at home', *BBC News*, 19th November 2017.

Moore, Sarah, and Breeze, Simon. 'Spaces of male fear: The sexual politics of being watched', *British Journal of Criminology* 52/6 (2012), pp. 1172–91.

Penner, Barbara. 'A world of unmentionable suffering: Women's public conveniences in Victorian London', *Journal of Design* 14/2 (2001), pp. 35–43.

Reneau, Annie. 'This university's transgender bathroom signs are on point', *Upworthy*, 21st Februaru 2019. Online at <https://www.upworthy.com/this-university-s-transgender-bathroom-signs-are-on-point>

Quinn, Karl. 'Now I use the men's bathroom, but it's still uncomfortable', *The Age*, 27th February 2021. Online at <https://www.brisbanetimes.com.au/lifestyle/gender/now-i-use-the-mens-bathroom-but-its-still-uncomfortable-20210227-p576d4.html>

Saul, Jennifer. 'Politically significant terms and philosophy of language', in Sharon L. Crasnow and Anita M. Superson (Eds.) *Out from the Shadows: Analytical Feminist Contributions to Traditional Philosophy* (Oxford: Oxford University Press, 2012).

Smith, Matthew. 'Where does the British public stand on transgender rights?' *YouGov*, 16th July 2020. Online at <https://yougov.co.uk/topics/politics/articles-reports/2020/07/16/where-does-british-public-stand-transgender-rights>

Stock, Kathleen. *Material Girls: Why Reality Matters for Feminism* (UK: Little, Brown, 2021).

Stock, Kathleen. 'Not the social kind: Anti-naturalist mistakes in the philosophical history of womanhood', manuscript as at 24th February 2020. Online at <https://philpapers.org/rec/STONTS>

Watson, Lori. 'The woman question', *Transgender Studies Quarterly* 3/1 (2016), pp. 248–55.

III
SPEECH

7
Is 'TERF' a Slur?[1]

There's a spirited contemporary literature on slurs (e.g. Anderson and Lepore 2013*a*, 2013*b*; Bach 2014; Bolinger 2015; Camp 2013; Cepollaro 2015; Croom 2011, 2015; Hedger 2012; Hom 2008; Jeshion 2013, 2016; Marques and Garcia-Carpintero 2020; Nunberg 2017; Richard 2008; Saka 2007; Swanson, forthcoming; Williamson 2009; Whiting 2013), but it tends to proceed on the basis of confidence about particular terms being slurs,[2] and build theories that focus on providing accounts of how it is that these terms function as slurs. This is all very well if we already know which things are slurs, and just want to compare candidate theories of those things. But what if we come to the literature with a genuine question: *is this term a slur?* In this paper I work in reverse, starting from theories of slurs offered which accommodate central cases, and asking whether they would also accommodate the particular term that I'm interested in: 'TERF'. I do this not only because I genuinely want to know *whether* 'TERF' is a slur, but also because I think it's an interesting reflection on the literature on slurs if it lacks classificatory power, that is, if existing theories cannot deliver novel verdicts about uncertain cases.

The term 'TERF'—originally an acronym for 'trans-exclusionary radical feminist' and now often functioning as a word in its own right—has become a source of controversy in contemporary debates over women's liberation and trans rights. In light of increased public debate on issues surrounding how best to recognize and protect gender identity (including debate on reforms to the Gender Recognition Act in the United Kingdom, the proposed Equality Act in the United States, and the Births, Deaths, Marriages and Relationships Registration Act in New Zealand), news outlets have found themselves grappling with the question of

---

[1] An earlier version of this paper was co-authored with Jane Clare Jones, Mary Leng, Sophie Allen, Elizabeth Finneron-Burns, Rebecca Reilly-Cooper, and Rebecca Simpson. It was titled 'On an alleged case of propaganda: Reply to McKinnon', and has been archived at PhilPapers since the 23rd September 2018. See <https://philpapers.org/rec/ALLOAA-3>. Since we first started thinking about whether 'TERF' was a slur, gender-critical feminists have partially reclaimed the term, which has taken some of the sting out of its usage. But none of the accounts discussed in Sections 7.3.1–7.3.2 depend on the targeted group's feelings about the slur alone, so this partial reclamation does not undercut the need for an analysis of the term.

[2] For example, Croom (2015, p. 31) works with the n-word, and also *cracker, kraut, kike, chink, bitch, slut*, and *faggot*; Hom (2008, pp. 416–17) works with *chink*, and the n-word; Jeshion (2013, p. 232) works with *chink, kike, dyke, queer, Spic*, the n-word, *and faggot*; Nunberg (2017, p. 255) works with a range of terms but interestingly includes those used by non-hegemonic subgroups, including *haole* (used by Hawaiians), *honky* (used by African Americans), *gringo* (used by Hispanics), and *shiksa* (used by American Jews).

how and whether to use this contested term. In a series of invited essays around the theme of transgender identities in 2018, *The Economist* banned the use of the term 'TERF', noting that while it 'may have started as a descriptive term [it] is now used to try to silence a vast swathe of opinions on trans issues, and sometimes to incite violence against women' (Joyce 2018). On the other hand, an article in the *New York Times* in 2019 took a different view on the use of the term, bemoaning the rise of 'TERFism' in the UK, presenting it as synonymous with transphobia and grounded in the UK's colonial history of racist 'othering' (Lewis 2019; see also the term's use in Hay 2019).

The question over the status of the term 'TERF' as a slur or derogatory term, on the one hand, or as a fair descriptor of a cluster of views, on the other, has also made its way into academic philosophy, with philosophers writing on trans issues expressing differing views on the appropriateness of the use of the term in philosophical contexts. Thus, for example, Bettcher (2017) counsels against use of the term for those who wish to engage in conversation,[3] noting that, 'It's clear that the term "TERF" has at least become offensive to those designated by the term and this raises questions around its use in such contexts.' She continues:

> With regard to 'TERF', it seems that caution should at least be deployed in case one wants to have a conversation across deep difference. This seems particularly important since much of trans politics is deeply committed to the importance of self-naming and respect for self-identities (Bettcher 2017, p. 7).

Jennifer Saul wrote in *The Conversation*: 'TERF is not a slur. Nonetheless, I don't use the word because it's inaccurate and misleading' (Saul 2020). She considers it inaccurate because of the '—RF'. She says 'I hesitate to attach the label feminist to any view that is committed to worsening the situation of some of the most marginalized women', preferring to describe those she thinks have this view as 'anti-trans activists'.

On the other hand, in a 2018 paper 'The epistemology of propaganda', in the well-regarded journal *Philosophy and Phenomenological Research*, Rachel McKinnon uses the term 'TERF' to characterize a collection of gender-critical views, dismissing the view that 'TERF' is a misogynistic slur as being 'ludicrous' and an example of 'TERF propaganda' (McKinnon 2018). Indeed, McKinnon has even claimed that "TERF' is not a slur on any modern account of slurs. It's not even a derogatory term'.[4] Jason Stanley also uses the term in his reply to McKinnon (Stanley 2018). The journal's decision to publish McKinnon's paper using the term 'TERF', as opposed to a more neutral counterpart, was publicly questioned by a number of philosophers including myself, stating that we were 'concerned

---

[3] See also (Watson 2016, p. 252).
[4] This was posted to McKinnon's Twitter account @rachelvmckinnon at the time—19th August 2018. The account's tweets have since been deleted and the account itself locked.

about the normalization of this term in academic philosophy, and its effect in reinforcing a hostile climate for debate on an issue of key importance to women' (Allen et al. 2019; see also Flaherty 2018).

There is, then, interest in the status of the term 'TERF', and concern about its usage, both inside and outside of academic philosophy. But to the best of my knowledge, there has been no extended philosophical interrogation of the claim that 'TERF' is a slur in light of the extensive philosophical literature on slurs (although Davis and McCready 2020 do discuss the term). Here my strategy will be to present a range of different theories of slurs, and make the case that 'TERF' counts as a slur on each of them. (I aim to be indicative of a range of approaches to slurs, rather than exhaustive of the literature, which is a task too big for a single chapter.)

7.1 General features of slurs

Let's start with some general features of slurs, before getting into specific accounts.

Adam Croom identifies two basic facts about slurs, which are that they depend on the descriptive attributes of those they target (e.g. race or sex), and they are considered to be the most offensive expressions language makes available (Croom 2015, p. 31). So for example, in a particular context a person might be identified as having markers of being a lesbian, and called *dyke*. There are other, less offensive expressions the person making the utterance could have used; they chose the most offensive on offer. A term can be an impolite way to refer to someone; it can be a morally inappropriate way to refer to someone; and it can be used in a speech act that derogates someone. Only the last category are candidates for the most offensive expressions language makes available.

Christopher Hom, who focuses particularly on racial epithets, identifies nine general features of how such epithets function. They convey hatred and contempt of those they target; how derogatory they are depends on the specific term; their derogatory meaning is independent of the speakers' attitudes or intentions; their use is taboo, or at the very least norm-violating; sentences containing these terms are generally meaningful; the meaning of the terms changes over time and with social attitudes; targeted groups may appropriate these terms in order to change their meaning; it is possible to use the terms in ways that are neither derogatory nor appropriated (such as pedagogical contexts); and such terms have derogatory force across identity categories e.g. race, sex, and religion (Hom 2008, pp. 426–30).

While Hom draws on racial epithets for his examples, he suggests that his account should generalize to other epithets, and it certainly seems that the features he identifies apply more broadly to slurring terms. For example, *dyke* conveys hatred and contempt of lesbians; *dyke* is more derogatory than *rug-muncher*;

someone can use 'dyke' without knowing its derogatory meaning and still convey that meaning (a notable version of this in the context of race might be the 16-year-old girl who used the slurring term *ape* in reference to Aboriginal Australian footballer Adam Goodes, as documented in the documentary *The Australian Dream* (2019)); it is generally taboo to refer to lesbians as *dykes*; the term *dyke* was more derogatory in e.g. the 1950s when homosexuality met with greater social disapprobation; some lesbians and lesbian groups have appropriated the term, and use it to self-refer (it may be seen on badges or T-shirts at PRIDE, for example); we can talk in the classroom about the fact that lesbians have been targeted with terms like *dyke* and what that has meant for lesbian communities; and, finally, the way terms like *dyke* function are not limited to sexual orientations, but are common across a range of descriptive attributes relating to things like race, sex, class, and religion.

Finally, Robin Jeshion takes it to be fundamental to slurs that they 'function to derogate or dehumanize...to signal that their targets are unworthy of equal standing or full respect as persons, that they are inferior as persons' (Jeshion 2013, pp.; although see Nunberg 2017, esp. pp. 254–5, for criticism of this claim). When someone calls a lesbian *dyke* they signal that she is inferior to heterosexual women, or to heterosexual people more generally.

Relative to these general criteria, does 'TERF'[5] look like a plausible candidate for being a slur? There's a fair amount of anecdotal evidence suggesting that the term is used to derogate or dehumanize. Usages from Twitter and other online platforms are documented at a Google photos page called 'TRA[6] violent Tweets',[7] and the website terfisaslur.com. To give a selection of representative examples of derogatory uses of the term in 2019, the year following the UK's consultation over changes to the Gender Recognition Act which put the issue of trans activism into the public debate in multiple countries: 'Someone find me a terf I'm mad and ready to fistfight'; 'Punch a terf y'all'; 'If every TERF on the planet could set themselves on fire that'd be appreciated. Thanks!'; 'anyways, punch all nazis and every terf in their disgusting faces <3'; 'Nerf a terf, Kill a terf'; 'friendly reminder, if youre a terf im Going to slice your throat actually i Will run a knife through you and Sever your spinal cord uwu'; 'ARE YOU KIDDING ME. TBIS WAS MONTHS AGO. FUCK YOU IF YOURE A TERF. YOU REALLY SHOULD GO K*LL YOURSELF'; 'Punch a terf'; 'All TERFs deserve to be shot in the head'... (readers

---

[5] Alternatively 'Terf' and 'terf'—both which suggest it is moving away from being an acronym to being its own word.
[6] 'TRA' stands for 'Trans Rights Activists'. Note that these people are often self-declared *allies* of trans people, rather than trans people themselves.
[7] <https://photos.google.com/share/AF1QipOM9J_ZIrYtiMagVRr_jhagMR-XP59TBsJFLwNlcS13 iIUT4ovqKRN9zttevr0PmA?key=NmJuV1AyRnVSU3dOS2VObVhLSm1uNUkxRjRBSk9R>

are encouraged to consult the Google Photos page for corroboration and further examples).[8]

In Scotland, a prominent trans activist who attempted to assault feminist author Julie Bindel had earlier incited violence with the term 'TERF' when they tweeted: 'Any trans allies at #PrideLondon right now need to step the f**kup and take out the terf trash. Get in their faces. Make them afraid. Debate never works so f**k them up' (Davidson 2019). At an event in Vancouver, protesters at a talk by Canadian radical feminist Meghan Murphy showed up with a cardboard guillotine painted with the words 'Step Right Up! SWERFs[9] TERFs' (Christiansen 2019). At a protest against a talk in Melbourne, Australia, by a speaker assumed to be gender-critical (she wasn't), protesters turned up with a sign reading 'TERF graves are gender neutral bathrooms'. There's at least a *prima facie* case for 'TERF' meeting Jeshion's criterion, then.

There's room to move on Croom's criteria, because there's a question about whether 'TERF' targets identity features (being a woman, being a lesbian, more generally being a gender norm-violating woman) or something that is not a descriptive attribute but an ideological one. (We ordinarily think there's a qualitative difference between targeting people on the basis of arbitrary features like sex or sexual orientation, on the one hand, and targeting them on the basis of considered political or philosophical views, on the other).

There's also a question about whether 'TERF' is the *worst* that language has to offer when it comes to radical and gender-critical feminists. In a YouTube video with more than 3.5 million views, popular YouTube transwoman and social commentator Natalie Wynn (known online as ContraPoints) agreed that 'TERF' is derogatory (ContraPoints 2019).[10] But it could be a derogative, or a pejorative; it could be offensive, misogynistic, lesbophobic, and dismissive; all without being a *slur*. It's easy enough to prove that it's not *none* of these. Were it genuinely equivalent in both content and implicature to the neutral term 'gender-critical feminist', then those who wish to use the term in this neutral way should be happy to replace their uses of the term 'TERF' with 'gender-critical feminist'. The extent to which those who claim to use the term 'TERF' to express neutral content remain staunchly resistant to this proposed replacement suggests that their uses might not be as neutral as they wish to claim. I take this as some evidence that, at a minimum, the term 'TERF' has a derogatory implicature going beyond the

---

[8] In 2019, several of the authors of the original version of this paper (see fn. 1) were listed on the public Facebook page 'This Trans Eats TERFs' in a post tracking 'transphobes working in higher education' (14th March 2019); earlier in the year a post by the same account read 'Jesus fucking christ we need to do something about these trashy excuses for human beings. I would suggest arming trans women, but at the moment I'm too much of a risk to myself for that to be a good idea. Please send photos of dead TERFs' (4th January 2019).

[9] 'SWERF' stands for 'Sex Worker-Exclusionary Radical Feminist'.

[10] Views as of 25th October 2022.

descriptive content expressed by the term 'gender-critical feminist'. But it remains to be seen whether it counts as a slur in particular.

Finally, while many of Hom's criteria do seem to apply to 'TERF', there's one in particular that isn't obvious, namely that the use of 'TERF' is taboo, or norm-violating. Within trans and trans-allied subcommunities, the use of the term is commonplace. Gender-critical feminists are working to *make* it taboo, by protesting at the ways the term is associated with lesbophobia, misogyny, and incitement to violence against women. But in this cultural moment, the status of 'TERF' remains contested.

In what follows, I first briefly consider the claim that 'TERF' is merely a descriptive term, which would tell against its being a slur. I dismiss this claim, and then move into a broader exploration of whether 'TERF' is a slur in light of several interesting accounts of slurs.

7.2 'TERF' as a merely descriptive term

McKinnon claims of the term 'TERF' that it is 'meant as a descriptive phrase to separate radical feminists into those who accept transwomen as women, and those who don't' (McKinnon 2018, p. 484; cf. Reilly-Cooper 2016). While the term may indeed have been introduced only to pick out a particular radical feminist position, in its current usage (as outlined above) the term appears to pick out *any* individuals, feminist or otherwise, who take it to be politically and socially relevant in certain contexts that transwomen are not female.[11] Most of those people are not radical feminists. The term expresses a negative attitude toward such individuals. However, even if it were the case that those using the term in these ways were misusing the term (rather than using the term in accordance with its current evolved meaning) the claim that the phrase 'trans-exclusionary radical feminism' is merely descriptive of a section of radical feminist thought remains somewhat questionable. At least if 'trans-exclusionary' is taken to mean exclusionary of all transgender people, there are no 'trans-exclusionary' radical feminists, because, at the very least, radical feminists do not exclude transgender men. The phrase is not a meaningful description of any feminist politics; it is not accurately applied to a sub-group of people with radical feminist politics; and no feminist describes her own position in this way.

Radical feminism is concerned with challenging the oppression, under patriarchy, of women. To the extent that the scope of the term 'women' here is contestable, this raises the question of who is included in the scope of radical feminist

---

[11] As noted at the start of this book, some gender identity activists collapse the sex/gender distinction into gender and so argue that one can be female on the basis of gender identity. For example McKinnon, who is biologically male, claimed to be female in the *New York Times* (McKinnon 2019).

politics. An analysis of patriarchy that sees patriarchal oppression as targeted at women *qua* females, and grounded in material differences between male and female people (including differences relating to reproductive role), means that historically most radical feminists have taken their position to involve challenging the oppression of women *qua* female human beings. This means radical feminism includes transmen in the scope of feminism (however much transmen might wish it didn't, given that they generally won't like to think of themselves as being female),[12] and so is *not* 'trans-exclusionary' in any general sense; and simply has nothing to say about transwomen (because merely identifying as a woman, or taking 'cross-sex' hormones, doesn't make a male person female).[13] To say that this makes radical feminism primarily 'trans(women)-exclusionary' is thus equivalent to saying that a children-only swimming session is 'adult-exclusionary.' It's not technically inaccurate, but it is misleading: it replaces the determination to centre the needs of a certain group of people with the determination that the *purpose* of that centring is to exclude.

Whether a 'trans(women)-inclusionary radical feminism' is genuinely possible, as suggested by the alleged introduction of the term 'trans-exclusionary radical feminism' by self-described radical feminists who wished to include transwomen (*qua* women) in their feminism (and, presumably, exclude transmen, *qua* men, from the same), depends on whether one can make sense of an account of patriarchal oppression as targeted at classes of individuals based on their gender identity as opposed to their sex. Given that one's gender identity can be an entirely private matter, many radical feminists are sceptical that such an account could be made coherent. I am one of them. Nevertheless, it is notable that if one did propose to develop a radical feminism targeted at women understood as a gender identity category (as opposed to as a sex caste) then this form of radical feminism would remain trans-exclusionary, to the extent that it would exclude transmen from the scope of feminism (while including transwomen). Even, then, if we accept the potential for a divide in radical feminism based on whether one adopts a sex-based or a gender identity-based analysis of the term 'woman', it would not follow that 'trans-exclusionary radical feminism' would accurately describe those radical feminists who adopt a sex-based rather than gender identity-based analysis of women. Both forms of radical feminism would exclude some trans people.

Suppose, though, we were to concede that 'trans(women)-exclusionary radical feminism' was an accurate (if perhaps somewhat loaded) characterization of the gender-critical feminist position. It would still not follow that the term 'TERF',

---

[12] Davis and McCready deny that this move is open to such feminists, because it involves 'a denial of the agency and self-determined identity of trans men' (2020, p. 16, fn. 23.). I counter that fighting against the historical and ongoing structural oppression of female people is more important than this particular type of agency and self-determination.

[13] For a comprehensive survey of the role of the so-called 'sex hormones', and an argument that this is an unhelpful description, see (Jordan-Young 2010).

either as used by McKinnon in her paper, or in its current use more broadly, merely serves as an acronym to pick out this position. A quick survey of uses of the term 'TERF' should make clear that it has come to be used in a way that targets women who raise questions about issues relating to the adoption of self-identification as the sole criterion for legal change of sex, and women who question whether affording all self-identified transwomen the full legal status of woman/female in all contexts might have any detrimental effects on women's hard-earned rights. Indeed, a woman can be labelled a 'TERF' when she does not herself raise these questions, but simply supports the right of others to do so. Men can be labelled 'TERF' too.[14] Regardless of whether 'TERF' once was intended to apply as a merely descriptive term to pick out a particular form of feminism, the term has long since ceased to have (only) this meaning.

The label 'gender-critical feminism' has been proposed as a more accurate and less loaded descriptor of the feminist position outlined above. Gender-critical feminism is the form of radical feminism which, reclaiming the term 'woman' to pick out the female sex caste, and seeing feminism as concerned with challenging the oppression of that sex caste, excludes transwomen and includes transmen (see further discussion in Lawford-Smith 2022). I will use 'gender-critical feminism' rather than 'trans(women)-exclusionary radical feminism' to refer to this position.

7.3 (Some) contemporary philosophical accounts of slurs

Luvell Anderson and Ernie Lepore's view of slurs as prohibited words holds that a term is a slur if the group it refers to declare it to be one. They say:

> What's clear is that no matter what its history, no matter what it means or communicates, no matter who introduces it, regardless of its past associations, *once relevant individuals declare a word a slur, it becomes one* (Anderson and Lepore 2013a, p. 39, their emphasis).[15]

The authors go on to clarify that by 'relevant individuals' they generally mean the group targeted by the term: 'By and large, those relevant individuals are targeted members, but they needn't be' (p. 39). They note that in some cases the targeted group is unable to declare the word a slur—'We can imagine slurs for infants or

---

[14] In an interview for *The Times*, Graham Linehan described being at a protest for abortion rights, where protesters included the claim that the state should pay for trans people's operations alongside the claim that women need abortion rights. He said 'I couldn't understand why trans started to attach itself to the abortion fight. I was more puzzled and confused because then people who had fought beside us started calling me a "terf"...when my biggest crime was objecting to the word terf' (Wade 2021).

[15] The passage quoted here is taken from Anderson and Lepore (2013a), but also appears in Anderson and Lepore (2013b), where the authors quote their earlier paper.

the severely mentally disabled'—in which case 'relevant individuals' may involve those concerned with the interests of the group targeted by the term (p. 39 fn. 37).

Those targeted by the term 'TERF' overwhelmingly take it to be a slur, so this is an easy victory for the view that 'TERF' is a slur. Anderson and Lepore's account makes sense in light of what Geoff Nunberg calls the 'sweeping revision of the framework of civic virtue' beginning in the 1950s, which 'implied a doctrine of linguistic self-determination, which entails that every group should have the right to determine what it should—and, more important, should not—be called, with *slur* the name we now give to certain infractions of that doctrine' (Nunberg 2017, p. 238).

However, Anderson and Lepore's account is certainly not the only account available of slurring terms, and is something of an outlier in the literature on slurs. Thus it is important to consider some alternative approaches. I will consider six further accounts—three pragmatic (Nunberg 2017; Bolinger 2015; and Swanson, forthcoming), and three semantic/expressivist (Jeshion 2016; Davis and McCready 2020; and Camp 2013).

7.3.1 Pragmatic accounts

7.3.1.1 Nunberg: slurs as markers of in-group allegiance

Nunberg starts with the strong view of a slur as 'a kind of verbalized thoughtcrime: it perpetuates social inequities, infects even innocent minds, and undermines the conduct of public discourse' (Nunberg 2017, p. 239). It is arguable that the term 'TERF' does all of these things. It gives those who hear it an excuse to pigeonhole and dismiss the political concerns of female people, who have a long history of having their political concerns dismissed and trivialized, and in this way it perpetuates social inequity between male and female people. It infects 'innocent minds' by associating transphobia (obviously unacceptable) with political concerns about female interests (obviously acceptable). And it undermines the conduct of public discourse by classifying a multitude of divergent views as one homogenous group (namely 'transphobic'), and by encouraging those views to be treated as pure bigotry. This is stultifying for intellectual discourse and the negotiation of our shared political lives.

Nunberg's own account is pragmatic, focusing on slurs being markers of ingroup allegiance. This is not to say that slurs aren't weaponized against their targets, but it does mean that this is not the *only* thing going on with slurs. This is important because, as Nunberg points out, previous discussion has focused on the latter and overlooked the importance of the former:

> Writers focus almost entirely on what slurs convey about their targets and the insult or offense they give, not on what they have to say about the groups that coin and use them, though these group-identifying or group-affiliating uses are more prevalent, more universal, and arguably prior to their uses as terms of direct abuse. (Nunberg 2017, p. 241)

Instead of focusing on the semantics, Nunberg focuses on the socio-political importance of slurs (p. 242). With respect to the semantics, Nunberg denies that there's anything in the meaning of slurring terms that conveys disparagement (p. 244). Rather, slurring words carry a conversational implicature insofar as they violate a conversational maxim to use appropriate language (p. 244). The conventions of different social groups prescribe disparaging attitudes toward a class of others, and these attitudes are signalled by the use of a slurring term rather than a neutral term (Nunberg's example is 'redskin' instead of 'American Indian') (p. 243). He says:

> In a nutshell: racists don't use slurs because they're derogative; slurs are derogative because they're the words that racists use (Nunberg 2017, p. 244).

Nunberg says that the use of slurs by members of an in-group does all sorts of things, from creating solidarity through a shared sense of resentment against, or superiority over, those the slur targets, through enjoying the 'naughtiness' together of using terms that are offensive to those they target, to reaffirming and cementing the in-group's values. He says 'adolescent boys who threw the word *fag* around loosely aren't focused on disparaging homosexual men as such so much as communing with each other over their own macho heterosexuality' (p. 254). For Nunberg, the question is whether the members of the in-group who use the term view those targeted by the term with contempt (p. 277). If they do, the use of that term will conform to an in-group convention to signal that contempt.

All of this is extremely helpful for understanding the use of the term 'TERF'. Is there a particular in-group who tend to deploy the term? Is it plausible that this group have developed a convention of using this term, rather than a neutral counterpart, in order to signal contempt towards those the term targets, primarily as a means of shoring up in-group solidarity and underwriting in-group values? Yes! The in-group in question consists of gender identity activists. The use of the term 'TERF' signals a shared resentment against the collection of views they (rightly or wrongly) associate with gender-critical feminism. The fact that it is common knowledge that the women who hold some number of these views take the term to be a slur is presumably part of the thrill of using it, which might explain why those who continue to use the term wish to do so despite the availability of 'gender-critical feminist' as a proposed and currently neutral alternative.

The use of the term 'TERF' reaffirms the values of the in-group, including opposition to what they perceive as transphobia, and contempt for any political views that would deny to transwomen the full social and legal treatment accorded to female people (including access to female-only spaces). What Nunberg says about adolescent boys using the term 'fag' is entirely plausible as a description of gender identity activists using the term 'TERF'. Given the documented usages of 'TERF' given earlier—e.g. 'all TERFs deserve to be shot in the head'—it's clear that this term is used with contempt by members of the in-group against those who hold some number of the targeted political views. Thus 'TERF' has all the features of a slur on Nunberg's pragmatic account.

7.3.1.2 Bolinger: slurs as offensively chosen over neutral counterparts

Renee Bolinger (2015) also argues that the offensiveness of slurs is pragmatic, not semantic. Competent speakers of a language are aware not only of its vocabulary and grammar, but also of the norms and conventions concerning its use (Bolinger 2015, p. 447). For Bolinger, the offense comes from the fact that the person uttering the slurring term has made a 'contrastive choice', namely to utter that term *rather than* its neutral counterpart: '[f]or signals based in *contrastive choice*, the relevant behaviour is the free selection of a marked expression, and performance signals that the speaker endorses a cluster of attitudes associated with the term (or, more precisely, a high probability that the speaker shares some or all of the attitudes in this cluster)' (p. 447). Choosing to use the slurring term instead signals that one endorses the negative associations of the term.

The signal's strength depends on how well-known the negative association is. The example Bolinger gives is 'old lady' for 'mother', which in polite contexts is associated with disrespect. How much offense a person targeted with a slur is justified in taking depends on the severity of the negative attitudes conveyed by the term. These can range from 'bare contempt' to 'a willingness or desire to kill or inflict great suffering on the target' (p. 447). Because much of the abusive language associated with the term 'TERF' occurs on the internet, it is hard to assess the severity of the attitudes. Obviously there's a difference between the things we say to express anger and the things we would actually do to a person we're angry at.

One way to deny that 'TERF' counts as a slur on Bolinger's account of slurs, then, would be to deny that there's any neutral counterpart available. But this route is not available in the case of 'TERF', even if it may be available for other alleged slurs. As I have said already, a neutral counterpart of 'TERF' preferred by those targeted by the term is 'gender-critical feminist'. So long as speakers are aware of this, it's a pretty straightforward inference from their use of the term 'TERF' to the conclusion that 'TERF' is a slur. Given that it is widely used in derogatory contexts with derogatory associations, and given that those who utter it *could* use 'gender-critical feminist' instead, their persistent use of 'TERF' even when a neutral alternative is requested defeasibly signals that they intend its derogatory associations.[16]

Another way to deny it would be to appeal to the ignorance of the speaker, either that 'TERF' is associated with negative attitudes, or that there's a neutral counterpart available. At least some of those who use 'TERF' may sincerely believe it to be neutral, and so not see the need to use 'another' neutral synonym instead. This will be true of those who are new to the contemporary gender debate, or who merely follow the usage conventions of those they first encounter (assuming they first encounter the gender identity activists). For example, Ásta uses 'TERF' in her book *Categories We Live By*, and has said that she believed the term to be neutral at the time the book went to press (*p.c.*). In this case, offence is not warranted.

What about when the speaker knows that 'TERF' is associated with negative attitudes, but is not aware of 'gender-critical feminist' as a neutral counterpart? Bolinger says that whether offence is warranted in this case depends on a counterfactual: whether the speaker *would have refrained* from using the slurring term *had she known* that an alternative was available (Bolinger 2015, p. 448). We might push back against this, by saying that speakers can still *invent* neutral terms, or can use slurring terms but add a disclaimer that they do not have the negative attitudes associated with them. Nevertheless, even if we accept, with Bolinger, that offence isn't warranted if the relevant counterfactual holds, it remains the case that in very many of its uses, such 'excusing' conditions do not apply, as the users of the term are both aware of the derogatory associations of the term and are aware that a neutral alternative—preferred by the target group—is available.

On Bolinger's account, we can conclude that 'TERF' functions as a slur in at least all the cases where speakers know or can be reasonably expected to know (i) that it has negative associations, and (ii) that there is a neutral counterpart available. Most gender identity activists who choose to use the term 'TERF' know both of these things very well, even if newcomers to the debate do not.

7.3.1.3 Swanson: Slurs as Cues for Harmful Ideologies

The final pragmatic account of slurs I'll consider comes from Eric Swanson (forthcoming). Swanson argues that 'slurs and ideologies stand in mutually supporting relations to each other' (on the connection between slurs and ideologies see also Hom 2012). An ideology, on Swanson's account, is a 'temporally persistent and socially extended cluster of mutually supporting beliefs, interests, norms, values, practices, institutions, scripts, habits, affective dispositions, and ways of

---

[16] In some cases, particularly where groups feel their language or conduct has been heavily policed, there may be alternative explanations of their resistance to changing the terms they use.

interpreting and interacting with the world' (Swanson, forthcoming, p. 5).[17] Ideologies need not be transparent to those who consent to them, need not involve inaccurate representations of the world, and must involve a mutually supporting cluster of beliefs etc. that makes them socially and temporally persistent (p. 6). The use of slurs strengthens ideology by acting as a signal from the speaker that she consents to and endorses the ideology, and by encouraging the hearer to do the same.

Swanson is concerned with what he calls 'acceptability implicatures', which are the implications carried by the use of any word at all that it's acceptable to use that word (whether 'conversationally, legally, morally, prudentially, all things considered, and so on') (Swanson, forthcoming, p. 2). These implicatures can sometimes be cancelled, and sometimes not. On Swanson's view, slurs cue ideologies (p. 7), putting the ideology into position to do harm towards those disadvantaged by it. Swanson makes his point using the comparatively mild slur 'nerd'. Using 'nerd' cues an ideology that disparages and subjugates the class of people who are concerned with academic achievement, are socially awkward, are shy, are obsessive, etc. The ideology ranks this group low in the hierarchy of social groups (pp. 7–8).

The use of slurs strengthens ideologies in three ways: first, by emboldening the speaker (because if speakers are not challenged, they will believe that their use of the slur, and the cueing of the relevant ideology, is permissible) (Swanson, forthcoming, p. 12); second, by conversationally implicating the speaker's consent to the ideology; and third, by emboldening others to consent to and enact the related ideology (p. 13). Swanson takes the harmfulness of a slur to be proportional to the harmfulness of the ideology that it cues. If an ideology is not particularly harmful, then the use of the slur won't be particularly harmful. The ideology around 'nerd' is harmful to school kids, and not very harmful to adults. So the slur will be harmful for school kids, and not very harmful for adults. Swanson's account of slurs differs from many others to the extent that the terms used as slurs need not be connected by convention to the related ideologies (pp. 15–16).

The strong formulation of 'ideology' given by Swanson might initially seem to suggest that 'TERF' can't be a slur. Paradigm examples of mutually supporting clusters of beliefs etc. are things like racism and sexism—clusters of beliefs etc. about people of colour or about women that persist across time and space, in these cases over hundreds of years and in almost every country. Some cultural commentators place the argument between transwomen and radical feminists as beginning only about 60 years ago; and it's a culturally-specific argument in that those who would be trans people in a British, American, Canadian, Australian, or

---

[17] Page references are to a 2017 pre-print version of Swanson's paper, which was archived at his institutional webpage but is no longer available.

New Zealand (etc.) cultural context are considered to be 'third gender' people in other cultural contexts (such as Samoa, or Pakistan).

Still, one of Swanson's own examples was 'nerd', a slur which relates to an ideology nowhere near as old or as widespread as racism and sexism. The question becomes just how old and just how widespread a cluster of beliefs etc. has to be before it counts as an ideology. Certainly there is a cluster of mutually supporting 'beliefs, interests, norms, values, practices', 'habits, affective dispositions, and ways of interpreting and interacting with the world' (Swanson, forthcoming, p. 5) that make up gender identity activists' account of, and hostility toward, radical and gender-critical feminism. To the extent that these constitute an ideology, it's clear that the term 'TERF' relates to that ideology in a supportive way; uses of the term 'TERF' cue consent to and enactment of the ideology that 'TERFs' are bigoted, contemptible, deserving of hostility, etc. At minimum, I conclude that to the extent that gender identity activists' beliefs about and opposition to radical and/ or gender-critical feminism constitutes an ideology, 'TERF' also functions as a slur on Swanson's account.

What I have just said takes gender identity activists' hostility to radical and gender-critical feminism to be an independent ideology. But it is surely no accident that of all the people in the world who deny that transwomen are women (and that transmen are men), it is *feminists* who are specifically targeted. The more general term 'transphobe' does exist, but both terms are in play, and the term that is associated with incitement to violence, and with violent and abusive language, is 'TERF'. This term for the most part targets women, in particular lesbians. So there is reason to consider the relevant ideology to be misogyny more generally. In that case there's no question about whether this is an ideology: it is. 'TERF', then, is a slur on Swanson's account. (This same point can be made against Davis and McCready; see discussion in Section 7.3.2.3).

7.3.2 Semantic/expressivist accounts

7.3.2.1 Jeshion: slurs function to express dehumanization
Robin Jeshion (2016) offers an account on which people using slurs convey that those targeted are inferior, have lesser standing as human beings, are not deserving of the full respect we normally owe to humans. When we utter terms that express these attitudes, we dehumanize their targets (Jeshion comments that she thinks there is widespread agreement on this point among theorists of slurs, even if they tend to put it in terms of derogation rather than dehumanization—see p. 131, fn. 2). She's interested in how slurs are created and (later) neutralized (e.g. via appropriation), and in how slurs contribute to creating bigotry, not just maintaining bigotry that already exists.

Jeshion argues that a hybrid expressivist view of slurs can answer these two questions (see also Jeshion 2013; Richard 2008; Saka 2007). The semantics are the same as of a neutral counterpart; what makes the usage a slur is a 'contemptuous intonation', or being 'fronted by certain expletives or contempt-expressing adjectives' (Jeshion 2016, p. 132). So someone might say 'Andrea is a TERF', 'Andrea is a *radical feminist*' (in a contemptuous tone), or 'Andrea is a repulsive radfem'. In their semantics, these three utterances are the same. The semantics of the term pick out a particular group, the same as the neutral counterpart ('TERF' picks out the same women that 'gender-critical feminist' picks out). The difference between 'TERF' and 'gender-critical feminist' is the *expression* of contempt that comes along with the former. But this only works to dehumanize when the term classifies the person in a way that is ontologically significant: 'contemptuous regard for another person involves taking the properties of that basis as fundamental to the target's identity as a person' (p. 133). Jeshion's example is the slur 'kike' for a Jewish person, which picks out *being Jewish* as an aspect of 'what the target is' and which takes that aspect to be fundamentally negative. It is this aspect of the contemptuous expression that is dehumanizing.

It is straightforward that 'TERF' picks out a group, the same group as its neutral counterpart, and that its use (at least very often—see examples in Section 7.1) involves an expression of contempt toward those it targets. The more challenging question is whether 'TERF' classifies a person in a way that is ontologically significant. It is not clear that to be ontologically significant something must be an arbitrary/involuntary feature of a person like sex or race, because being Jewish can be understood as a matter of ethnicity, culture, religion, or a combination of these things (one can convert to Judaism). If religious views are appropriate targets then political or philosophical beliefs might plausibly be, too, at least if they are deeply-held commitments, as radical and gender-critical feminism are for many women.

Furthermore, as discussed above, there remains a question about whether to conceptualize 'TERF' as targeting women *qua* women (where women with the 'wrong views' about gender identity are policed as failing to conform to the norms of femininity, such as protecting the vulnerable, being kind, being inclusive, focusing on servicing others' needs rather than on their own political interests, etc.) or women *qua* radical and/or gender-critical feminists. If I'm right that it's the former, then there's a clearer path to establishing that 'TERF' is a slur on Jeshion's hybrid expressivist account.

Even if 'TERF' hits the target's identity as a person, it remains to be established that it dehumanizes. Jeshion explains that when we call people slurs, we 'induce shame...compel a self-representation or self-assessment as someone lesser, unworthy, undeserving of respect' (Jeshion 2016, p. 134). Even more saliently, these uses 'lower the target's worth in the eyes of others, and...define their social standing *as* lesser' (p. 134). I cannot establish the former without surveying a large number of the women who are targeted with the term 'TERF', but I note that the term is unlikely to induce shame in women who reject the ideology from which it springs (whether that is misogyny more generally, or gender identity ideology more specifically). But I do think there is significant anecdotal evidence suggesting that 'TERF' is functioning to lower targets' social standing in others' eyes, to inflict reputational damage and to deter others from either being targeted themselves or from becoming guilty by association.

What of the two questions Jeshion was concerned to answer, slur creation and bigotry formation? On her account, there is at least one 'basic and plausible mechanism' for creating slurs (even if there are others) (p. 134), which is that speakers begin to use a term either with a contemptuous intonation, or with a *unilateral lip curl* (a contemptuous facial expression). This transmits affect between interlocutors, and given the human tendency to imitation, causes the expression of contempt to 'crystallize' in the term. This also helps to explain how terms can become slurs quickly and easily, through a kind of affect contagion. For this same reason, slurs can also help to create rather than merely maintain bigotry, because through affect contagion contempt can 'go viral' (p. 136). This is helpful for thinking about 'TERF', which has had a swift ascendancy in use.

7.3.2.2 Davis and McCready: slurs as subordination by privileged group members

Davis and McCready (2020) offer a hybrid theory of slurs on which their offensiveness is built into the 'complex' of a term (the historical facts, prejudices, and social attitudes associated with it) and their derogatoriness is a function of the utterer's attitudes or intentions. That these two come apart allows for slurring speech acts to be offensive without being derogatory. On the authors' account, a slur targets a group on the basis of intrinsic properties; invokes social meaning capable of derogating that group; and the derogation subordinates the targeted group according to power relations supported by flawed ideology (Davis and McCready 2020, p. 1).[18] For these authors, derogation is *only* slurring when the target group is subordinated, and the person uttering the slur is a member of a privileged group. They do not consider 'TERF' to be a slur, but they reach this conclusion by considering the 'complex' of the term to be the use it has been put to by trans people,[19] rather than the history of male policing of women's self-determination, including their feminist theory and activism. For that reason, I'll work through each of their conditions again from this alternative perspective.

---

[18] Page numbers correspond to the November 19th 2018 open-access preprint archived at <https://semanticsarchive.net/Archive/2Y0NTg2Y/Davis-McCready-Instability_of_Slurs.pdf>

[19] They say: 'it invokes a complex of historical fact, the hostility toward trans people expressed by (some members of) this group, which can be used by trans-inclusive people to express anger or derogation toward this kind of trans-exclusionary person' (Davis and McCready 2020, p. 14).

It is important for Davis and McCready's view that targeted groups are defined by intrinsic properties. The examples they give in introducing the account are 'race/gender/sexuality/abledness' [sic] (Davis and McCready 2020). Those who reject the claim that 'TERF' is a slur may attempt to argue that it targets a *political* or *philosophical* view, rather than intrinsic properties of persons. Indeed, the authors themselves make this assumption, saying 'turning again to terms that target individuals on the basis of political and social beliefs, we can consider the term 'TERF'' (p. 13). According to Davis and McCready, it is because women/lesbians are radical feminists, or because radical feminism commits them to unpopular views about transwomen, that they are targeted with the term 'TERF', and not because they are women/lesbians. If they were women/lesbians who maintained that transwomen were women, there wouldn't be any targeting. On this view, *feminazi* wouldn't be a slur, because not all women are feminists, and being a feminist is a political or philosophical choice; and *bitch* wouldn't be a slur, because not all women are unkind, and unkindness is a choice.

To the contrary, Louise Richardson-Self (2018) argued that misogynistic speech counts as hate speech even when it targets only a subset of women rather than all women; it is part of how gender norms function that it is norm-violators and non-conformers who are targeted. It would be strange to argue that *slut* is not hate speech simply because it's only *some* women (the sexually liberated) that are targeted by it, rather than *all* women (including the chaste). Davis and McCready (2020) agree with this, saying 'as a gendered slur, *slut* canonically targets women' (p. 9, fn. 3). But by the same reasoning, it's no objection to 'TERF' being a slur that it targets some but not all women. To be a 'slut' or to be a 'TERF' are to be the wrong kind of woman from the perspective of the misogynist. The good woman has the right amount of sex (not none; but not too much), the good *feminist* woman accepts that 'trans women are women'. Overwhelmingly, those targeted by the term 'TERF' are women/lesbians, and these are intrinsic properties. Another way to think about this is in terms of indirect discrimination: if members of a particular racial group tend to subscribe to a particular religion, you can discriminate on the basis of race (intrinsic) by discriminating on the basis of religion (voluntary). So there's ultimately no problem on these grounds in taking Davis and McCready's account of slurs to vindicate the claim that 'TERF' is a slur, despite their own denial of this.

The second complication in applying their account is that it requires the person uttering the slur to be a member of a privileged group, and the group targeted by the slur to be subordinated within a structure of power relations that is supported by flawed ideology. It is only in this context that the term is subordinating: otherwise it may rather be an accusation (as when used by a member of a subordinated group against a member of a privileged group); an act of solidarity (when used between members of subordinated groups); or an act of complicity (when used between members of privileged groups) (Davis and McCready 2020, following McCready & Davis 2017). Presumably, what tells us which axes of privilege/subordination to look at is the term itself, for example if it's *dyke* that's at issue we'll be interested in male/female and heterosexual/homosexual. But what's complicated in the discussion of whether 'TERF' is a slur is that *both* groups contesting the term are subordinated along at least one axis, and sometimes people deploying the term have multiple identities which place them as privileged relative to one axis and subordinated relative to another.

The most committed users of the term 'TERF' are gender identity activists, who are either themselves trans, or who are allies of trans people. Where those allies are heterosexual males, we have a straightforward case of members of privileged groups (male, heterosexual) targeting members of subordinated groups (female, homosexual). So their use of the term might well be a slur. But what about when the person using the term is a transwoman, or a male nonbinary person? Is she (are they) privileged as male, or subordinated as trans? Does it not matter how many other axes the utterer is subordinated along, so long as relative to the term 'TERF', which targets sex and sexual orientation (and political belief) they are privileged? If so, then *all* heterosexual male deployers of the term may be slurring, regardless of whether they are trans. And what about when heterosexual women, or *other lesbian women*, use 'TERF'? If the subordinated group is women/lesbians, it looks like this would be classified as an act of solidarity on Davis and McCready's view, but that's clearly not the case. The term is used against those who dissent from gender identity ideology.

This need not be taken to scupper the view. After all, some women have internalized misogyny and are capable of deploying terms like *slut* or *dyke* or *bitch* against those women who fail to conform to gender norms. Identity politics can create factions within oppressed groups, who use such terms against each other. But it does suggest that 'privileged groups' and 'subordinated groups' need to be picked out in a more sophisticated way than mere intrinsic properties, which will be over-inclusive in the case of gender policing. This is arguably an artifact of the bulk of attention to slurs in the philosophical literature going into racial slurs as compared to misogynistic slurs, which function differently.[20]

7.3.2.3 Camp: Slurs as allegiance to a derogating perspective

In her (2013) paper, Elisabeth Camp is not focused on giving a full account of slurs, but rather setting aside a less controversial component of slurs (predication of extensional properties) in favour of focusing on a more controversial component. She argues that slurs conventionally signal allegiance to a derogating perspective (Camp 2013, p. 331).

---

[20] For an excellent discussion of misogynistic vilification as it relates to questions about the legal regulation of speech, see (de Silva 2020).

For her, a 'perspective' is a disposition to structure one's thoughts in a particular way, to notice and remember certain types of things, and to treat some things as central (e.g. as causes or explanations) (p. 336). In the context of a slur, a perspective is 'an integrated, intuitive way of cognizing members of the targeted group' (p. 335). It is not itself a feeling, but it will tend to motivate certain feelings. Political orientations are good examples of perspectives (p. 336).

In the case of slurs, the perspective on the targeted group is negative, and it is 'distancing': the speaker signals that he is not one of the targeted people, and that the targeted people are not worthy of respect (p. 338). Slurs are offensive either because the properties attributed to the targeted group under the perspective are not fair or correct, or because their presence doesn't merit the kinds of affective responses and evaluative attitudes they tend to be awarded (p. 338).

Although not the focus of her article, I have already noted in discussion of other accounts of slurs that it is straightforward to pick out the extension of 'TERF'. So whether 'TERF' is a slur on an account combining that feature with the idea about perspectives defended in her article will depend on whether there's a negative, distancing perspective that tends to underwrite uses of the term, and that is not warranted by the objective features of the targeted group.

I simply refer at this point to things I've said already, about ideology (Sections 7.3.2.2 and 7.3.1.3), about in-group allegiance (Section 7.3.1), and about 'complexes' of histories and attitudes (Section 7.3.2.2). Misogyny and gender identity ideology both look like decent candidates for 'perspectives', and 'TERF' clearly serves a distancing function, signalling that the speaker is *not like those women*, and that *those women don't deserve respect*.

I take it that the objective features of the targeted group—women who believe that a person's sex is sometimes politically relevant regardless of their gender identity—do not warrant the negative, dehumanizing inferences that 'TERF' appears to introduce. 'TERF' looks to have all the relevant features of a slur on Camp's account.

7.3.3 Taking stock

I've considered seven accounts of slurs: Anderson and Lepore's account which appeals to whether those targeted by the term take it to be a slur; Nunberg's account on which slurs signal in-group membership; Bolinger's account on which the choice to use a slurring term rather than its neutral counterpart signals endorsement of the term's negative associations; Swanson's account on which slurs cue harmful ideologies; Jeshion's account on which slurs express dehumanization; Davis and McCready's account, on which slurs are used by privileged group members to subordinate; and, finally, Camp's account, which takes slurs to be a negative, distancing perspective on targeted groups.

I've argued, in each case, that the features that the accounts pick out as characteristic of slurs apply equally well to the term 'TERF', so that there is a good case for taking 'TERF' to be a slur on *all seven* of the accounts surveyed. Of course, this article is not an exhaustive survey of all the various accounts of slurs, so it is left open that there might be some accounts of slurs for which 'TERF' is not a slur. But I hope to have shown, at the very least, that the term 'TERF' plausibly counts as a slur on a range of contemporary philosophical accounts.

One might object to the discussion so far that I've made a mistake in reasoning from accounts of slurs that accommodate pre-given slurring terms, to terms that happen to have the features of these accounts and yet are not slurs. That is to say, it might be that all the authors discussed here have been concerned to *explain* known slurring terms, which has resulted in an account of slurring terms that is not yet intended to provide necessary and sufficient conditions for *being* a slurring term. If that's right, then there could—at least in principle—be terms that have all the same features stipulated by the account, without actually being slurs.

This takes us back to the point I made at the start of the chapter, which was that it's an interesting reflection on the literature on slurs if it can't *answer questions* about whether a particular term is a slur. When we have two words that both function in the way the account describes, and the first is accepted to be a slur while the second's status as a slur is contested, what settles the matter? It is surely a goal of understanding the semantics and pragmatics of slurs, how they work and what they do (including how they offend and how they derogate), that we can distinguish slurs from non-slurs.

There are two moves that can be made at this point. The first is to take it as a further desirable feature of an account of slurs that it can settle the matter on contested terms. Some of the accounts surveyed here seem to offer more resources to do this than others, e.g. Davis and McCready's account appears to have more classificatory power than Swanson's. At the very least, then, my attempt to *apply* accounts of slurs, in order to settle the question of whether 'TERF' is a slur, might contribute to further reflection by the authors working in the literature on slurs about how to move from accommodating known cases to classifying contested terms.

The second move is bolder: it involves pushing the burden of proof back on the author of an account of slurring terms to explain why, when there are two words that both function in the way the account describes, one is and one isn't a slur. It would surely be surprising if we found a term that met all the conditions of an account—e.g. semantically invoked a misogynistic complex which could be used to derogate women; the derogation of women functioned to subordinate them within the structure of patriarchal power relations—which is itself a flawed ideology that places male people in a hierarchy above female people; and targeted women on the basis of an intrinsic property, in this case either their sex or their sexual orientation, *à la* Davis and McCready (2020)—and yet *wasn't* a slur. In this case, the author owes us some debunking explanation of those terms that have all the features of slurs and yet which are not slurs.

Until such an explanation is provided, I think it's reasonable to proceed on the assumption that terms that have the relevant features are indeed slurs, which means that we're justified in proceeding on the assumption that 'TERF' is a slur.

7.4 Conclusion

Despite its alleged introduction as a neutral acronym for a version of radical feminism, in its current usage the term 'TERF' has evolved so that it has become derogatory in at least its implicature if not its content. The term is widely used to apply to those who hold that the sex category 'female' has social and political relevance in certain contexts regardless of gender identity. The term is almost exclusively used in derogatory and dehumanizing ways, and often accompanied by violent imagery, by those who are critical of people who take such a view. On seven different accounts of slurs, 'TERF' appears to meet the criterion for counting as a slur.

References

Allen, Sophie, Finneron-Burns, Elizabeth, Jones, Jane Clare, Lawford-Smith, Holly, Leng, Mary, Reilly-Cooper, Rebecca, and Simpson, Rebecca. 'Derogatory language in philosophy journal risks increased hostility and diminished discussion' *Daily Nous*, 27th August 2019. Online at <http://dailynous.com/2018/08/27/derogatory-language-philosophy-journal-hostility-discussion/>

Anderson, Luvell, and Lepore, Ernie. 'Slurring words', *Nous* 47/1 (2013a), pp. 25–48.

Anderson, Luvell, and Lepore, Ernie. 'What did you call me? Slurs as prohibited words', *Analytic Philosophy* 54/3 (2013b), pp. 350–63.

Bach, Kent. 'Loaded words: On the semantics and pragmatics of slurs', *American Philosophical Association Pacific Division*, San Diego, 19th April 2014.

Bettcher, Talia Mae. 'Trans feminism: Recent philosophical developments', *Philosophical Studies* 12/11 (2017), pp. 1–11.

Bolinger, Renee. 'The pragmatics of slurs', *Nous* 51/3 (2015), pp. 439–62.

Camp, Elizabeth. 'Slurring perspectives', *Analytic Philosophy* 54/3 (2013), pp. 330–49.

Cepollaro, Bianca. 'In defence of a presuppositional account of slurs', *Language Sciences* 52 (2015), pp. 36–45.

Christiansen, Rebecca. 'Victory for free speech: Gender talk held In Vancouver despite threats of violence', *The Post Millenial*, 3rd November 2019. Online at <https://www.thepostmillennial.com/the-wrong-kind-of-feminism-meghan-murphy-speaks-in-vancouver/>, accessed 26th November 2019.

ContraPoints. 'Gender critical', *YouTube,* 31st March 2019. Online at <https://youtu.be/1pTPuoGjQsI>

Croom, Adam. 'Slurs', *Language Sciences* 33 (2011), pp. 343–58.

Croom, Adam. 'The semantics of slurs: A refutation of coreferentialism', *Ampersand* 2 (2015), pp. 30–8.

Davis, Christopher, and McCready, Elin. 'The instability of slurs', *Grazer Philosophische Studien* 97/1 (2020), pp. 63–85.

Davidson, Gina. 'Feminist speaker Julie Bindel "attacked by transgender person" at Edinburgh University after talk', *The Scotsman*, 6th June 2019.

de Silva, Anjalee. 'Addressing the vilification of women: A functional theory of harm and implications for law', *Melbourne University Law Review* 43/3 (2020) [early view].

Flaherty, Colleen. '"TERF" war', *Inside Higher Ed*, 29th August 2018. Online at <https://www.insidehighered.com/news/2018/08/29/philosophers-object-journals-publication-terf-reference-some-feminists-it-really>

Hay, Carol. 'Who counts as a woman?' *The New York Times*, 1st April 2019. Online at <https://www.nytimes.com/2019/04/01/opinion/trans-women-feminism.html>

Hedger, Joseph A. 'The semantics of racial slurs: Using Kaplan's framework to provide a theory of the meaning of derogatory epithets', *Linguistic and Philosophical Investigations* 11 (2012), pp. 74–84.

Hom, Christopher. 'The semantics of racial epithets', *Journal of Philosophy* 105 (2008), pp. 416–40.

Hom, Christopher. 'A puzzle about pejoratives', *Philosophical Studies* 159 (2012), pp. 383–405.

Jeshion, Robin. 'Expressivism and the offensiveness of slurs', *Philosophical Perspectives* 27/1 (2013), pp. 231–59.

Jeshion, Robin. 'Slur creation, bigotry formation: The power of expressivism', *Phenomenology and Mind* 11 (2016), pp. 130–9.

Jordan-Young, Rebecca. *Brain Storm* (Massachusetts: Harvard University Press, 2010).

Joyce, Helen, 'Transgender identities: A series of invited essays', *Economist* June 29th 2018, <https://www.economist.com/open-future/2018/06/29/transgender-identities-a-series-of-invited-essays>

Lawford-Smith, Holly. *Gender-Critical Feminism* (Oxford: Oxford University Press, 2022).

Lewis, Sophie. 'How British feminism became anti-trans', *New York Times*, 7th February 2019, <https://www.nytimes.com/2019/02/07/opinion/terf-trans-women-britain.html>

Marques, Teresa, and Garcia-Carpintero, Manuel. 'Really expressive presuppositions and how to block them', *Grazer Philosophische Studien*, 97/1 (2020), pp. 138–58.

McCready, Elin. & Davis, Christopher. 'An invocational theory of slurs', *Proceedings of LENLS14* (2017).

McKinnon, Rachel. 'The epistemology of propaganda', *Philosophy and Phenomenological Research* XCVI/2 (2018), pp. 483–9.

McKinnon, Rachel. 'I won a World Championship. Some people aren't happy', *The New York Times*, 5th December 2019. <https://www.nytimes.com/2019/12/05/opinion/i-won-a-world-championship-some-people-arent-happy.html>

Nunberg, Geoff. 'The social life of slurs', in Daniel Fogal, Daniel Harris, and Matt Moss (Eds.) *New Work on Speech Acts* (Oxford: Oxford University Press, 2017).

Reilly-Cooper, Rebecca. 'The word "TERF"', <https://rebeccarc.com>, 4th December 2016.

Richard, Mark. *When Truth Gives Out* (New York: Oxford University Press, 2008).

Richardson-Self, Louise. 'Woman-hating: On misogyny, sexism, and hate speech', *Hypatia* 33/2 (2018) [online first].

Saka, Paul. *How to Think about Meaning* (Berlin: Springer, 2007).

Stanley, Jason. 'Replies', *Philosophy and Phenomenological Research* XCVI/2 (2018), pp. 497–511.

Saul, Jennifer. 'Why the words we use matter when describing anti-trans activists', *The Conversation* 6th March 2020.

Swanson, Eric. 'Slurs and ideologies', in Robin Celikates, Sally Haslanger, and Jason Stanley (Eds.) *Ideology* (Oxford: Oxford University Press, forthcoming).

Wade, Mike. 'Graham Linehan interview: "Gender row is an onslaught on rights, returning women to pre-suffragette era"', *The Times*, 4th September 2021. Online at <https://www.thetimes.co.uk/article/graham-linehan-interview-gender-row-is-an-onslaught-on-rights-returning-women-to-pre-suffragette-era-wfjcdc07w>

Watson, Lori. 'The woman question', *Transgender Studies Quarterly* 3/1–2 (2016), pp. 248–55.

Whiting, Daniel. 'It's not what you said, it's the way you said it: Slurs and conventional implicatures', *Analytic Philosophy* 54/3 (2013), pp. 364–77.

Williamson, Timothy. 'Reference, inference and the semantics of pejoratives' in Joseph Almog and Paolo Leonardi (Eds.) *The Philosophy of David Kaplan* (Oxford: Oxford University Press, 2009).

8
Is Gender-Critical Speech Hate Speech?

8.1 Gender-critical speech

Is gender-critical speech hate speech? Some gender identity activists say that it is;[1] gender-critical feminists say that it is not. In this chapter I'll consider the case for saying that it is, and argue that it isn't. In Chapter 9, I'll take up the related, but weaker, claim that gender-critical speech is merely harmful speech.

In order to assess whether gender-critical speech is hate speech, we need to know what counts as gender-critical speech. This is delicate: if we count too much as gender-critical speech, then we're virtually guaranteed to find some of it hate speech; if we count too little as gender-critical speech, then we're virtually guaranteed not to. We need a conception of gender-critical speech that doesn't count just anything a person self-describing as 'gender-critical' says, but also doesn't let gender-critical feminists off the hook for commonplace speech that is made in the name of their movement. The broadest way to understand gender-critical speech would be as any speech that articulates, advocates for, or defends, a gender-critical position. To fill in the details of this understanding, we'd need only to know the details of the gender-critical position. I take it to be a cluster of views centring on the importance of sex and sex-based rights, asserted in the context of ongoing debate over social and legal changes to the understanding and recognition of sex and gender categories.[2] This cluster of views include:

- There are two sexes, male and female.
- It is impossible to change your sex.
- Sex characteristics cluster into a bimodal distribution and intersex people are not outside of the two main clusters.

---

[1] To give just one example, the National Tertiary Union in Australia has for the last two years been being lobbied to pass an 'Emergency Motion' put forward by its QUTE network ('Queer Unionists in Tertiary Education') which included 'The NTEU should publicly affirm its opposition to transphobic hate speech, including "gender-critical ideology".' The person who moved an amended version of the motion in late 2022 said in their speech '"gender-critical" ideology...is a genocidal hate movement operating in tertiary spaces which contributes to the climate of violence which kills people like me.' The amended motion, which passed, contains the slightly more temperate 'NTEU believes..."Gender-critical ideology" is a term that is used to defend transphobic ideology and when used to do so is not consistent with academic freedom', and later, 'NTEU will...Campaign and educate members about hate speech and the impact that it has on others, especially our LGBTIQA+ members.' See also discussion by Osbaldiston (2022).

[2] For more detail see Lawford-Smith (2022).

- Sex matters politically and women's sex-based rights should be protected.
- Female-only spaces, services, and provisions are important to women and girls and should not be offered on the basis of self-identified sex/gender identity.
- Self-identification, statutorily declared, is an inadequate basis for legal sex.
- A subjective sense of one's 'identity' does not trump all others' interests in conflict cases.
- Transwomen are male and transmen are female, and if they weren't they wouldn't be trans.
- Gender is not gender identity.
- Sex is not gender identity.
- Gender is sex caste by way of gender norms, explained by or built on top of sex difference.
- Gender (as previously defined) should be abolished.
- Everyone is 'nonbinary' (relative to the previous definition of gender) so no one is.
- The terms 'female' and 'male' should refer to sex.
- The terms 'woman' and 'man', 'girl', and 'boy' should refer to either or both of sex and gender (as previously defined).*
- 'Lesbian' and 'gay' are sexual orientations, and thus refer to and depend on sex.[3]

These are general commitments that anyone self-describing as gender-critical is highly likely to have.

There are some idiosyncratic or eccentric views that gender-critical women have and which are not thereby 'gender-critical views'. For example, some radical feminists active in the gender-critical feminist movement are separatists, who think women should withdraw from the society of men. But separatism is not a commitment of gender-critical feminism.

What about views that are not shared by all or most gender-critical feminists, and yet also cannot be classed as idiosyncratic or eccentric? I put an asterisk on the second-to-last claim in the list to note this kind of complexity. There is reasonable disagreement among gender-critical feminists over the question of whether the terms 'man' and 'woman' are sex terms and so synonymous with 'male' and 'female', or gender terms and so dependent for their meaning on whichever is the correct conception of gender.[4] Most gender-critical feminists maintain a sex/gender distinction in some form, but some use 'female' and

---

[3] This list also appears in Chapter 9.
[4] See discussion in Byrne (2020) and Bogardus (2020). Byrne talks about the ordinary meaning of the so-called 'gender terms', while Bogardus argues against the sex/gender distinction, which has the effect of collapsing the so-called 'gender terms' back into sex terms.

'woman' synonymously for sex and use 'femininity' for gender, while others use 'female' for sex and 'woman' for gender. Some believe the former is technically accurate but think norms of politeness require referring to people as they want to be referred to, or that the ship has sailed on 'woman' and we should focus on fighting to retain 'female' (Reilly-Cooper 2018). Others insist that we work to reclaim 'woman'.[5] This means there is considerable diversity in how the words 'man' and 'woman', along with their accompanying pronouns, are deployed. There is also considerable conflict between gender-critical women on this point.[6]

Despite this disagreement, there are many gender-critical feminists who endorse (and advocate for) the idea that 'woman' means 'adult human female'. Given that the core commitments of gender-critical feminism include that transwomen are male, and that it is impossible to change your sex, if 'man' is synonymous with 'male' it follows that transwomen are men. So calling transwomen 'men', or using 'he'/'him'/'his' pronouns to refer to them, should count as gender-critical speech, *even though* it is not the case that all or even most gender-critical feminists do this.[7] This understanding of gender-critical speech should be broad enough to capture most of what has been accused of being hate speech, without being so broad as to unfairly impugn a whole movement for idiosyncratic individual views.

8.2 Gender-critical speech as hate speech

I'll understand 'speech' as synonymous with 'expression', so that it covers communicative acts not limited to those that are verbal (see e.g. Ely 1974–5). So while what gender-critical feminists say both online and offline will be a central concern, I'll also include things like the wearing of T-shirts, the putting up of billboards, flags, and posters, and the distribution of stickers and flyers, all containing gender-critical slogans, messaging, or imagery.

There are real-world examples of all of these things being treated as hate speech or similar (at least, speech that deserves suppression, merits punishment, or justifies compensation to its targets). There have been legal cases in the United Kingdom and Australia turning on whether gender-critical comments made on Twitter justified the termination of an employment relationship, or gender-critical

---

[5] The best-known campaign is likely Kellie-Jay Keen's. See e.g. the merchandise on sale in her shop (<https://www.standingforwomen.com/>), or the T-shirts she generally appears in during her YouTube livestreams (<https://youtube.com/c/KellieJayKeen>).

[6] For example, when Kathleen Stock's book *Material Girls* was published in May 2021, some gender-critical women expressed anger about her choice to use preferred pronouns to refer to transwomen in the book.

[7] This does not mean that all 'misgendering' is gender-critical speech, even when done by a gender-critical person. It matters whether it is done in order to express gender-critical beliefs, as opposed to being done in order to insult or offend.

comments made on Facebook counted as vilification on the basis of gender-identity, respectively.[8] The high-profile Spanish feminist Lidia Falcón was accused of hate speech and had to go to court (Sánchez 2020). A gender-critical transwoman was accused of hate speech after wearing a T-shirt that read 'Trans women are men. Get over it!' (Lyons 2019). A woman was thrown out of a pub in Cheshire, England, for wearing a T-shirt that read 'woman/wʊmən/noun/adult human female' (Birchall 2019). A billboard featuring the same words was removed from a site in Liverpool, England, after protest by trans activists (BBC 2018). Stickers in the shape of pink penises featuring the words 'women don't have penises', distributed around Liverpool, were accused of 'trans hatred' (Pidd 2018).[9] A billboard reading 'I ♥ JK Rowling' was removed from Edinburgh Waverley railway station in Scotland for being 'too political' (Hay 2020). An event at the University of Melbourne, Australia called 'The Future of Sex-Based Rights', featuring a number of radical and gender-critical feminist speakers, was subject to attempted deplatforming on the basis that by providing a venue for the event, the university was 'putting transgender and gender non-conforming students and staff at risk.'[10] Gender-critical feminists have been banned from Twitter under its 'Hateful Conduct' policies.[11] Reddit banned the popular subreddit r/GenderCritical, which had over 64,000 members (Kearns 2020).

These are just a few examples; the point is that there's clearly a public perception, at least among some parts of the population, that gender-critical speech is hate speech. The question for the rest of this paper is, *is it*?

---

[8] The United Kingdom case was (Maya Forstater vs CGD Europe, 2019). The Australian case, heard in the Australian Capital Territory, was (Clinch v Rep (Discrimination), 2020, ACAT 13).

[9] Pidd reports for *The Guardian* that 'The stickers were condemned by a coalition of women's groups... In an open statement addressed to "our trans siblings", the groups said: "In our city there's no room for hate against trans people. We condemn the behaviour, hate and transphobia of "Liverpool Resisters"/ We condemn their appalling stickers and we absolutely will not tolerate transphobia in our city."

[10] <https://equalityaustralia.org.au/open-letter-to-the-university-of-melbourne/>

[11] Meghan Murphy and Graham Linehan are among the most prominent (BBC News 2019; Blackall 2020). My own account has been banned too. To give an example of what is considered to be 'hateful conduct' under this policy, my first suspension was for referring to a self-identified transwoman with he/him/his pronouns, and my second was for saying directly to a self-identified transwoman that they are not female. ('@saltyfemst @RipTaraWB @MaggioAlex @annaloiuseadams @unimelb just for the record, i've blocked tara so cannot see his tweets but can see him tagged here. he has been harassing both me & my employer on facebook and twitter. i have not made any public comment against surgery for trans people. if you're a rad fem, i recommend blocking.') (@sasha4th when you say 'transgender female' do you mean that you're a trans man? if so, you're very welcome in female-only spaces, there's no issue. if you mean trans woman, then you're not female, and the reasoning applies to you. it doesn't matter that *you* appreciate the spaces.' 6.00 p.m. 28th April 2019). There are screenshots at my website: <https://wordpress.com/page/hollylawford-smith.org/2174>

8.3 Hate speech

The standard way to proceed in thinking about *free* speech is to work through the underlying justifications and check whether a particular category of speech is protected in relation to them (Howard 2019, fn. 21); (Yong 2011, pp. 389–94). We might take the same approach to *hate* speech here, figuring out the underlying harms and working out whether that means gender-critical speech belongs in that category or not. Unfortunately, there has been no convergence upon a definition of hate speech, either in the popular discussion or in the academic discussion. There are at least nine different academic definitions (Simpson 2017). Here are some examples: Jeremy Waldron and Steven Heyman characterize hate speech as an assault on dignity;[12] Waldron because it denies recognition of common humanity (Waldron 2012), Heyman because it denies recognition of status as a rights-bearer (Heyman 2009; discussed in Simpson 2013, pp. 710–14). Robert Simpson characterizes hate speech as speech that 'convey[s] the idea that belonging to a particular social group warrants someone's being held in or treated with contempt' (Simpson 2013, p. 702). Rae Langton, Catharine MacKinnon, and Mari Matsuda have all focused on the way that some speech can undermine equality, by subordinating or marginalizing (see discussion in Schwartzmann 2002, p. 421), silencing (MacKinnon 1987; Langton 1990; Langton 1993), or defaming or discriminating against (MacKinnon 1991), people from oppressed groups.[13] Gail and Richard Murrow connect hate speech to dehumanization, and dehumanization to reduced response to the targeted group's suffering (Murrow and Murrow 2015; see also discussion in Simpson 2016). Caleb Yong identifies a category of hate speech, targeted vilification, intended to wound, insult, or intimidate its targets (Yong 2011, p. 394).

Let's just pick one of these, to illustrate how this approach might go. Waldron, for example, accounts for the harm of hate speech in terms of assaults upon human dignity, understood in terms of the 'security and assurance' had by members of a society. He thinks all members of society deserve 'protection from the most egregious forms of violence, exclusion, indignity, and subordination' (Waldron 2012, pp. 82–3). Hate speech denies security and assurance over these things to members of particular groups. On Waldron's view, dignity is about

---

[12] For further examples of authors who tie hate speech to dignity, see (Simpson 2013, p. 707, fn. 11). Simpson takes the main reason to take a dignity-based approach to be that 'the targets of identity-based hate speech are vying to secure a position of esteem and recognition within a wider social and cultural ecosystem, and that this aspiration is what is being opposed – both maligned, and also, some authors claim, impaired – in the hate speaker's verbal conduct' (p. 709).

[13] Matsuda talks about racist hate speech (Matsuda 1989). Mackinnon says that pornography is 'hateful', 'propaganda', 'a hate literature', 'group hate', and 'group hate propaganda'—which is close enough to saying that it is hate speech (against women) (MacKinnon 1991, pp. 803 and 807–10). Langton defends MacKinnon's earlier claim that pornography subordinates and silences women (MacKinnon 1987; Langton 1993).

humanity, about 'the sorts of beings human persons are' (p. 86). Everyone is owed equal *recognition* respect, respect in virtue of their humanity. But it is not the case that everyone is owed equal *appraisal* respect, which takes into account their 'virtues, vices, crimes, views, merits, and so on' (pp. 82–3). As Simpson explains, for Waldron, hate speech is 'group defamation', and we should restrict it in order to protect public order. Public order depends on 'a widely-shared understanding and acceptance among the populace of the status-respect that we all owe, and are owed, as fellow members of society' (Simpson 2013, p. 719; following Waldron 2010, pp. 1604–5).

To be helpful in answering the question of whether gender-critical speech is hate speech, the account must allow us to settle novel cases. This is worth saying, because many discussions of hate speech make use of uncontroversial examples of hate speech, directed toward social groups whose classification as oppressed is generally not regarded as controversial. Neither of these things are the case when it comes to gender-critical speech. Trans people, the alleged targets of gender-critical speech, are not one of the social groups usually talked about in connection with hate speech—the paradigm cases are race and religion. And we're not looking for an explanation of *why* certain gender-critical expressions are hate speech, but rather for an answer to *whether* they are. So our question, framed in terms of Waldron's account of hate speech, would be something like: does gender-critical speech assault trans people's human dignity, denying them the security and assurance owed to all members of society?

Some certainly think that it does. Judith Butler, one of the main proponents of gender identity ideology, said in an interview with *New Statesman* that 'trans women['s]...abiding and very real sense of gender ought to be recognized socially and publicly as a relatively simple matter of according another human dignity. The trans-exclusionary radical feminist position attacks the dignity of trans people' (Ferber 2020).[14] The judge in Maya Forstater vs CGD Europe 2019—a case determining whether the termination of Forstater's employment relationship because of her gender-critical feminist tweets was a violation of her rights because gender-critical speech is protected as a 'philosophical belief'—found that her tweets failed at the fifth condition for a philosophical belief, namely that it 'must be worthy of respect in a democratic society, not be incompatible with human dignity and not conflict with the fundamental rights of others'.[15] (The judge's verdict was later overturned).

---

[14] 'Trans-exclusionary radical feminist', or 'TERF', is gender identity activists' preferred term for gender-critical feminists. See also Chapter 7.

[15] (Maya Forstater vs CGD Europe, 2019), p. 16. Because the fifth condition has three elements, it is technically possible that the judge found Forstater's tweets to be not worthy of respect in a democratic society, or to conflict with the fundamental rights of others, rather than to be incompatible with human dignity. But there is some evidence in the judgement to suggest that this is not the case. First of all, there is a reference to P v S and Cornwall CC, 1996, 795, a European Court of Justice case in which a person was fired for undergoing sex reassignment surgery, quoting 'To tolerate such discrimination

These claims are not, of course, sufficient to establish that gender-critical speech is, in fact, incompatible with human dignity. For Waldron, assaulting dignity means denying a person's security and assurance, failing to accord them equal recognition respect in virtue of our common humanity. But nothing about denying that males can be or become female, and vice versa, requires denying the equal humanity of a trans person. Humans have sexes; someone is not less human because they're one sex or the other. (Or at least, that is what we are morally committed to as social egalitarians; in practice, if one sex is treated as less than fully human, it's females, not males).[16] Perhaps a transwoman confronted with a 'women don't have penises' sticker in a public space might feel excluded, specifically from the category 'women', but Waldron's concern is exclusion *from society*, not from a specific social concept. As Kathleen Stock has argued, concepts—like 'woman'— are not tools of exclusion or inclusion, they're tools for tracking features of the world and the interests humans have in them (Stock 2021, Chapter 5).

When there is something that a person wants, for people to refuse to give it to them may be undermining of their 'security' or 'assurance' that they will get it. When male people desire to be recognized, acknowledged, treated as women, it undermines their security and assurance that they will be when there are women on the streets wearing T-shirts proclaiming 'woman / wʊmən / noun / adult human female'. But Waldron is unlikely to think that *any* undermining of security and assurance amounts to a violation of dignity and a failure of recognition respect. After all, he said very clearly that we did not owe all people equal appraisal respect. If there are valid reasons for saying things that someone wants you not to say, or refusing to say things that someone wants you to say (e.g. saying that a woman is an adult human female, refusing to call a male person a 'woman'), then that refusal does not count as a violation of that person's dignity. There are two high-profile cases, both tied to desires that relate to identity, where the widespread public response was to refuse rather than to assent to an individual's desires. Rachel Dolezal wanted to be treated as black, Emile Ratelband wanted to be treated as twenty years younger (Aitkenhead 2017; Boffey 2018). There are valid reasons for refusal in the case of gender-critical speech, namely the feminist

---

would be tantamount, as regards such a person, to a failure to respect the dignity and freedom to which he or she is entitled, and which the Court has a duty to safeguard' (para. 66, p. 19). Second, there is a reference to the Equality Act, which defines harassment among other things as violating a person's dignity (para. 73, p. 21). Finally, in the analysis, the judge says 'I consider that the Claimant's view, in its absolutist nature, is incompatible with human dignity and fundamental rights of others' (para. 84, p. 24); 'people cannot expect to be protected if their core belief involves violating others' dignity and/or creating an intimidating, hostile, degrading, humiliating or offensive environment for them' (para. 87, p. 25), and 'the Claimant is absolutist in her view of sex and it is a core component of her belief that she will refer to a person by the sex she considered appropriate even if it violates their dignity and/or creates an intimidating, hostile, degrading, humiliating or offensive environment. The approach is not worthy of respect in a democratic society' (para. 90, p. 25).

[16] See e.g. Catharine MacKinnon's book *Are Woman Human?* (2007), in particular the eponymous essay from (1999).

ends served by being able to articulate a conception of women as a political class, and argue for that group's legal, political, social, and economic interests.

One problem with this response is that opponents of gender-critical feminism are likely to simply disagree. They may deny that feminist ends are ends we should care about, or insist that these ends can be met in a 'trans-deferential' way (meaning, deferring to trans people's self-identifications). Or they may allow that there are valid reasons for refusing to say (or not say) certain things, but say that when it comes to sex/gender identifications, these trump all other interests. Maybe not all desires to be recognized, acknowledged, or treated in a particular way should be met on pain of violating human dignity, but trans people's desires to be recognized, acknowledged, or treated according to their sex/gender identifications should. If these specific desires are frustrated, then that is a violation of dignity and a failure of recognition respect.

At this point, we end up in a stalemate. Gender-critical feminists say that calling a male a man is not a violation of dignity, because the person is a man (the defences being truth, and freedom of opinion),[17] and there are compelling feminist reasons for them to call males 'men' (the defence being the moral and political importance of sex-based justice). Opponents say that calling a male (who identifies as a woman) a man is a violation of dignity, because of the overriding importance of sex/gender identifications. Where to from there?

The risk of working through accounts of hate speech to see whether they classify gender-critical speech as hate speech (in the same way that we worked through accounts of slurs to see whether they classified 'TERF' as a slur in Chapter 7) is that we will inevitably end up in this kind of stalemate. To someone already convinced of the absolute and overriding importance of 'gender identity', a sticker saying 'women don't have penises' will seem to assault dignity, convey contempt, undermine equality, dehumanize, and vilify (see above). To those not already convinced of this, including gender-critical feminists but not limited to them, it will not. We're left none the wiser about who is right, because whether gender-critical speech counts as hate speech according to any of these accounts ultimately depends on the prior question of how important 'gender identities' are, and whether they do trump all other interests.[18]

Some of those who have thought hard about hate speech think this problem is a general one. Stanley Fish, for example, says '[i]t could just as well be said that one man's hate speech is another man's (or woman's) speaking of truth to a world

---

[17] As formalized in the United Nations' Universal Declaration of Human Rights, Article 19: 'Everyone has the right to freedom of opinion and expression; this right includes freedom to hold opinions without interference and to seek, receive and impart information and ideas through any media and regardless of frontiers'.

[18] We end up in structurally similar stalemates considering whether criticism of Islam, or of Israel, is hate speech; for those two, the disagreement depends on the prior question of how we're understanding Islam, or Israel.

that needs to hear it. Only if the content of hate speech were self-identifying—if upon hearing an instance of it, a *universal* chorus would explain in unison, "That's hateful"—would it stand still long enough to become the object of principled regulation. But if it is a moving target, as the endless, inconclusive discussions of it amply show, any regulation of it—or of what some persons take "it" to be—will be *ad hoc* and political. In the end, then, hate speech can be defined only as speech produced by persons whose ideas and viewpoints you despise and fear. *Hate speech is what your enemy says loudly*' (Fish 2019, p. 51, his emphasis).

If Fish is right, and the problem generalizes, then attempting to pin down the 'correct' account of hate speech in the first place, in order to ask whether gender-critical speech fits the description, is futile. There is no correct account, on this view; there is just disagreement, and the naming of some of what we each disagree with as 'hate speech'. Opponents of gender-critical feminism will call gender-critical speech hate speech because it is what their enemy says loudly. Gender-critical feminists could just as well start calling gender identity activists' speech hate speech, on the basis of its dismissive and trivializing attitude towards female people's rights and protections.

Whether the problem generalizes or not, it's a problem when it comes to gender-critical speech. The underlying issue, relating to the importance of 'gender identities', remains unsettled. Is failing to acknowledge a person's 'gender identity', that is, their subjective sense of themselves as being a man or a woman, a violation of recognition respect, or not?[19] It is important to keep in mind that the parties to the disagreement use these terms differently. Hold fixed that 'man' and 'woman' are gender terms for both parties. For those who think that gender is sex caste, transwomen are not women because they are not female, and transmen are not men because they are not male. Gender identity is literally beside the point. For those who think that gender is identity, transwomen are women because they have a 'woman' gender identity, and transmen are men because they have a 'man' identity. Sex is literally beside the point. So the issue is not whether trans people have the gender identities they say they do, in which case it would be *obviously* disrespectful to deny that. Denial would involve presuming greater authority than the trans person over how they feel about themselves. Rather, the issue is whether

---

[19] A reviewer made the interesting suggestion that denying a person's self-conception might helpfully be understood as akin to telling someone that they have an adaptive preference, or are in the grip of false consciousness. This looks especially plausible in the case of gender identity, a self-conception that is the product of an ideology, where denying the self-conception is the result of rejecting the ideology. This is certainly fraught, but it need not be a violation of recognition respect. The same kind of tension would appear between, say, a radical feminist and a liberal feminist sex worker, where the latter has a self-conception as sexually liberated and empowered, and the radical feminist is denying the accuracy of that self-conception on the grounds that she thinks the sex worker is in the grip of patriarchal ideology that positions women as empowered when they act in the service of men's sexual interests.

the dispute between gender identity activists and gender-critical feminists over what gender is *must* be settled in favour of gender as identity. If it's not the case that it must, then it cannot be that failing to acknowledge gender identity is a failure of recognition respect.[20]

Whether failing to acknowledge a person's 'gender identity' is a violation of recognition respect is a moral question currently being debated in the public sphere, and while gender identity activists tend to treat it as settled, it is not a matter of general consensus—even merely among progressives—in anything like the way it is for e.g. contemptuous comments about whole racial groups. The gender-critical position is the *mainstream* position outside of the activist left in wealthy liberal countries. Anti-racist goals don't impinge on any other identity group's legitimate political interests, whereas gender identity activists' goals do impinge on both women's and lesbian, gay, and bisexual people's interests. While the question remains actively contested, it will not be settled by an account of hate speech, even if some other instances of speech may be. So we should not take the approach of identifying the correct account of hate speech and then working out whether it classifies gender-critical speech as hate speech.

In the rest of the paper, then, we should ask a slightly different question: should gender-critical speech be suppressed?[21] We can answer this question by thinking more directly about the harm that gender-critical speech does (if any), and how these harms (if any) balance out against the interests that gender-critical speech is advancing.[22] I will assume that there is some threshold level of harm that would make it appropriate to suppress gender-critical speech regardless of whether it advanced some interests. For example, if gender-critical speech involved a direct incitement to physical violence, then it would cross this threshold. Below that threshold, I will allow that whether it can be suppressed depends on the balance of the harms done by the speech against the interests served by the speech. For example, if gender-critical speech causes low-level emotional suffering

---

[20] One might be tempted to wonder why we can't have both gender concepts: caste and identity. We can, but it doesn't help, because what gender identity activists want is that 'trans women are women!' and 'trans men are men!', and they wouldn't get that from a compromise solution in which transwomen are women in one sense but men in another; transmen men in one sense but women in another. I am also sceptical that a compromise could be reached by conceding the terms 'man' and 'woman', because too many gender identity activists also contest the terms 'male' and 'female', and there wouldn't be much benefit in gender-critical feminists having a sense of gender as sex caste yet with no words left to refer to the people in the caste.

[21] Related questions include: should those who express gender-critical ideas be punished/sanctioned? Do the targets of gender-critical speech deserve compensation? For an intriguing approach to compensation for hate speech see (Meyers 1995).

[22] Robert Simpson takes a similar approach, albeit still in pursuit of a category of hate speech: 'a harm-prevention framework—in which our principal aims are to characterize the harms that may be caused by hate speech, and ascertain whether hate speech does in fact cause those harms—should be adopted for assessing the legitimacy of legal restrictions on hate speech' (Simpson 2013, p. 703). Just substitute the words 'gender-critical speech' for 'hate speech'.

(e.g. insecurity, self-doubt), then it will not cross the threshold, and so depends on the balance of harms done against interests served.[23]

In Section 8.3.1, I briefly consider the claim that gender-critical speech *constitutes* harm, and argue that this is subject to the same problems as looking for an account of hate speech to settle the matter was. In Section 8.3.2 I follow Jeff Howard and ask whether gender-critical speech is 'dangerous speech', arguing that in virtue of its political purpose, and in light of demographic considerations about the population alleged to be targeted by it, it is not.

8.3.1 Constitutive harm

It has been standard to make a distinction between speech that *causes* harm, and speech that *constitutes* harm, when thinking about the relation between speech and harm.[24] MacKinnon, for example, has argued that pornography itself does harm: it defames and discriminates against women (MacKinnon 1991; 1993). Langton defends MacKinnon's conclusion, saying more about what it is for pornography to constitute harm. Some speech is not merely a 'saying' but a 'doing'. Speech *acts* are expressions that do things. For example, saying 'look out!' *warns* someone, saying 'I promise you' *promises* someone, saying 'I now pronounce you husband and wife' (when you have the requisite authority and are in the right context) *marries* two people, saying 'shoot her' *urges* someone to shoot (Langton 1993, p. 295; following Austin 1962). What harm has speech been said to 'do', in this way? Constitutively harmful speech may humiliate, threaten, or legitimate someone's violation (De Silva 2020, pp. 41–2); it may offend, insult, or intimidate (p. 43); it may subordinate or silence (p. 44). Langton develops the idea that pornography silences because the powerful can do more with words than the powerless, and one of the things they can do is 'silence the speech of the powerless' (Langton 1993, pp. 298–9). Pornography does this to women by making women's refusal of sex and sexual violence unspeakable (p. 324).

Is this a useful idea for thinking about the harm gender-critical speech does, if any? One problem with the examples given above is that there are always causal harms in the vicinity. Saying 'shoot her' urges someone to shoot, but if that person shoots then it also causes her to be shot (and if they don't shoot, it still causes her to be at risk of being shot). Pornography silences women by making sexual refusal unspeakable, but if a woman's refusal is not given uptake in a specific case,

---

[23] This may seem to licence gender-critical feminists to engage in targeted harassment of trans people, so long as this 'only' causes low-level emotional suffering. I am only saying here that such speech wouldn't be a clear candidate for suppression. I take up the separate question of harmful speech in Chapter 9.

[24] For further discussion of constitutively harmful speech as it relates to legal protections against vilification see (De Silva 2020).

it also causes rape (and if it does not cause rape in the specific case, it still causes her to be at risk of being raped). And so on. If we're really worried about the rape rather than the silencing itself, then we might consider pornography as causal harm (incitement to rape), rather than as constitutive harm (silencing). To really test whether it's constitutive harm rather than causal harm we care about, we'd have to find a case of constitutive harm without causal harm.[25]

Here's an attempt to try to pull the two apart. Suppose there is a society in which people are very much committed to treating people as equals. A small group of people in this society subscribe to a particular religious view, and are inculcated into this view through family lines. Everyone else in the society thinks that these people are intellectually inferior, because the religious beliefs they subscribe to are so implausible. But they never discriminate. There is no material difference, in this society, between members of that religious group and others in terms of life expectancy, health, employment, income, and so on. People are not less cordial with members of the religious group. In a society like this, the expression of the belief that this group of people are intellectually inferior does not cause anyone to treat the members of the group any differently.

In this context, suppose two people from outside the religious group are filming a live political debate for a local television channel, and while they are perfectly friendly with the members of the religious group working on set, during their debate one mentions the group and the other makes the remark 'a cockroach has more intelligence than those people'. By *those people* he refers to the religious group. By drawing a comparison between cockroaches and a particular social group, he dehumanizes them, positioning them as inferior in relation to other people. This is a failure of recognition respect, in Waldron's terms. This is an excellent candidate for constitutively harmful speech, in that it dehumanizes and subordinates. But we are assuming that this public speech will not affect any individual members of the group in any way in terms of their material outcomes, or put them at risk of being affected in this way, so robust are the citizens' commitments to equal treatment. So it is not a candidate for causally harmful speech. Should this speech nonetheless be suppressed? I think it should not, and I think this shows that our opposition to constitutively harmful speech comes from the close relationship it normally has with causal harm.

This case is exaggerated relative to our purposes: gender-critical speech does not dehumanize or subordinate trans people. There is no entailment from any of the gender-critical commitments outlined in Section 8.1 to the denial of trans persons' moral equality. Many of those expressing gender-critical ideas go

---

[25] An alternative, not covered by the thought-experiment to follow, is that we care about constitutive harm only when there's causal harm, but that we do care about it *additionally* to the causal harm. We might think the causal harms (perlocutionary effects) are made worse by the constitutive harms (illocutionary effects).

to great lengths to make clear their commitment to trans rights and anti-discrimination protections. What is at issue is not whether trans people are social equals, but whether males who identify as women/female *are women/female*, and females who identify as men/male *are men/male*. This is a disagreement over concepts (what gender is) and terms (whether 'woman' and 'man' are sex terms or gender terms). But there are plenty of disagreements in the world, over both concepts and terms, that do not produce accusations of hate speech. The case is useful not for the content of its speech, but for its quarantining of constitutive harm.

What the case helps to show is that when we are careful to separate constitutive harms from causal harms, it is much less obvious that constitutively harmful speech is harmful, or if we prefer to grant that it is, that this particular kind of harmful speech should be suppressed. It is likely that those already committed to the overriding importance of respecting 'gender identities' will consider it a constitutive harm (perhaps 'denial of first-personal authority')[26] while those not so committed will not. We end up back in the stalemate we were in when attempting to settle the issue with reference to accounts of hate speech. For this reason, I'll set the possibility of gender-critical speech being constitutively harmful aside, and focus on the possibility of it causing harm.

8.3.2 Dangerous speech

Jeff Howard argues that 'we have an enforceable moral duty to refrain from speech that incites the incontrovertible violation of others' rights' (Howard 2019, p. 237).[27] The violation does not have to be imminent (p. 211). He thinks that 'incendiary speakers can render themselves morally liable to coercion' (p. 211). This is a reorientation of discussions of free speech and hate speech, drawing on the resources of just war theory (p. 212). When speech will impose harm, we can ask whether that harm is narrowly proportional—which means, whether those targeted by it are morally liable to suffer the harm—and whether it is widely proportional—which means, whether those who are not morally liable to suffer the harm will suffer harm, and what the effects of that will be. This distinction allows us to account for the wider consequences of suppressing speech, as well as of not suppressing it. We can also ask whether suppression meets a necessity condition, which means that 'no more force, or harm, than necessary to defuse a

---

[26] See Bettcher (2009), and further discussion in Chapter 3.
[27] While this wording suggests it's the *violation* that's incontrovertible, he is clear earlier in the paper that it's the *rights* that must be incontrovertible. Dangerous speech is speech that incites violation of incontrovertible rights, not speech that incontrovertibly incites the violation of rights (Howard 2019, p. 215).

threat is permissible' (p. 248). Listing all of your housemate's character flaws until he cries so that he stops interrupting you when you are trying to read would violate the necessity condition applied to expression.

Establishing that speech incites a clear violation of others' rights will be enough to show that the speaker has violated an enforceable duty, which means that in principle her speech can be suppressed (she can be made to do what she should have done). But Howard treats whether we should in fact suppress it as a separate question that depends on wide proportionality and necessity (p. 213). This helps to show that counter-speech is sometimes preferable to suppression, because when counter-speech would work to eliminate the harm, suppression will violate the necessity condition (pp. 248–54).

In focusing on 'dangerous speech', Howard is limiting his focus to speech that advocates (whether explicitly or implicitly) or justifies a course of action; where that course of action will violate rights that are incontrovertible, such as the right to life; and where that speech 'dangerously incites' the course of action, meaning that it puts people at risk by advocating or justifying the particular course of action (pp. 215–16). In order to apply this idea in the case of gender-critical speech, it will be useful to consider some of the examples he gives of incendiary speakers, or speech that incites the violation of others' rights. He mentions online extremists advocating a duty to kill, in one an Islamic cleric advocating the killing of Americans, in the other a Norwegian white supremacist advocating the killing of Muslims (pp. 208–9). He also mentions a Ku Klux Klan member calling for 'revengeance' against black and Jewish Americans (p. 209), and a hypothetical case in which a speaker addressing an audience 'argues that members of [a] religious group are vile scum who deserve to be killed', after which time one member of the audience attacks another who is a member of that religious group (p. 216).

A hypothetical case which does *not* count as dangerous speech is also provided, in which a woman addresses an audience with an argument for atheism, and in response a group of religious fanatics murder her and others (p. 218). Howard writes 'she is engaging in activity that she, intuitively, has every presumable moral right to engage in: the promulgation of her reasonable convictions on matters of religious truth' (p. 218). Because her speech is valuable we should protect her from the violence of those provoked by it, rather than suppressing her speech to avoid that violence (pp. 218–19).

I think it's more or less obvious that gender-critical feminists are like the woman arguing for atheism, who has the bad luck of antagonising a group of religious fanatics. Gender-critical speech is feminist speech, uttered by women as part of a good faith attempt to explain the history of women's oppression, articulate why women are a class, say what women have in common, and provide a coherent justification of, and vision for, feminism. As a historically oppressed group women have every right to do this, and as a group of people whose self-determination has been severely impacted by men, they have every right to do that without men.[28]

But I'm a gender-critical feminist, so I would say that. And in any case, that won't satisfy the opponent of gender-critical feminism, who is likely to see it as more like the first hypothetical case. So instead let's ask, what's the strongest case we can make that gender-critical feminists are 'incendiary speakers', whose speech incites the violation of trans people's incontrovertible rights? If we can establish this, then—supposing that Howard is right—we can show they've violated an enforceable duty not to do so, and we can ask whether enforcing that duty by suppressing their speech would be widely proportionate and necessary.

Because the rights in question have to be incontrovertible, we can't pin the harm to anything that is at issue between gender-critical feminists and their opponents, like an alleged right that people believe that one's gender identity determines one's sex/gender.[29] We're dealing with things like the right not to be killed, or physically assaulted, or raped, for example.[30] The opponent of gender-critical speech can work with this, however, by referring to violence against trans people, including the murders, assaults, and rapes that are perpetrated against them. Dangerous speech will be speech that incites the violation of trans people's rights to life, and rights against physical violence. Now that we are clear on what the rights are, we can ask whether gender-critical speech advocates for, or justifies, the perpetrating of murder, physical assault, or sexual assault.

Who perpetrates these harms? It's useful to establish this, in order to figure out whether there's a plausible connection between those people and gender-critical speakers. In Howard's hypothetical examples, there were speakers directly addressing audiences, and either members of the audience or members of the public aware of the events were incited. In the two real cases of terrorism, there was online content (the Islamic cleric's YouTube channel, and the white supremacist's manifesto), which the terrorists had consumed directly. So once we know

---

[28] By this I mean that ideas about womanhood and femininity have largely been constructed by men to benefit men, which we can see most clearly when we consider the history of women from around the invention of agriculture through to the early 1960s, when feminism finally started to take off. Because of this egregious and long-lasting violation of self-determination (at the level of the whole group, but impacting on every individual woman) it is especially pressing that women begin to rewrite what it means to be a woman/female without men's input, that is, that *women decide this for themselves*. I cannot think of any other historically oppressed social group that is in a comparable situation. See also Hacker (1951).

[29] I say this, rather than 'alleged right to have one's gender identity respected', because even if there were this right, it wouldn't settle anything between the gender-critical feminist and her opponents. She can accept that you identify as a woman without accepting that your identification makes you a woman, or female.

[30] These are all physical harms. This should not be taken to imply that I don't think psychological harm counts as harm. I do, but I don't think there are incontrovertible rights against psychological harm, precisely because psychological harm is more subjective, and harder to prove. Thus I bracket it in this paper, and take it up in Chapter 9.

who perpetrates the relevant violence against trans people, we can ask about the possible connections between those people and gender-critical feminists.

There are some cases in which trans people are murdered by their sexual partners. The 'trans panic' defence is a version of the 'gay panic' defence in which criminal defendants try to argue temporary insanity, diminished capacity, provocation, or self-defence to get their charges reduced. As Cynthia Lee describes it, 'the defendant claiming trans panic tries to blame the transgender victim by claiming the victim's deceit provoked him ("if he hadn't lied about being a woman, I wouldn't have killed him")' (Lee 2008, p. 478). Although she doesn't provide data for trans murders in particular, Lee notes one study on violence against lesbians and gay men finding that 67% of perpetrators were white and 94% male; and another on violence against lesbians, gay, bisexual and transgender people finding that 47% were white and 82% were male (Lee 2008, p. 512, fn. 202).

It's hard to be precise about the other perpetrator groups, because there isn't much data. In Lee's paper only one case involving the trans panic defence is mentioned, but she also writes that the defence was 'a fairly recent modification of the gay panic defence', so there may have been more cases attempting to use it in the intervening twelve years (p. 478). The United States does not collect systematic data on trans homicides (Stotzer 2017), but Alexis Dinno attempted an estimate for the years 2010–2014. He found that 'the overall homicide rate of transgender individuals was likely to be less than that of cisgender individuals', but that 'the homicide rates of young transfeminine Black and Latina residents were almost certainly higher than were those of cisfeminine comparators' (Dinno 2017). Estimates of the transgender homicide rate during this period were between 3.66 people per 100,000 and 110 people per 100,000. (The smaller number came from assuming the Transgender Day of Remembrance and National Coalition of Anti-Violence Programs homicide figures were not undercounted, and that there was a larger transgender population; the higher number came from assuming the figure undercounted so that four in every five homicides were not reported, and that the transgender population was smaller) (Dinno 2017). In Australia, there are just two deaths on record in the last decade, for death by murder, suicide, or drug overdose (Lavopierre 2019).

Wilfred Reilly, in an attempt to investigate frequent news headlines claiming an 'epidemic' of trans murders, looked into the Human Rights Campaign's (HRC) database for transgender individuals killed by violent means in America,[31] and found that it was 29 in 2017, 26 in 2018, and 22 in 2019 (Reilly 2019). (Unfortunately the HRC does not usually note information about the perpetrators. But we do know as a general matter that most murders are committed by men. For example in the United States in 2019, there were 10,335 murders

---

[31] <https://www.hrc.org/resources/violence-against-the-transgender-community-in-2017>

by men, and 1,408 murders by women[32]—although there were also 4,502 murders marked as 'unknown' (Statista 2019).) Reilly looked into some of the cases tracked by the HRC, and found that many were not accurately classified as hate crimes. One, for example, was killed in the course of trying to intervene in a physical altercation between family members. Reilly reports on another author's review of around half of the cases recorded by the HRC, who found that 37 were due to domestic violence, 24 involved sex workers (and related to the dangerous conditions of illegal sex work), a few were random acts of violence, and 'exactly four of the perpetrators were clearly motivated by "anti-trans bias", animus, or hatred' (Reilly 2019; see also Greene 2019). Reilly also reports that transgender murders were usually perpetrated between people of the same race. Seven of the nine killers of white trans people were white, and 34 of the 37 killers of black trans people were black, during 2015–2019.

We have a somewhat unclear perpetrator pool here. It is likely to be mostly, if not entirely, men (as in Lee 2008, discussed above). It contains men who react violently to a perceived threat to their heterosexuality, or who actively target gay or trans people. It contains men who perpetrate domestic violence, men who use sex workers, and a few men—four, as far as we can be sure—with bias, animus, or hatred towards transgender people. It's hardly credible to try to track domestic violence, violence against sex workers, or acts of random violence back to gender-critical feminist speech. The first two are important social issues that radical and gender-critical feminists stand *against*. We could use the figure of four hate crimes in a five-year period in a country with a population of 328 million, come up with a plausible estimate for the world with some generous overestimating, and this would still be a very small number of men. If we multiply the United States' population by 23 we get the population of the world, so that's roughly 92 men, and if we generously exaggerate that by 5 (the overestimate used by Dinno for trans homicides) we get 460. The question that remains is, *is it plausible that these 460 men were incited to murder by gender-critical feminists?*[33]

Bear in mind that none of the gender-critical feminist claims discussed in Section 8.1 had any connection to advocating for, or attempting to justify, violence against trans people. All could be held perfectly consistent with advocating a zero tolerance policy on all forms of violence. So there is certainly no direct incitement. Could there be indirect incitement, instead? Might gender-critical feminists say 'men shouldn't be allowed to compete in women's sports' and men *hear* 'you should murder the next transwoman you see?' That is

---

[32] An analysis of women who killed in Victoria, Australia between 1985 and 1995 ($n = 86$) found that 40% of the female perpetrators killed a partner or ex-partner, and that 59% of those women killed in response to their partner's or ex-partner's violence (Kirkwood 2003; see also discussion of female offenders in Lawford-Smith, forthcoming).

[33] We can collect the relevant evidence, and ask the appropriately modified question, for other incontrovertible rights like the right against physical assault, or rape.

possible, but it looks more like the atheist talking to the audience and coming up against the religious fanatics than it does the speaker arguing that a particular religious group are vile scum who deserve to be killed. Perhaps opponents of gender-critical feminism will argue that gender-critical feminist ideas influence 'the culture', and the culture influences whether trans people are accepted in their chosen gender/sex categories. If we all thought transwomen were really women, then there would be no 'trans panic', because it would be fine, and indeed expected, for a woman to have a penis. If we all thought transwomen were really women, there wouldn't be any trans hatred, and so no hate-motivated murder, assault, or rape. So maybe gender-critical feminists aren't directly inciting this violence, but they're inciting it indirectly, by feeding ideas into the culture which fail to work for the acceptance of gender identities as determinants of sex/gender.

I am sure that Howard would not classify such an indirect causal claim as 'dangerous incitement'. This looks less like incitement and more like extremely diffuse causal contribution, on a par with the role one person's greenhouse gas emissions might play in climate change, or the role purchasing one sweatshop T-shirt might play in global labour injustice. Gender-critical feminists do contribute to the lack of acceptance of gender identities determining sex/gender classification, but that is because they object to such acceptance on political grounds, finding sex classification important. It is perfectly possible for us to think sex is real and can't be changed, that women are adult human females, and that transwomen are men/male, while also thinking that violence against anyone on the basis of how they choose to present themselves or how they choose to think of themselves is unacceptable. If acceptance of gender identity as determining sex/gender classification was the only way to end violence against trans people, then a case could be made against everyone who contributes to a lack of this acceptance that they were endangering trans people's lives (albeit to a lesser degree than non-trans people's lives are endangered). Then we'd be dealing with a collective action problem, but it would be possible to argue that as outspoken contributors to this lack of acceptance, gender-critical feminists had a particularly strong responsibility.

But there is no evidence that this would be the only way to end violence against transgender people. Indeed, surely as strategies go it is a bad one, because it involves science denial (making false claims about what sex is and how it can be changed) and a major shift in interrelated terms and concepts that is unlikely to be easily mainstreamed. The words that pick out sex/gender exist in every language, and connect up with words describing particular roles, like 'mother', and sexual orientations, like 'lesbian'; and not only the terms but the self-conceptions that relate to them, for example thinking that in order not to be 'transphobic' everyone had better start thinking of themselves as attracted to gender identities, or as pansexual. So long as there is a better way to end violence, then gender-critical feminists are not even causal contributors to violence against trans people along with everyone else who doesn't buy into gender identities, and in that case we don't even need to move to the second stage of asking whether we should enforce gender-critical feminists' duty to not incite rights-violations by suppressing their speech. We should not, because they haven't violated any such duty. Gender-critical feminist speech is not dangerous speech.

References

Aitkenhead, Decca. 'Rachel Dolezal: 'I'm not going to stoop and apologize and grovel', *The Guardian*, 25th February 2017. Online at <https://www.theguardian.com/us-news/2017/feb/25/rachel-dolezal-not-going-stoop-apologise-grovel>

Austin, J. L. *How To Do Things With Words* (London: Oxford University Press, 1962).

BBC News. 'Woman billboard removed after transphobia row', *BBC News*, 26th September 2018. Online at <https://www.bbc.com/news/uk-45650462>

BBC News. 'Twitter-ban feminist defends transgender views ahead of Holyrood meeting', *BBC News*, 22nd May 2019. Online at <https://www.bbc.com/news/uk-scotland-48366184>

Bettcher, Talia Mae. 'Trans identities and first-person authority', in Laurie Shrage (Ed.) *You've Changed: Sex Reassignment and Personal Identity* (Oxford: Oxford University Press, 2009).

Birchall, Guy. 'Getting shirty. Mum banned from pub for wearing T-shirt saying "Woman: human female" in case it upset transgender people', *The Sun*, 6th January 2019. Online at <https://www.thesun.co.uk/news/8131093/banned-pub-t-shirt-woman-human-female-trangender/>

Blackall, Molly. 'Twitter closes Graham Linehan account after trans comment', *The Guardian*, 27th June 2020. Online at <https://www.theguardian.com/culture/2020/jun/27/twitter-closes-graham-linehan-account-after-trans-comment>

Boffey, Daniel. 'Dutch man, 69, starts legal fight to identify as 20 years younger', *The Guardian*, 8th November 2018. Online at <https://www.theguardian.com/world/2018/nov/08/dutch-man-69-starts-legal-fight-to-identify-as-20-years-younger>

Bogardus, Tomas. 'Evaluating arguments for the sex/gender distinction', *Philosophia* 48 (2020), pp. 873–93.

Byrne, Alex. 'Are women adult human females?' *Philosophical Studies* 177 (2020), pp. 3783–803.

de Silva, Anjalee. 'Addressing the vilification of women: A functional theory of harm and implications for law', *Melbourne University Law Review* 43/3 (2020), [early view].

Dinno, Alexis. 'Homicide rates of transgender individuals in the United States: 2010-2014', *American Journal of Public Health* 107/9 (2017), pp. 1441-7.

Ely, John Hart. 'Flag desecration: A case study in the roles of categorization and balancing in First Amendment analysis', *Harvard Law Review* 88 (1974-5), pp. 1482-509.

Ferber, Alona. 'Judith Butler on the culture wars, JK Rowling and living in "anti-intellectual times"', *New Statesman*, 22nd September 2020. Online at <https://www.newstatesman.com/international/2020/09/judith-butler-culture-wars-jk-rowling-and-living-anti-intellectual-times>

Fish, Stanley. *The First: How to Think About Hate Speech, Campus Speech, Religious Speech, Fake News, Post-Truth, and Donald Trump* (New York: Simon & Schuster, 2019).

Greene, Chad. 'I crunched the data. The violence "epidemic" against transgender people is a myth', *The Federalist*, 4th November 2019. Online at <https://thefederalist.com/2019/11/04/the-left-is-lying-about-a-hatred-and-violence-epidemic-against-transgender-people/>

Hacker, Helen Mayer. 'Women as a minority group', *Social Forces* 30/1 (1951), pp. 60-9.

Hay, Katharine. 'JK Rowling: Billboard at Edinburgh Waverly station in support of author removed', *The Scotsman*, 30th July 2020. Online at <https://www.scotsman.com/news/politics/jk-rowling-billboard-edinburgh-waverley-station-support-author-removed-2928241>

Heyman, Steven. 'Hate speech, public discourse, and the First Amendment', in Ivan Hare and James Weinstein (Eds.) *Extreme Speech and Democracy* (Oxford: Oxford University Press, 2009).

Howard, Jeffrey. 'Dangerous speech', *Philosophy & Public Affairs* 47/2 (2019), pp. 208-54.

Kearns, Madeleine. 'Reddit bans gender-critical views', *National Review*, 17th July 2020. Online at <https://www.nationalreview.com/corner/reddit-bans-gender-critical-views/>

Kirkwood, Deborah. 'Female perpetrated homicide in Victoria between 1985 and 1995', *The Australian and New Zealand Journal of Criminology* 36/2 (2003), pp. 152-72.

Langton, Rae. 'Whose right? Ronald Dworkin, women, and pornographers', *Philosophy and Public Affairs* 19/4 (1990), pp. 311-59.

Langton, Rae. 'Speech acts and unspeakable acts', *Philosophy and Public Affairs* 22/4 (1993), pp. 293-330.

Lavoipierre, Angela. 'Why is it so hard to work out how many transgender people have been murdered in Australia?' *ABC News*, 20th November 2019. Online at <https://www.abc.net.au/news/2019-11-20/today-is-transgender-remembrance-day-australia-acknowledge/11718366>

Lawford-Smith, Holly. *Gender-Critical Feminism* (Oxford: Oxford University Press, 2022).

Lawford-Smith, Holly. 'Female offenders', in Jesper Ryberg (Ed.) *Oxford Handbook of Punishment Theory and Philosophy* (Part 5, 'Punishment and Special Offenders') (New York: Oxford University Press, forthcoming).

Lee, Cynthia. 'The gay panic defense', *University of California Davis Law Review* 42/471 (2008), pp. 471–566.

Lyons, Izzy. 'Transgender woman accused of "hate speech" after wearing T-shirt stating she is still biologically male', *The Telegraph*, 22nd December 2019. Online at <https://www.telegraph.co.uk/news/2019/12/22/transgender-woman-accused-hate-speech-wearing-t-shirt-stating/>

MacKinnon, Catharine. 'The sexual politics of the First Amendment', in *Feminism Unmodified* (Massachusetts: Harvard University Press, 1987), pp. 206–13.

MacKinnon, Catharine. 'Pornography as defamation and discrimination', *Boston University Law Review* 71/5 (1991), pp. 793–815.

MacKinnon, Catharine. *Only Words* (Massachusetts: Harvard University Press, 1993).

MacKinnon, Catharine. *Are Women Human?* (Massachusetts: Harvard University Press, 2007).

Matsuda, Mari. 'Public response to racist speech: Considering the victim's story', *Michigan Law Review* 87/8 (1989), pp. 2320–81.

Meyers, Diana. 'Rights in collision: A non-punitive compensatory remedy for abusive speech', *Law and Philosophy* 14 (1995), pp. 203–43.

Murrow, Gail., & Murrow, Richard. 'A hypothetical neurological association between dehumanization and human rights abuses', *Journal of Law and the Biosciences* (2015), pp. 1–29.

Osbaldiston, Nick. 'Whither academic freedom?' <https://nickosbaldiston.substack.com>, 17th October 2022.

Pidd, Helen. 'Sticker protest on Antony Gormley's beach statues accused of 'trans hatred'', *The Guardian*, 20th August 2018.

Reilly, Wilfred. 'Are we in the midst of a transgender murder epidemic?' *Quillette*, 7th December 2019. Online at <https://quillette.com/2019/12/07/are-we-in-the-midst-of-a-transgender-murder-epidemic/>

Reilly-Cooper, Rebecca. 'A woman's place is a sanctuary: Rebecca Reilly-Cooper (15 March 2018)', 25th May 2018. Online at <https://www.youtube.com/watch?v=qXoZIcc1nFM>

Sánchez, Raquel Rosario. 'Sobreviví la dictadura franquista en Espana. Ahora me persigue el colectivo trans', *elCaribe*, 14th December 2020. Online at <https://www.elcaribe.com.do/panorama/pais/sobrevivi-la-dictadura-franquista-en-espana-ahora-me-persigue-el-colectivo-trans/>. Translated by Woman's Place UK as 'Lidia Falcón: "Women are being erased from the law and public policy"', 13th December 2020. Online at <https://womansplaceuk.org/2020/12/13/lidia-falcon-women-erased-from-the-law-and-public-policy/>

Schwartzmann, Lisa. 'Hate speech, illocution, and social context: A critique of Judith Butler', *Journal of Social Philosophy* 33/3 (2002), pp. 421–41.

Simpson, Robert. 'Dignity, harm, and hate speech', *Law and Philosophy* 32/6 (2013), pp. 701–28.

Simpson, Robert. 'Is the term "hate speech" a useful one?' Talk presented in the Melbourne Applied Philosophy Seminar, 6th September 2017.

Statista. 'Number of murder offenders in the United States in 2019, by gender', *Statista*, 1st October 2019. Online at <https://www.statista.com/statistics/251886/murder-offenders-in-the-us-by-gender/>

Stock, Kathleen. *Material Girls* (UK: Fleet Reads, 2021).

Stotzer, R. L. 'Data sources hinder our understanding of transgender murders', *American Journal of Public Health* 107/9 (2017), pp. 1362–1363.

Waldron, Jeremy. 'Dignity and defamation: The visibility of hate', *Harvard Law Review* 123 (2010), pp. 1596–657.

Waldron, Jeremy. *The Harm in Hate Speech* (Cambridge, MA: Harvard University Press, 2012).

Yong, Caleb. 'Does freedom of speech include hate speech?', *Res Publica* 17 (2011), pp. 385–403.

9
Is Gender-Critical Speech Harmful Speech?

9.1 Gender-critical speech

Gender-critical feminists are routinely accused of hate speech, harmful speech, and more recently, transphobic dogwhistles. For example, the Cambridge University Students' Union Women's Campaign website lists a document 'How to spot TERF ideology', which includes the claim 'Terf ideology uses a lot of the same phrases and tropes [as transmisogyny], which often seem innocuous on the surface but are actually being used as dogwhistles for transphobia and transmisogyny. Overall, terf ideology hides itself in feminist language, often claiming to support trans rights while actually working to undermine them'.[1] A guest post at the philosophy blog *Daily Nous* by three anonymous philosophers in 2019 claimed that gender-critical feminists 'like other activists...will denigrate or vilify their opponents, make use of dogwhistles, appeal to people's baser emotions to increase support for their cause, and ignore inconvenient facts', and that their writings 'express demeaning and offensive ideas about trans people' (Weinberg 2019). They go on to identify the terms 'male', 'men', and 'biological male' as transphobic dogwhistles, claiming that these are used in order to demean, denigrate, disrespect, sexualize, objectify, and 'threaten trans people's access to public goods'. A recent article for *Vice* describes the UK Labour party as using a 'TERF dogwhistle' in their manifesto when they promise to protect the Equality Act 2010's exemptions for single-sex spaces (Smith 2019). *Pink News* accused a birth coach of using a 'transphobic dogwhistle' when she objected to Cancer Research UK's campaign directed at 'everyone aged 25–64 with a cervix', denying that she was a 'cervix owner', a 'menstruator', or a 'feeling', and insisting instead 'I am a woman: an adult human female' (Parsons 2019).

Usually, these types of claims are simply asserted. Occasionally, the author will gesture at the harm that the speech is alleged to bring about. Jennifer Saul, for example, emphasizes how marginalized transwomen are, stressing that 'an absolutely key component of this marginalization and discrimination is the denial of trans women's identity as women' (Saul 2020). Katharine Jenkins does something similar, pointing first to the marginalization of trans people—'[i]t will be relevant to my arguments that trans people in general are a severely disadvantaged and

---

[1] The CUSU Women's Campaign. 'How to spot TERF ideology'. Online at <https://www.womens.cusu.cam.ac.uk/how-to-spot-terf-ideology/accessed>, 24th June 2021.

marginalized group in society, suffering oppression and injustice in multiple respects including discriminatory denial of goods such as employment, medical care, and housing; consistently negative portrayals in the media; and particularly high risks of violence' (Jenkins 2016, p. 396)—and then asserting that '[f]ailure to respect the gender identifications of trans people is a serious harm and is conceptually linked to forms of transphobic oppression and even violence' (Jenkins 2016 p. 396; citing Bettcher 2007).

Before we can settle the question of whether gender-critical speech is harmful speech, we need to set the parameters of what counts as gender-critical speech. (Those who have already read Chapter 8 should skip ahead to the next section). There's a difference between speech uttered by any person who claims to be gender-critical or signals affiliation with the gender-critical movement, and speech that asserts core commitments of the gender-critical feminist view. If we're talking about the former, it's plausible that examples of harmful speech abound, as they do in any online community where accountability is low. But that's hardly a surprising or interesting conclusion. The latter is more interesting.

I'll focus on a cluster of views centring on the importance of sex-based rights, frequently asserted by academics, journalists, lawyers, and other professionals who self-describe as gender-critical. There is plenty of reasonable disagreement among gender-critical feminists about other things, but these are commitments that anyone self-describing as gender-critical is likely to have: there are two sexes, male and female; it is impossible to change your sex; sex characteristics cluster into a bimodal distribution and intersex people are not outside of the two main clusters; sex matters politically and women's sex-based rights should be protected; female-only spaces, services, and provisions are important to women and girls and should not be offered on the basis of self-identified sex/gender identity; self-identification, statutorily declared, is an inadequate basis for legal sex; a subjective sense of one's 'identity' does not trump all others' interests in conflict cases; transwomen are male and transmen are female, and if they weren't they wouldn't be trans; gender is not gender identity; sex is not gender identity; gender is sex caste by way of gender norms, explained by or built on top of sex difference; gender (as previously defined) should be abolished; everyone is 'nonbinary' (relative to the previous definition of gender) so no one is; the terms 'female' and 'male' should refer to sex; the terms 'woman' and 'man', 'girl', and 'boy' should refer to either or both of sex and gender (as previously defined); 'lesbian' and 'gay' are sexual orientations, and thus refer to and depend on sex. (This same list of claims appeared in Chapter 8).

Some people who use 'men' as a gender term think gender is gender identity. To them, 'transwomen are men' will be heard as a denial of a transwoman's gender identity. It would only take granting that denying identity is harmful to land on the conclusion that gender-critical speech is harmful speech. That's why it's important to note how gender-critical feminists and their opponents sometimes talk past each other because of their different concepts of gender. For gender-critical feminists, identity is beside the point. According to the cluster of views just given, transwomen are male, and it's impossible to change sex, and gender is sex caste by way of gender norms, and 'man' is either or both of a sex or a gender term (on these understandings). It follows from these views that all/only male people are men, and so that 'transwomen are men' is true. Still, if such gender-critical claims are reasonably understood as denials of identity, perhaps because gender as identity is the dominant conception of gender and gender-critical feminists do not take sufficient steps to be clear about what they mean, then the phrases 'transwomen are men' and 'transmen are women' may be good candidates for being harmful speech. I'll argue later that a correlate of these claims, namely 'woman: adult human female', is a good candidate for gender-critical speech being harmful speech.

I'll start by considering the claim—less common in the public discussion but of interest in the philosophical discussion—that gender-critical speech involves transphobic figleaves. Then I'll move on to the claim that gender-critical speech involves transphobic dogwhistles.

9.2 Harmful speech: figleaves and dogwhistles

Saul has presented accounts of both figleaves and dogwhistles in the context of racist political speech.

Figleaves. Saul describes racial figleaves as 'utterances that provide just enough cover to give reassurance to voters who are racially resentful but don't wish to see themselves as racist' (Saul 2017, p. 97), made in addition to utterances that are more explicitly racist (p. 103). Racial resentment is a cluster of negative ideas about a racial group that fall short of explicit racism, for example believing that they get 'special favours' (p. 99); that they no longer face much discrimination (Saul 2018, p. 365); that their disadvantage is mainly explained by facts about them, like a poor work ethic (p. 365); that 'they are demanding too much too fast' (p. 365); and that they have been given more than they deserve (p. 365). A classic example is the 'denial figleaf': 'I'm not a racist, but…' (Saul 2017, p. 103).[2]

---

[2] Saul also lists the 'friendship assertion figleaf' ('some of my best friends are black, but…'), the 'mention figleaf' ('what I feel like saying is…'), and one she doesn't name but we could call the 'generics figleaf' ('not all black people, but…') (Saul 2017, p. 104-6). She also toys with the notion of a *human figleaf*, a person from a social group who says something that seems to be undermining of that group's equality (p. 107, fn. 17). Gender-critical transsexuals may be a good example here: in virtue of being trans themselves, audiences will be reluctant to understand their utterances as 'transphobic'. (In fact this is not how things go; gender-critical transsexuals are subject to particular abuse, including the slur 'truscum'). John Turri notes that Saul's discussion of figleaves is left-biased, focusing on 'statements made by conservative politicians, commentators, and their supporters' (Turri 2022, p. 6). Turri attempts a corrective, offering some examples of liberal figleaves including the 'Humpty Dumpty

Most of this is easily transposed from race to trans status, e.g. 'trans people are demanding too much too fast', 'trans people have gotten more than they deserve', 'trans people get special favours', 'trans people no longer face much discrimination', and 'any disadvantage trans people face is mainly explained by facts about them'. There may also be more specific resentments that are specific to trans status. The denial figleaf for trans would be 'I'm not transphobic, but...' (this was in fact the title of a prominent blogpost written against gender-critical feminists—see Finlayson et al. 2018).

Acceptance of these claims would be a sign of 'trans resentment', falling short of explicit transphobia. Saul follows Tali Mendelberg in thinking there's a 'norm of racial equality', which rules out explicitly racist speech (Saul 2017, p. 99). Is there a 'norm of trans equality'? If there isn't, then it doesn't make sense to try to run the parallel—we could just look directly at explicitly transphobic speech. While a lot of speech is *accused* of transphobia, it's clear that in progressive circles in many countries today there is a norm of trans equality. Indeed, the chapters in this book are *about* the way the enthusiastic policing of that norm has caused problems for feminism. So 'trans resentment' is the phenomenon of people who nominally conform to the norm of trans equality nonetheless having attitudes that are not entirely egalitarian.[3]

One issue here is that stating 'trans resentment' in parallel to race smuggles in the assumption that trans people as a social group are in the same kind of position as disadvantaged racial groups, and that is not at all obvious. As groups, they have very different histories, their disadvantage has a different explanation, and its ongoing form has a different shape (e.g. how and by what/whom it is sustained). This formulation makes it seem like anyone who agrees that 'trans people have gotten more than they deserve' has trans resentment, when it is perfectly possible that trans people *have* in fact gotten more than they deserve. (For example, transwomen deserve social equality, but have gotten women's rights). So it would need to be established independently that all of these claims were indicators of *unjustified* resentment, in order for us to be worried about gender-critical

---

figleaf', which stipulatively redefines bigoted words in the mouths of certain utterers (pp. 7–8), the 'force figleaf', which reduces the force of a bigoted remark by saying that it's merely imitating its opponents (p. 9), and the 'stipulative figleaf', which denies that an utterance is bigoted by pointing to the lack of power of its utterer (pp. 9–10). His examples, respectively, include '#KillAllMen' when uttered by feminists on Twitter, an Asian American woman posting to social media 'fuck white women lol', and the claim that the same Asian American woman couldn't be bigoted against white people because it's white people who have been bigoted against Asians in the past (pp. 9–10).

[3] While I formulate the norm in terms of equality here so that it has some content, Saul's formulation of the norm of *racial* equality is left open, simply 'don't be racist', with that allowing different people to plug in their different understandings of what that means (Saul 2017, p. 100). The problem with taking the norm in the trans case to be 'don't be transphobic' is that the gender identity activist community has a very expansive conception of what counts as 'transphobia', incompatible with a feminist commitment to the importance of sex and sex-based rights. More on 'transphobia' in Section 9.2.1.

utterances that give reassurance to those that are trans resentful but don't wish to see themselves as transphobic. Women resenting their rights being appropriated is hardly unjustified.

Let's assume for the sake of argument that there's a good parallel to be made between racism and transphobia, and racial resentment and trans resentment. In this case, gender-critical speech could be characterized as a 'figleaf' whenever it provided cover to trans resentful people who didn't want to see themselves as transphobic. This kind of speech would be fundamentally denying the moral equality of trans persons, but in a way that is palatable to people who nominally uphold a norm of trans equality. This might be seen as an intrinsic wrong; but Saul herself links racist figleaves to the outcomes of 'corrupt[ing] not just our political discourse but our culture more broadly' (Saul 2017, p. 97); blocking self-understanding (because the figleaf disguises racism that would otherwise be called out; p. 110); and potentially causing racist behaviour, up to the point of contributing to genocidal violence (pp. 101 and 112).

The problem for running the parallel argument is that nothing in the core commitments of gender-critical feminism denies the moral equality of trans persons. There is no denial of humanity, or moral status; no assertions of inferiority, or lesser worth. There is no denial that trans people should be protected from discrimination, or that their social disadvantage matters. What gender-critical feminists deny is that it is possible to change sex, that 'woman' is a subjective identity, and that a theory and movement about sex caste should cede a coherent and useful definition in order to be 'inclusive'. But all of these commitments are perfectly compatible with trans equality. If gender-critical speech doesn't deny moral equality then it doesn't involve transphobic figleaves, and if it doesn't involve transphobic figleaves then it can't be linked to the harmful outcomes of that speech that may exist in parallel cases of racist figleaves. So the figleaves claim is a non-starter.

Dogwhistles. Perhaps we'll get more traction with the claim that gender-critical speech is harmful speech by thinking about gender-critical dogwhistles. Saul writes that dogwhistles 'are a disturbingly important tool of covert political manipulation...one of the most powerful forms of political speech, allowing for people to be manipulated in ways that they would resist if the manipulation was carried out more openly' (Saul 2018, p. 362). A dogwhistle is speech that communicates different things to different audiences, usually one thing to people 'in the know' and another thing to everyone else. The neutral example she gives of this is children's cartoons, which sometimes contain more sophisticated references or jokes for the parents who may be watching along (p. 363). But her main interest is in political dogwhistles, which can be used to manipulate voters.

She distinguishes four types of dogwhistle: overt intentional, covert intentional, overt unintentional, and covert unintentional. A dogwhistle is overt when its meaning is right there on the surface for those in the know, and covert when it taps into prejudices those in the know have but isn't transparent about doing so. A dogwhistle is intentional when its utterer wants to communicate different things to different audiences, and unintentional when she merely repeats it without understanding that it will do.

Saul takes the most important type to be the overt intentional dogwhistle. She gives two examples. The first is the phrase 'wonder-working power' as used by George W. Bush in concealed communication with Christian fundamentalists. She says it works in two ways, first by being a 'favoured phrase' to refer to the power of Christ, so that fundamentalists will hear it as a religious reference while others will simply hear 'fluffy political boilerplate' (p. 363); second, by signalling that Bush shares in their idiolect, and so is one of them. The second example is Bush's statement of opposition to an outdated legal decision denying citizenship to black persons, as a concealed communication to those on the right that he opposes abortion. This may 'trigger allusions for those in the know', because the decision is so often referenced in discussions about abortion, or may work by conversational implicature—*everyone* opposes that decision, so something else must be being communicated (p. 364).

A *covert* intentional dogwhistle is one that people 'fail to consciously recognize' (p. 366). It is consistent with norms of moral equality, while tapping into resentment. Saul's example is a campaign against a prison furlough programme, which centred on a particular individual who had committed violent crimes while out on furlough. The campaign was on the surface 'only' about preventing crime, but because the individual who perpetrated those crimes was black, it was also covertly racist. Saul notes that the campaign was initially very successful—causing the politician whose programme it was to fall in the opinion polls—but then was accused of racism, and the politician began to recover (p. 367). She thinks this supports the view that the dogwhistle only worked *because* covert, because people are nominally committed to racial equality and so will reject overt racist messaging (see also the experimental work done by Tali Mendelberg (2001) on this point).

What about the *unintentional* types? Saul says 'a crucial fact about the way that dogwhistles do their work in the world is...they can be unintentionally passed on, with identical effects to the original dogwhistle' (Saul 2018, p. 368). Others who are not aware of the dogwhistle can repeat it, and it can keep doing its work. She gives the example of reporters and TV producers covering the campaign against prison furlough, and thus unintentionally disseminating the racist dogwhistle to a much bigger audience. Their coverage functions as a dogwhistle, but they do not intend it to do so, unlike the original campaigners. These can be referred to as 'amplifier dogwhistles' (p. 369). This is a useful concept given that much gender-critical speech happens online and across social media. We might liken the creators of gender-critical content to the original politicians in Saul's examples, and those who help to disseminate that content online—by liking it, sharing it, commenting on it, or repeating it—to the reporters and TV producers.[4]

Saul thinks dogwhistles are perlocutionary speech acts, 'the acts of making utterances with certain effects' (Saul 2018, p. 377).[5] Those that are covert rather than overt cannot succeed if the hearer recognizes that a particular effect is intended by the speaker. Dogwhistles can 'pose problems for democracy' (p. 379), either because they undermine the democratic mandate for particular policy positions in virtue of only some voters recognizing their true meaning (see also Goodin and Saward 2005), or because they work to exclude certain perspectives from the democratic debate, or undermine reasonableness (see also Stanley 2015). The dogwhistle 'inner city', functioning to mean *black*, has been found in experimental work to have a significant effect on the answers subjects gave to a question about public spending. The question asked about directing funding towards new prisons, or spending it on anti-poverty projects for crime prevention, and varied between using the words 'violent criminals' and 'violent inner city criminals'. Regardless of subjects' existing racial attitudes, there was no difference in answers in the 'violent criminals' condition, but in the 'inner city' condition, racial conservatives favoured prison spending, racial liberals favoured anti-poverty spending (Saul 2018, p. 368; see also Hurwitz and Peffley 2005).[6]

Saul's inclusion of this empirical evidence is significant for two reasons: one, it supports her claim that dogwhistles are perlocutionary speech acts by identifying specific negative effects; two, it suggests such evidence is necessary. Saul herself allowed that there are non-harmful dogwhistles, e.g. the content for parents in children's television shows. So it's not enough to merely establish that there are gender-critical dogwhistles: we also have to show that there are gender-critical dogwhistles with harmful effects. It is noteworthy that no one, including Saul herself, has provided any empirical evidence for the claim that gender-critical speech has harmful perlocutionary effects.

Saul's discussion was focused on racist dogwhistles. We're interested in (genuinely) transphobic dogwhistles, if there are any. There are many questions to ask. What's the parallel to racism in the case of transphobic dogwhistles? What are the

---

[4] There is complexity here about whether sharing/retweeting is 'saying' or merely 'amplifying'. Some seem to understand it as 'saying', an implicit endorsement or repetition of content. Others seem to understand it as 'amplifying' or even merely sharing for comment, sometimes critically. Suppose someone shares/retweets a gender-critical dogwhistle. If that is 'saying' then it may be classed as an overt or covert *intentional* dogwhistle, if it is 'amplifying' then it will be classed as an overt or covert *unintentional* dogwhistle.

[5] The usual distinctions are between the semantics (what the words mean: locution), the speech act (what is done with the words, e.g. *marrying* two people, or *silencing* someone: illocution), and the downstream effects (the consequences of the words being said: perlocution).

[6] Saul used 'racial conservatives' and 'racial liberals' to distinguish answers to questions about racial stereotypes and the racial fairness of the justice system (Saul 2018, p. 368).

specific phrases in gender-critical speech that are meant to be dogwhistles, in the same league as 'inner city' or 'wonder-working power'? Are gender-critical feminists supposed to be the engineers of these dogwhistles, corresponding to the conservative politicians who use the racist dogwhistle phrases, or are they supposed to be the amplifiers or otherwise unintentional repeaters of these phrases? If the latter, whose dogwhistles are they, serving what interests? And finally, what are the negative consequences of gender-critical feminists' alleged transphobic dogwhistles, corresponding to the undermining of democracy by, or the voting practices of, those influenced by racist political dogwhistles? I'll take each of these questions in turn.

9.2.1 Parallel to racism

In the case of racist dogwhistles, the dogwhistle taps into racial prejudice. What there was in the racial case was a value judgement about the comparative moral worth of people of different races. Most types of prejudice, like homophobia, classism, xenophobia, or ageism, tend to involve both generalizations and value judgements: those people are all [*negative description*]; those people are all [*negative judgement*]. The concept 'transphobia' exists, so maybe this gives us what we need.

But we have to be careful here, because this concept has been inflated by activists, to include not just the assignment of negative traits to trans people as a group, but also any instance of a refusal to validate subjective identity claims. You can be accused of transphobia for not using a person's preferred name or pronouns, for dismissing the claim that sex is a social construct, for denying that single-sex services should be offered on the basis of gender identity, and for insisting that sexual orientation tracks sex, not gender identity. You can be accused of transphobia for thinking that being born and raised female under patriarchy makes a meaningful difference to your experiences as a woman. You can even be accused of transphobia for thinking that laws dealing with pregnancy and breastfeeding, or charities dealing with breast cancer and cervical cancer, should keep using the word 'woman' instead of switching to 'pregnant people' or 'people with cervixes'.[7] If transphobia is going to be like all the other -phobias and -isms, then we need to

---

[7] In case it's not immediately obvious why this *isn't* transphobic, note that the 'default male' has been a longstanding assumption against which women have fought for recognition (and that this assumption has caused real material harm, e.g. in the making of personal protective equipment to fit a standard male body, or the understanding of the symptoms of heart attack coming from the standard male experience of heart attack—for this and many other examples see Criado-Perez 2019). Naming women, acknowledging women's difference, and advocating for its accommodation, are important feminist projects, which are undermined by the push by gender identity activists to return to gender-neutral language, which will ultimately mean a return to the default male (see also discussion in MacKinnon 1987).

eliminate the inflation and focus on genuine prejudice against trans people as a group.

But then it will need to be shown that gender-critical speech in fact taps into (and in the best case, of overt intentional dogwhistles, *intends to* tap into) genuine prejudice against trans people. Let's return to the examples in the anonymous *Daily Nous* post, claiming that 'male', 'man', and 'biological males' are all transphobic dogwhistles used by gender-critical feminists. These are not value judgements, but statements of fact. There need be no prejudice involved in saying that a transwoman is a 'biological male' or is 'male'; the transwoman *is* in fact both of those things (and many transwomen themselves are perfectly happy to admit this).[8] There need be no prejudice involved in saying that a transwoman is a 'man', if you think 'man' is synonymous with 'male', or if you think that being male is a necessary and sufficient condition of being a man. Gender-critical feminists generally think one or both of these two things.

Males/men are the *superior* category in the sex hierarchy under patriarchy, not the inferior category, which makes it difficult to see how being referred to as a man can be demeaning or disrespectful. Indeed, calling a man a 'woman' (or a 'girl') is a way to *disrespect* him. Calling a transwoman 'male' or a transman 'female' might be a way to disrespect that person *as an individual* if it is done in the service of no other aim but to insult or offend; but gender-critical feminists don't have that as their aim, their aim is the protection of women's sex-based rights. Going forward, we'll need to look for gender-critical speech that taps into genuine prejudice against, or can be argued to cause real harm to, trans people.

9.2.2 Which phrases?

Let's start with an example that plausibly *does* count as tapping into the prejudices just mentioned, even though it's not an example of core gender-critical speech in the sense circumscribed in Section 9.1.

'Predators' and 'paedophiles'. In August 2019, an email went out to all staff at the University of Melbourne. It was from the Vice-Chancellor, and it read 'I have recently become aware of some highly offensive stickers and posters appearing on campus which vilify transgender and gender diverse people. Campus security have removed the material and made contact with Victoria Police.' As part of the campaigning against the Births, Deaths, and Marriages Registration Amendment

---

[8] See e.g. these tweets by high-profile transwoman Blair White, each of which feature a sexualized/revealing picture of White with the comments 'Men, what's stopping you from looking like this?' (August 19th 2020, 3:45 a.m.), and 'This is the ideal male body. You may not like it, but this is what peak performance looks like' (May 8th 2020, 3:16 a.m.). <https://twitter.com/MsBlaireWhite/status/1295778746566184960?s=20> and <https://twitter.com/MsBlaireWhite/status/1258445512266493953?s=20>

(BDMRA) Bill 2019 (the bill that proposed moving to self-identification for change of legal sex), someone had put two different posters up in various buildings around the university campuses of Melbourne.[9]

One said in large print 'COMING SOON! To a toilet with you. Ms #WaxMyBalls', laid over a picture of Jessica Yaniv,[10] and in smaller print 'If the births deaths and marriages registration Amendment bill 2019 passes predators like Jessica/ Jonathan Yaniv will be able to use female toilets And it will be illegal to protest'. Another had a picture of Karen White, and said 'This is Karen White. This 52 year old transgender woman is a convicted paedophile. HE was placed in a female prison and sexually assaulted female inmates. THE BIRTHS DEATHS AND MARRIAGES REGISTRATION AMENDMENT BILL 2019 WILL ALLOW VIOLENT SEX OFFENDERS LIKE WHITE TO SELF IDENTIFY INTO FEMALE PRISONS, SHELTERS, AN [sic] BATHROOMS. THANK A STATE LABOR POLITICIAN TODAY.'

These posters aim to get readers to resist the BDMRA Bill, and they do so by reminding their audience of two of the *worst* transgender people that exist in the public imagination, namely Jessica Yaniv and Karen White. Both Yaniv and White are linked online to paedophilia, Yaniv through widely circulated screenshots of inappropriate comments about pre-pubescent girls, and White through White's criminal record. This taps right into the 'sexual deviant' prejudice,[11] and it encourages generalization, along the lines that because we wouldn't want to share female-only spaces with Yaniv or White, we shouldn't want to share them with any transwoman. This looks like a classic case of generalizing from 'one bad apple' to a whole social group. Imagine if we heard a politician assert that we should disallow immigrants from Bulgaria, for example, on the basis that *one Bulgarian*

---

[9] This was reported a couple of years later in Melbourne newspaper *The Age*, in the context of protests against gender-critical research and teaching at the University of Melbourne (Carey 2021).

[10] Yaniv is a Canadian transwoman who took a number of immigrant home-based beauty therapists to court for discrimination when they refused to perform a Brazilian wax (Yaniv has male genitalia)—(see discussion at Murphy 2019, and Slatz 2019).

[11] There was a concerted attempt by opposition to the campaign for gay rights to link same-sex attraction in men up with sexual deviancy, in particular paedophilia. Prejudice against gay men often revealed itself through people making this connection. (Although this association gained some credibility through the fact that for a period gay rights campaigners did actually advocate for paedophiles—see discussion in de Castella and Hayden 2014). Whether this association with sexual deviancy is a prejudice is more complicated in the case of transwomen, for two reasons. One is that what is at least an uncommon sexual interest—autogynephilia, the attraction to oneself as a woman—*is* the cause of at least some transwomen's identification as women (see e.g. Blanchard 1989; Blanchard 2005; Lawrence 2013; Lawrence 2017; Zucker et al. 2016; and further discussion in Lawford-Smith 2022, pp. 107–9, p. 243 fn. 92, and p. 244 fn. 99). Another is that some transwomen are upfront about being attracted to women's sexual subordination (e.g. Andrea Long Chu's notorious claim that sissy porn made her trans—Chu 2019). So the 'prejudice' then can't be the projecting of incorrect ideas about sexual deviancy onto transwomen, but only either *generalizing* from autogynephilic or subordination-attracted transwomen to all transwomen, or considering autogynephilia or subordination-attraction 'deviant' rather than ordinary.

man raped one Australian woman. The inference from one rapist to all of his co-nationals is absurd.

Is it just as absurd in the case of transwomen? Gender-critical feminists think sex matters politically. That means they think *being male* matters. They don't distinguish transwomen from other male people in that regard; they are concerned with male violence, and with male sexual entitlement, and with other socialized male behaviours, and while they don't think that *all men are violent* (sexually entitled, etc.) they think that *we don't know which males are violent* (sexually entitled, etc.) and this gives us precautionary reasons to protect female-only spaces, services, and provisions. The fact that a law is being proposed that would allow *any male person* no matter who he is to self-identify into female-only spaces is a serious threat to those interests. But this point could have been made using a poster featuring a violent male person who wasn't trans.

Given that there are negative stereotypes of transgender people as being predators and/or paedophiles, and given that the case against self-identification for sex could have been made by referring to any male person, the choice of two transwomen to feature on the posters does look to be harmful. Whoever made the posters was probably reasoning that it's transwomen who are *contesting* women's spaces, not other males. But that doesn't change the fact that the point could have been made in a less harmful way. These posters did contain genuine prejudice against trans people. But while these posters were likely speech by a gender-critical *person*, what they say is not part of the core set of gender-critical commitments. So they do not suffice to establish that gender-critical speech is harmful speech.

'*Clownfish*'. In a segment for *Good Morning Britain* about the backlash against J. K. Rowling's gender-critical essay (Rowling 2020), India Willoughby said:

> ...there's some very oblique terms in that long essay that J. K. Rowling did, I mean there's a reference there to clownfish, now clownfish are amazing, clownfish can actually change sex naturally, incredible! But it's used in certain areas as an insult towards trans people, so on the face of it, I mean there's an innocent reference to clownfish, but J. K. Rowling knows the weight that clownfish carries, yet she used that thing (Good Morning Britain 2020).

While Willoughby doesn't use the word 'dogwhistle', that's what she's describing here—'clownfish' is used *in certain areas*, i.e. among people 'in the know', to communicate particular content. Whether or not this content is as strong as to be 'an insult towards trans people' is debateable, but it is true that the clownfish is well-known and frequently-discussed among gender-critical feminists. This began as part of the social media fight between gender-critical feminists and gender identity activists over whether it's possible for humans to change sex, with some social media users on the gender identity side contributing examples of plants and animals being able to change sex. Gender-critical feminists found this highly amusing—the obvious response, of course, being *what does the clownfish have to do with us?* From there, 'clownfish' became a sort of meme.

When J. K. Rowling writes about clownfish, then, she's using an idiolect that signals to gender-critical feminists *we are on the same team,* and to gender identity activists that she is with the gender-critical feminists. But it's not clear if it is an insult. If it is, the content is the fairly mild 'some gender identity activists are a bit stupid because they think the clownfish has implications for human sex categories', rather than anything more severe. Perhaps it isn't a direct insult, but rather an indirect insult, by way of signalling membership in the gender-critical community. But for that to be true, it would have to be established independently that this community has harmful views, so that signalling membership in it is a way of referring to those views. But this is precisely what is at issue.

'*Adult human female*'.[12] Here's a better candidate: asserting the dictionary definition of 'woman'. In 2018, the gender-critical activist Kellie-Jay Keen, better known as Posie Parker from the organization *Standing for Women*, placed a billboard in Liverpool featuring the following text:

woman
wʊmən
noun
adult human female

A man describing himself as 'an ally of the transgender community' made a complaint about the billboard which lead to its being taken down, saying that the billboard was a 'symbol that makes transgender people feel unsafe' (BBC 2018). The definition is printed on T-shirts and stickers that are worn and distributed as part of the gender-critical campaign against self-identification for legal sex status.

This is a great candidate for a gender-critical dogwhistle for several reasons. First, it is likely to operate as covert, at least for many people. It's the *dictionary definition*—so what's the problem? Second, those not 'in the know' are unlikely to understand its full implications. They may simply see a T-shirt stating an obvious truth.[13] But 'woman: adult human female' or even just '#AHF'[14] is a sex-based

---

[12] A related candidate would have been 'women don't have penises', which appeared on stickers that were widely distributed as part of a gender-critical campaign in the UK (Pidd 2018). But this is surely *less* offensive to transwomen than 'adult human female', given that it allows in principle that transsexual women are women, so I will not discuss it separately here.

[13] A recent article about Sheila Jeffreys, in connection with the publication of her memoir, uses the sentence 'She has no patience for the idea that depilation—like heels and lipstick and Botox and lesbian pornography—is a legitimate choice made by adult human females and therefore none of her business' (Overington 2020). This would be grammatically unusual in any other piece, but in an article about Jeffreys, one of the highest profile radical feminists, it functions as a hat tip to radical feminist and gender-critical women.

[14] All of these variations are widely used; I'll use the shorter version for brevity.

definition of 'woman', which includes *all* female people and excludes *all* male people. That means it counts trans men and female nonbinary people as 'women', and transwomen and male nonbinary people as *not* women. It *reclaims* the term 'woman' for female people, from those feminists and gender identity activists who use it to refer to the gender identities of a mixed sex category of people. #AHF is in tension with gender identity activism.

Whether this is enough to establish that it is a dogwhistle, and an example of harmful speech, depends on two things. One is the perlocutionary effects of the speech, what it causes in the world. I'll take this up in Section 9.2.4. The other is the relative social power of the speakers. We're more likely to agree that something is harmful speech when there is a power asymmetry. For example, the film *The Australian Dream* presents the story of Adam Goodes, an indigenous Australian footballer subject to racist abuse throughout his career.[15] A young white girl in the crowd at one of his matches called him an 'ape', and Goodes had security remove her from the stadium, which caused the public to turn against him—he was booed at matches for the next several years. As an Aboriginal Australian living in a country with a violent colonial history, no serious attempt at reparations for historical injustice, and ongoing structural, institutional, and individual racism, Goodes was in a subordinate social position *as* indigenous, being slurred by a white Australian. But being insufficiently attuned to this social group relation, what much of the Australian public 'saw' was a high-profile footballer targeting a young girl; perhaps being too easily offended by 'mere words'. There is no question that 'ape' is a slur in this context.[16] Is #AHF plausibly like 'ape'?

The two cases have something in common, which is that there are two ways to see them: in the Goodes case, the first is race (white against black), the second is celebrity/power (AFL player against young fan). In the #AHF case, the first is gender identity (non-trans against trans), the second is sex (female against male). The difference between the two cases is that in the Goodes case, Goodes was *responding to* racial abuse when he had the girl removed from the stadium, and the girl was targeting Goodes directly with racist abuse for no other reason than to insult him. This means the race framing has a stronger claim to being how the incident should be understood. In the #AHF case, women are asserting a specific view of 'woman' for feminist purposes, to protect their legal rights, and as a corrective to mainstream feminism which has ceded any possibility of a coherent definition of 'woman'. At best, their project has negative side effects for trans people. Yet gender identity activists respond as though the only purpose of such feminism could be to exclude trans people—as though #AHF is a direct attack on trans people. So #AHF cannot be considered as the parallel of a direct slur.

---

[15] 'The Australian Dream' (2019). Online at <https://iview.abc.net.au/show/australian-dream>
[16] For theories of slurs, see Chapter 7.

But the parallel is helpful, because gender identity activists' response to #AHF is a bit like the Australian public focusing on the celebrity/power dimension of the 'ape' incident. It reveals insufficient awareness of feminist issues, as though the only reason women might have to define themselves as a class is to be unpleasant towards trans people. In focusing on the non-trans/trans dimension of the case, they overlook the significance of the male/female dimension. Men have defined women for thousands of years of male-dominated history;[17] women have literally become what men wanted them to be (see discussion in MacKinnon 1987, p. 59).[18] Women have the moral right to push back on this, to define *themselves*. 'Woman: adult human female' is the definition that makes the most sense to gender-critical women, and gives them what they want for feminist politics, namely a coherent class with a demonstrable history of oppression. There should be a high bar on anyone's attempting to override this self-definition in their own interests. You cannot pretend to respect a woman's right to self-define while simultaneously telling her which definitions are acceptable. And yet this dimension of the issue is seldom acknowledged. No such defence can be offered of a young white Australian's right to yell 'ape' at an indigenous footballer.

For this same reason, the claim that 'woman: adult human female' is harmful speech because it denies transwomen's identities doesn't go through. It relies on *agreement* that 'woman' is a gender term and gender is gender identity, the latter of which, at least, gender-critical feminists deny. Only if it were common ground that woman is a gender term and gender is gender identity, would 'woman: adult human female' constitute a denial of transwomen's identity claims. Gender-critical feminists have nothing to say about trans identity claims, they're interested in sex, which isn't an identity but a material fact. To people who accept gender identity ideology, 'transwomen are male' and 'transwomen are men' might sound like hateful/harmful speech, *because* they sound like denials of trans identity. But this is nothing more than talking past each other, based on using the same words to mean different things. And both sides know this: both use words in their preferred way as part of a political strategy to retain the meaning/bring the words to mean what they want (gender-critical feminists to retain 'female' as a sex term and 'woman' as a sex or gender (as caste) term; gender identity activists to bring 'woman' and in some cases 'female' to refer to gender as identity). If the widespread social understanding was that 'woman' is a gender term and gender is gender identity, then the burden would be on gender-critical feminists to make their meaning clear in order to avoid misunderstanding and possible insult. But it

---

[17] For a very early discussion of this, see (Pizan [1405] 1999, Part I). Much later, Simone de Beauvoir wrote: 'Humanity is male, and man defines woman, not in herself, but in relation to himself' (Beauvoir [1949] 2011, p. 5).

[18] See also the matriarchal utopia imagined in *Herland*, which is an extended commentary on the extent of women's having been shaped by men (Gilman 1915).

is not. Rather, they are using words in the ordinary way, *refusing to* use them in accordance with a political minority's revisionist project with which they disagree.[19]

9.2.3 Whose phrases?

In a recent special issue of *The Sociological Review*, a group of co-authors claimed that gender-critical feminists criticize 'social developments such as LGBTIQ-inclusive school education and positive media representation of trans people', and that they 'argue that such developments result from what they call 'gender ideology"' (Pearce et al. 2020, p. 681). The authors then go on to identify the term 'gender ideology' as originating 'in anti-feminist and anti-trans discourses among right-wing Christians, with the Catholic Church acting as a major nucleating agent' (p. 681). They write that this term has been 'increasingly adopted by far-right organizations and politicians', who 'position gender egalitarianism, sexual liberation and LGBTQ+ rights as an attack on traditional values by 'global elites"' (p. 681). It is not uncommon for detractors to link gender-critical feminism to conservative groups, although the most common form is to simply suggest 'alliances', exploiting left ideological purity in order to discredit gender-critical feminists. But this claim is more dramatic, suggesting that gender-critical feminists are merely disseminating someone else's agenda, in this case the religious right's.

If this were correct then gender-critical feminists would not be the creators of the dogwhistle—at least not in the case of the phrase 'gender ideology'—but mere amplifiers. This would be an unintentional dogwhistle, rather than an intentional one (it is hard to believe that feminists would have any interest in opposing gender egalitarianism, sexual liberation, or LGBTQ+ rights). But whether or not the authors give a fair reconstruction of the history of 'gender ideology', it is much more common for gender-critical feminists to refer to gender *identity* ideology, specifically picking out the worldview of those who advocate for the replacement of sex with gender identity. For example, a search for 'gender identity ideology' at *Feminist Current*, the most popular and prominent radical feminist website, turns up nine articles with the phrase 'gender identity ideology' in the title, three with 'trans ideology', and only one with 'gender ideology'. Jason Stanley defines ideological beliefs as those that are resistant to revision, even when good evidence is presented (Stanley 2015, p. 178). Beliefs about gender identity fit this description, so there's a good reason for feminists to use phrases like 'gender identity ideology', or 'trans ideology'. 'Gender ideology' may be a simple shorthand for these,

---

[19] See discussion in Section 9.2.4 below of one further phrase, 'gender (identity) ideology'.

although if it *is* a religious-right dogwhistle then it can still do its work despite those who use it not intending it in that way.

9.2.4 Negative effects

As I said above, in the racism examples there are real outcomes that can and have been tracked in experimental work, such as causing people to choose different policies for public spending. What is the parallel in the case of gender-critical speech? I'll discuss three possibilities: counterfactual harm; causal contribution to collective harm; and the incitement of violent men.

Counterfactual harms. When Saul describes gender-critical feminists polemically as 'anti-trans activists', saying we 'fight against the key demands of trans women' and are 'committed to worsening the situation of some of the most marginalized women' (by which she means transwomen), she points immediately to transwomen's marginalization, mentioning suicide attempts, the lack of anti-discrimination laws, and the proportion of anti-LGBTQ hate crimes directed at them (Saul 2020). It is not plausible that gender-critical speech is the direct cause of suicide attempts or hate crimes (it is not incitement to violence or self-harm).[20] Saul may be making a counterfactual causal claim, something like, *but for gender-critical feminists, transwomen's demands would be granted* (or, their situation would be better). Or she may be pointing to transwomen's marginalization in order to justify a prioritarian claim, something like *transwomen are the worst-off women, so we should be focusing our efforts on helping them, and gender-critical feminists are failing to do that*. Gender-critical feminists are failing to do something they ought to be doing, and this creates another counterfactual: were they doing it, transwomen would be better off. Both of these interpretations of what Saul is saying give us a 'negative effect' of gender-critical speech, although less direct than we might normally have in mind when we worry about the perlocutionary effects of speech acts.

Are either of these counterfactuals plausible? The prioritarian claim can't get us very far, given that it begs the question. At issue between gender-critical feminists and feminists of some other kinds is *whether* transwomen are women. Gender-critical feminists think they are not. If transwomen are not women, then they cannot be 'some of the most marginalized women'. If it's not true that they're some of the most marginalized women, then it's not true that gender-critical feminists are failing by their own lights as feminists in not helping them. (Escaping this

---

[20] Decisions about suicide are extremely complex and don't have a single cause. Trans communities have disproportionately high rates of autism, mental health issues, and same-sex attraction—which itself correlates with high suicide ideation—all of which may exist *prior to and separate from* the individuals' identification as trans, and in some cases may explain that identification (see also discussion in Lawford-Smith 2022, Chapter 5).

conclusion might also have been achieved by rejecting prioritarianism). Is it true that 'but for' gender-critical feminists, transwomen's demands would be granted, or their situation would be better? That is quite possible. Gender-critical feminists are sometimes the only voices speaking up in opposition to legal changes that are being pitched as good for trans people. But whether fighting against these 'key demands' actually explains transwomen being worse off than they otherwise would have been is unclear. That's because it is perfectly possible for there to be a reasonable compromise between transwomen and women, such that *both* sex and gender identity are legally protected. It is unfair for transwomen to demand *women's rights* and then for allies like Saul to complain that women are making transwomen worse off by refusing their demands. If they had have simply demanded *trans rights* in the first place, we wouldn't be in this situation.

Causal contribution to collective harm. There's another way in which gender-critical speech might be argued to do harm, which is as a causal contributor, rather than a cause. Climate change is caused by many different people's greenhouse gas emissions, and it's impossible to pick anyone in particular out as 'the cause' of devastation from an extreme weather event, but we can point to everyone who emits greenhouse gases as a causal contributor. Similarly, we might say that transwomen's marginalization is caused by many different people's attitudes towards them (e.g. not believing that they are what they say they are), and it's impossible to pick anyone in particular out as 'the cause' of there not being better legal protections, but we can still point to everyone who doesn't support particular legal reforms as a contributor. In cases like these, it might seem a bit unusual to single out one group of contributors. But just as some people emit a lot and spend a lot of time advocating for high-emissions activities, so too some people work hard to make sure there aren't particular legal reforms. It doesn't seem inappropriate to single out those who contribute more than others.

Gender-critical feminists do work hard to make sure particular legal reforms pitched as good for trans people don't go through. Sex self-identification is one such reform, eliminating gatekeeping requirements on change of legal sex. Conversion therapy and hate speech (vilification) laws are others, the first aimed at preventing the change or suppression of a person's gender identity, the second aimed at adding gender identity as a protected characteristic against which there can be hate speech (vilification). I have personally campaigned against all three of these legal reforms in my own state: sex self-identification because it undermines single-sex provisions (see also Chapters 4 and 5); prohibitions on conversion therapy (specifically talk therapy for gender identity) because they effectively mandate an 'affirmation-only' approach to trans identification which cannot sort out who is genuinely trans; and expanded vilification protections because they are likely to have the effect of suppressing feminist speech in the name of protecting gender identity (enabling gender identity activists to bring complaints against feminists). Gender-critical feminists are loud about these issues, and they are unique in including leftists that oppose these laws—often the only leftists who do.

The problem with this attempt to establish harm is that the legal reforms being opposed by gender-critical feminists exist in countries where trans people are already legally well-protected, and where the proposed reforms create a genuine conflict of interests with women by encroaching on sex-based rights (or undermining the adequate clinical care of trans-identifying children, or threatening feminist speech). Gender-critical feminists are not opposing laws that protect trans people from housing and employment discrimination, or that secure their access to adequate healthcare. Rather they are opposing laws that they see as going too far in protecting one group at the expense of another. If the proposed laws are unreasonable, promising gains to trans people at the expense of women and girls (and lesbian, gay, and bisexual people), then it cannot fairly be said that in opposing those laws, gender-critical feminists are causal contributors to transwomen's marginalization. It isn't 'marginalization' for an already well-protected group not to have bad law passed.

An even more indirect argument for gender-critical speech being a causal contributor to harm involves linking gender-critical speech in other countries to the situation in the United States. The United Kingdom is frequently acknowledged as having the largest and most active gender-critical movement, but there are also gender-critical groups in Australia, New Zealand, Canada, and other countries too.[21] Gender-critical feminist speech is largely emanating *from these countries,* where trans protections are extremely good, and rates of violence are extremely low. But perhaps it could be argued that the speech in those countries causes harm to trans people in the United States, where the protections for trans people are significantly worse. Due to social media, the feminist discussion is global, so ideas anywhere can influence ideas everywhere.

While there may be some cultural influence between countries just due to the internet and the free flow of ideas, this is not obviously more or less than for any other issue, and in any case not a sufficient reason for gender-critical feminists to give up advocating for women's rights. What is at stake is important, and what is risked is far from certain. There's no reason to think that women in the United States couldn't take account of the differences in context, making clear that in opposing the conflation of sex with gender identity in the Equality Act, they're not opposing equal anti-discrimination protections etc. for trans people. So this is insufficient to establishing that gender-critical speech causes harm.

Incitement of violent men. Finally, perhaps the things gender-critical feminists say make it into mainstream awareness, say via popular media coverage of the

---

[21] The Declaration on Women's Sex-Based Rights has signatories from 119 countries, suggesting that whether or not there are active groups, there are at least gender-critical women in a majority of countries. See <https://www.womensdeclaration.com/en/>, 26th June 2021.

dispute between these feminists and gender identity activists, and from there influence the ideas of violent men. Let's return to the posters put up at the University of Melbourne for a moment. Suppose (contra fact) that a newspaper ran a story on this incident and printed a photo of the posters, then some men who saw the article became angry and protective of the women they cared about who, if the BDMRA Bill passed, would then be sharing a bathroom with predators and paedophiles (according to the poster). There is a long tradition of (some) men enacting violence against (other) men in the name of protecting women, most famously in the cases of white men lynching black men for sleeping with white women (see e.g. Crenshaw 1989, p. 158, fn. 49). I have already said that the speech in the poster wasn't core gender-critical speech, but this example helps to illustrate the link from the speech to potential negative impacts. Could core gender-critical speech—particularly that stressing the *safety* issues arising from transwomen's inclusion in women's spaces—feed into protectiveness that men feel for women, and thus be an indirect cause of male violence against transwomen?

Perhaps it could; we need empirical evidence. But violence against transwomen is usually committed by intimate partners, and often as a result of homophobia (the male partner reacting to the transwoman as a 'trap').[22] That means the violent man *sees the transwoman as male and feels his attraction to be a threat to his heterosexuality*. This kind of reaction is about male insecurity with sexuality, not about gender-critical feminists triggering his protectiveness toward women. There is also violence towards trans people within the sex industry, but violence against sex workers is rife, so this is not a trans issue in particular, and is not plausibly connected with gender-critical feminism given that it long preceded the emergence of the gender-critical feminist movement.

Psychological harm. Perhaps gender-critical speech does not cause physical harm, whether violence, or the physical impacts created by lack of adequate legal protections (e.g. no recourse for having experienced violence, or inadequate healthcare), but rather causes psychological harm. We should distinguish emotional reactions like distress, grief, fear, and anger from psychological harm, which is something more serious and more sustained, for example anxiety, depression, post-traumatic stress disorder, and panic attacks. As with suicide ideation and suicide attempts, these psychological harms have complex causes which are unlikely to be reducible to the political speech acts of gender-critical feminists. It could be that in a world in which the ideology of gender identity was common ground, there would be a lower incidence of these psychological harms in transgender populations. It is not implausible that someone who feels strongly about being treated in line with their identity may become depressed when

---

[22] There's an entertaining discussion of 'traps' in the ContraPoints video 'Are Traps Gay?' (Wynn 2019).

consistently not treated that way, and when seeing no hope of coming to be treated that way. But gender-critical feminists are far from the only people who reject the ideology of gender identity, and they reject it for good reason, namely that it conflicts with their underlying feminist commitments. (So: probably they don't cause psychological harm; where they do they are at worst causal contributors; and they have an excuse). It is also not clear that there would be less psychological harm in the world where gender identity ideology was common ground, for this would make women's sex-based marginalization inarticulable, and that in turn may lead to psychological harms for a much larger group.

What about emotional reactions? This point should be conceded. Gender-critical speech can cause distress, grief, fear, and anger. Consider a transsexual person, born male but who transitioned medically and surgically at the earliest age possible in their country, who has 'lived as' a woman and been treated by others as a woman for a significant period of time, and whose self-conception is as a woman. It may be deeply distressing to such a person to hear themselves referred to as 'male', or worse, 'a man'. They may sincerely believe that their sex has changed, whether only that they are 'not male' (any more), or that they are (now) 'female'. They may believe that others relate to them as a woman, and gender-critical speech may cause them to question these relations, creating insecurity and self-doubt. Friends and family of trans individuals react to gender-critical speech with outrage precisely because they want to shield their loved ones from these impacts. So if the 'harm' at issue in the claim that 'gender-critical speech is harmful speech' is emotional, then the claim is at least sometimes true. (This may be what is meant by gender identity activists or allies when they claim that gender-critical speech has made trans people 'unsafe'. For a recent example see ABC 2022.)

There are two complexities, however. The first is that the trans community is a large and heterogeneous group. Very few of its members are transsexual, and not all have experienced gender dysphoria. Some have social or political motivations for identifying as trans.[23] It is implausible that having their sex acknowledged will cause distress, grief, fear, anger etc. to all members of this group, and that might even be true for *most* of its members. The second is that if something causes harm without creating any counterbalancing benefit, or if the counterbalancing benefit is frivolous, then we might want to say that the harm should be prevented. That would mean suppressing or silencing gender-critical speech *because* of the harm it does. But gender-critical speech does have a counterbalancing benefit, namely that it allows women to pursue the feminist theory and movement that makes the most sense to them. The freedom of thought, freedom of expression, and freedom of political belief lying behind this speech is clearly not frivolous, but at the heart

---

[23] On political motivation see e.g. Dembroff (2018); Butler (1990); on social motivation see Littman (2018); Schrier (2020); Marchiano (2017).

of political life. And it is unavoidable: there is no more polite way for gender-critical feminists to say what they need to say that would avoid this harm. Some gender identity activists may be tempted to deny this, and say that feminists can concede the words 'woman', 'female', 'mother', 'lesbian', 'breastfeeding', etc. without losing the ability to discuss and defend sex-based experiences and sex-based rights. But I do not see how this is possible. The replacements currently on offer fragment women's issues as though they apply to numerous different groups (as though the 'cervix-owners' aren't the same people as the 'menstruators'), and obscure sex-based issues (as though it's 'people' who need abortions, making abortion an 'everyone' issue, rather than 'women', making abortion a women's issue). Unless and until there is a way for feminism to proceed with the language it needs to articulate its issues, feminists have the right to refuse to concede feminist language to gender identity activists. So there is no case for saying the harm should be prevented. At best, it should be regretted as an unfortunate (and unintended) side effect of feminist speech.

The first three routes to establishing that gender-critical speech causes harm were unsuccessful, and the fourth had only limited success. For gender-critical speech to be harmful in virtue of involving transphobic dogwhistles, it had to be established that the dogwhistles in fact caused harm to trans people. At most, we've seen that it causes negative emotional reactions in *some* trans people, and while this is regrettable, it is also unavoidable.

9.3 Conclusion

We've considered whether gender-critical speech is harmful in virtue of involving transphobic dogwhistles or 'trans resentful' figleaves, and discussed several examples including posters linking transwomen to predators/paedophiles, the reference to 'clownfish' as an organism capable of changing sex, the campaign slogan 'woman: adult human female', and the phrase 'gender ideology'. We've also considered possible harms that gender-critical speech might be linked to, including a lack of legal protections and the incitement of male violence. Because a dogwhistle is not necessarily harmful, we had to establish whether gender-critical speech involves *transphobic* dogwhistles, and this required looking at whether it can be demonstrated to do harm (physical or psychological). I argued that there is no plausible case for this.

References

ABC. 'ACON & the ABC', *ABC Media Watch*, 17th October 2022. Online at <https://www.abc.net.au/mediawatch/episodes/acon/101544378>

BBC News. 'Woman billboard removed after transphobia row', 26th September 2018. Online at <https://www.bbc.com/news/uk-45650462>

Beauvoir, Simone de. *The Second Sex*. Trans. Constance Borde and Sheila Malovany-Chevallier (Paris: Vintage [1949] 2011).

Bettcher, Talia Mae. 'Evil deceivers and make-believers: On transphobic violence and the politics of illusion', *Hypatia* 22/3 (2007), pp. 43–65.

Blanchard, Ray. 'The concept of autogynephilia and the typology of male gender dysphoria', *Journal of Nervous and Mental Disease* 177 (1989), pp. 616–23.

Blanchard, Ray. 'Early history of the concept of autogynephilia', *Archives of Sexual Behaviour* 34/4 (2005), pp. 439–46.

Butler, Judith. *Gender Trouble* (Abingdon: Routledge, 1990).

Carey, Adam. 'Transgender debate a free speech stress test for Melbourne University', *The Age*, 18th June 2021. Online at <https://www.theage.com.au/national/victoria/transgender-debate-a-free-speech-stress-test-for-melbourne-university-20210617-p581r8.html>

Crenshaw, Kimberlé. 'Demarginalizing the intersection of race and sex: A black feminist critique of antidiscrimination doctrine, Feminist theory and antiracist politics' *The University of Chicago Legal Forum* 139 (1989), pp. 139–67.

Criado-Perez, Caroline. *Invisible Women: Exposing Data Bias in a World Designed For Men* (London, Chatto & Windus, 2019).

de Castella, Tom, and Heyden, Tom. 'How did the pro-paedophile group PIE exist openly for 10 years?' *BBC News*, 27th February 2014. Online at <https://www.bbc.com/news/magazine-26352378>

Dembroff, Robin. 'Why be nonbinary?' *Aeon*, 30th October 2018. Online at <https://aeon.co/essays/nonbinary-identity-is-a-radical-stance-against-gender-segregation>

Finlayson, Lorna, Jenkins, Katharine, and Worsdale, Rosie. '"I'm not transphobic, but...": A feminist case against the feminist case against trans inclusivity', *Verso Books*, 17th October 2018.

Gilman, Charlotte Perkins. *Herland* (New York: The Forerunner, 1915).

Goodin, Robert, and Saward, Michael. 'Dogwhistles and democratic mandates', *Political Quarterly* 76/4 (2005), pp. 471–6.

Good Morning Britain. 'Is the JK Rowling anti-trans backlash fair?' *YouTube*, 16th June 2020. Online at <https://www.youtube.com/watch?v=QXKSVWnyOSM>

Hurwitz, Jon, and Peffley, Mark. 'Playing the race card in the post-Willie Horton era: The impact of racialized code words on support for punitive prison policy', *The Public Opinion Quarterly* 69/1 (2005), pp. 99–112.

Jenkins, Katharine. 'Amelioration and inclusion: Gender identity and the concept of Woman*', *Ethics* 126 (2016), pp. 394–421.

Lawford-Smith, Holly. *Gender-Critical Feminism* (Oxford: Oxford University Press, 2022).

Lawrence, Anne. *Men Trapped in Men's Bodies: Narratives of Autogynephilic Transsexualism* (New York: Springer, 2013).

Lawrence, Anne. 'Autogynephilia and the typology of male-to-female transsexualism', *European Psychologist* 22/1 (2017), pp. 39–54.

Littman, Lisa. 'Parent reports of adolescents and young adults perceived to show signs of a rapid onset gender dysphoria', *PLoS ONE* 13/8 (2018), pp. 1–44.

Long Chu, Andrea. *Females* (New York: Verso Books, 2019).

MacKinnon, Catharine. *Feminism Unmodified* (Cambridge, MA: Harvard University Press, 1987).

MacKinnon, Catharine. 'Difference and dominance', in *Feminism Unmodified* (Massachusetts: Harvard University Press, 1987), pp. 32–45.

Marchiano, Lisa. 'Outbreak: On transgender teens and psychic epidemics', *Psychological Perspectives* 60/3 (2017), pp. 345–66.

Mendelberg, Tali. *The Race Card: Campaign Strategy, Implicit Messages, and the Norm of Equality* (Princeton, NJ: Princeton University Press, 2001).

Murphy, Meghan. 'Women warned you: Yaniv's human rights case is the inevitable result of gender identity ideology', *Feminist Current*, 18th July 2019.

Overington, Caroline. 'When choosing to become a lesbian was a radical act', *The Weekend Australian*, 5th September 2020.

Parsons, Vic. 'Birth coach resigns from national industry organisation Doula UK for using "transphobic dogwhistle"', *Pink News*, 5th November 2019.

Pearce, Ruth, Erikainen, Sonja, and Vincent, Ben. 'TERF wars: An introduction', *The Sociological Review Monographs* 68/4 (2020), pp. 677–98.

Pidd, Helen. 'Sticker protest on Antony Gormley's beach statues accused of "trans hatred"', *The Guardian*, 20th August 2018. Online at <https://www.theguardian.com/society/2018/aug/20/sticker-protest-on-antony-gormleys-beach-statues-accused-of-trans-hatred>

Pizan, Christine de. *The Book of the City of Ladies*. Transl Rosalind Brown-Grant (London: Penguin, [1405] 1999).

Rowling, J. K. 'J.K. Rowling writes about her reasons for speaking out on sex and gender issues', 10th June 2020. Online at <https://www.jkrowling.com/opinions/j-k-rowling-writes-about-her-reasons-for-speaking-out-on-sex-and-gender-issues/>

Saul, Jenny. 'Why the words we use matter when describing anti-trans activists', *The Conversation*, 6th March 2020.

Saul, Jennifer. 'Dogwhistles, political manipulation, and philosophy of language', in Daniel Fogal, Daniel Harris, and Matt Moss (Eds.) *New Work on Speech Acts* (Oxford, Oxford University Press, 2018), pp. 361–82.

Saul, Jennifer. 'Racial figleaves, the shifting boundaries of the permissible, and the rise of Donald Trump', *Philosophical Topics* 45/2 (2017), pp. 97–116.

Schrier, Abigail. *Irreversible Damage* (Washington: Regnery Publishing, 2020).

Slatz, Anna. 'Jessica Yaniv loses cases against women who wouldn't "wax her balls", *The Post Millenial*, 23rd October 2019.

Smith, Reiss. 'LGBTQ rights: What are the Tories, Labour and Lib Dems promising?', *Vice*, 10th December 2019.

Stanley, Jason. *How Propaganda Works* (Princeton: Princeton University Press, 2015).

Turri, John. 'Figleaves right and left: A case-study of viewpoint diversity applied to the philosophy of language', *Journal of Controversial Ideas* 2/1 (2022), pp. 1–13.

Weinberg, Justin. (Guest post by three anonymous philosophers). 'Recognizing gender critical feminism as anti-trans activism (guest post)', *Daily Nous*, 6th August 2019. Online at <http://dailynous.com/2019/08/06/recognizing-gender-critical-feminism-anti-trans-activism-guest-post/>

Wynn, Natalie. 'Are traps gay?' *YouTube*, 16th January 2019. Online at <https://www.youtube.com/watch?v=PbBzhqJK3bg&t=1s>, accessed 29th March 2020.

Zucker, Kenneth, Lawrence, Anne, and Kreukels, Baudewijntje. 'Gender dysphoria in adults', *Annual Review of Clinical Psychology* 12 (2016), pp. 217–47.

Index

Andelin, Helen 11
Anderson, Luvell 156–7
Argentina, sex self-identification 79, 102
aspirational argument for 'trans women are women' 66
Atkinson, Ti-Grace 67, 68, 69

Bach, Theodore 56
Bailey, Michael 38
bathrooms, *see* public bathrooms
Belgium, sex self-identification 79
Bettcher, Talia Mae 53, 61, 65, 150
Bindel, Julie 153
biological sex:
   bodily differences 103
   and legal concept of sex 102–3
   political significance 82–3, 103
   understandings of 113–14 n.22
Blackwell, Olivia 24
Bolinger, Renee 159, 160
Briggs, R. A. 66
Bush, George W. 199

cages, genders as 3, 5–6
Cameron, Deborah 68
Camp, Elizabeth 166–7
Canada, sex self-identification 102
Carter, W. Burlette 127, 128–9
Cavanagh, Sheila 128
child marriage 105
clownfish 204–5
comfort of women:
   assurance in women-only spaces 107
   as rationale for women-only spaces 86–7, 94
Convention on the Elimination of All Forms of Discrimination against Women (CEDAW) 82
conversion therapy 210
Croom, Adam 151, 153

Daly, Mary 66
dangerous speech 184–90
Darwall, Stephen 70
Davis, Christopher 164–6, 168
Dembroff, Robin 14, 47, 54–5, 59 n.15

Denmark, sex self-identification 102
de Pizan Christine 30–1
dignity of women:
   assurance in women-only spaces 107
   as rationale for women-only spaces 6, 86–7, 94
dogwhistles:
   explained 198
   racist dogwhistles 199–201
   transphobic dogwhistles 202, 204, 208
   types 198–200
Drummond, Alex 108 n.11

Facebook 153 n.8, 175
fairness for women, as rationale for women-only spaces 87, 96
Falcón, Lidia 175
females:
   sexual objectification 32, 57–8, 106–7
   socialization 35–9, 48, 106
   see also women
femininity:
   decoupled from woman herself 32–3
   devaluing of 48
   norms of 3, 4
   presentational cues by males 109–10
feminism:
   gender-critical feminism 5, 8, 46, 54, 63 n.21, 64, 156, 195–6
   as an idea 68
   and inclusivity 49
   as intellectual framework 68–9
   lack of consensus regarding gender 46
   materialist feminism 40
   as political project 55–6, 68
   radical feminism 14, 33, 63 n.21, 154–5
   second wave feminism 32
   third wave feminism 41
figleaves:
   racist figleaves 196–7
   transphobic figleaves 197–8
Fine, Cordelia 35
Firestone, Shulamith 3
first-personal authority argument for 'trans women are women' 65
Fish, Stanley 179–80

INDEX

Forstater, Maya 69, 177–8 n.15
Fraser, Ben 103–4
Fricker, Miranda 57
Frye, Marilyn 3, 39

gender:
  cage metaphor 3, 5–6
  conceptual divide 30
  distinguished from sex 9, 32–3
  as identity 13–14, 40, 41–7, 49
  as sex caste 33–9, 41, 43, 45–6, 47, 48–9
  as social class 40–1
  social enforcement of 34–9, 48–9
  social position theories 13
  as a spectrum 16
  universal gender identity 80 n.4
gender abolition:
  feminist project of 39–46
  as pathway to ending sex-based oppression 9–12, 23, 24
gender-critical feminism 5, 8, 46, 54, 63 n.21, 64, 156, 195–6
gender-critical speech:
  broad understanding of 172–4
  causal contribution to collective harm 210–11
  counterfactual harms 209–10
  as dangerous speech 186–90
  as feminist speech 185–6
  as harmful speech 194–5, 204
  as hate speech 174–5
  incitement of violent men 211–12
  psychological harm 212–14
  transphobic dogwhistles claim 202
  transphobic figleaves claim 197–8
gender dysphoria:
  diagnosis as requirement for legal change of sex 115–17
  prevalence 21 n.21, 22
gender identity activists:
  hostility to radical and gender-critical feminism 153, 160, 162
  use of term TERF as slur 162
gender identity ideology:
  on intersectional disadvantage 56–7
  misogyny 160
  use of term by feminists 208
gender ideology 208–9
gender norms:
  explained 3, 33 n.9
  policing of 3–4, 39
  radical feminist concept of 14
  violation of 7
gender socialization:
  enforcement of sex stereotypes 34–9, 48–9

females 35–9, 48, 106
males 20, 35–9, 45, 48–9
masculine socialization of transwomen 45
George, B. R. 66
Goodes, Adam 206
Green, Richard 35

harmful speech:
  causal contribution to collective harm 210–11
  counterfactual harms 209–10
  dictionary definition of 'woman' as 205–8
  gender critical speech as 194–5, 205
  incitement of violent men 211–12
  psychological harm 212–14
Haslanger, Sally 39–40, 41
hate speech:
  constitutive harm 182–4
  dangerous speech 184–90
  definition 183
  dignity-based approach to 176–9
  gender critical speech as 174–5
  as group defamation 176–7
  vilification laws 210–11
  as violation of recognition respect 177, 183–4
Hauskeller, Michael 63
hermeneutical injustice, argument for 'trans women are women' 57–60
heteronormativity 63
Heyman, Steven 176
Home, Christopher 151
homophobia 62 n.20, 187, 212
Howard, Jeff 184–5, 189

identity theories of gender 13–14, 40, 41–6, 49
ideologies:
  use of slurs to strengthen 160–2
  see also gender identity ideology; gender ideology
intersex people 109 n.12
intimate partner violence 105
Ireland, sex self-identification 79, 102

Jeffreys, Sheila 84, 126, 128, 130–1
Jenkins, Katharine 41–2, 49, 53, 60, 194–5
Jeshion, Robin 152, 153, 162–4
Jones, Jane Clare 84 n.10
justice for women, as rationale for women-only spaces 87, 94, 96

Kogan, Terry 126

Langton, Rae 176, 182
Lee, Cynthia 187

Lepore, Ernie 156–7
libertarian self-determination argument for 'trans women are women' 63–4
Linehan, Graham 156 n.14, 175 n.11
Long Chu, Andrea 10

MacKinnon, Catharine 32, 41, 176, 182
male superiority 33
males, socialization 20, 35–9, 45, 48–9
Mallon, Ron 55
Malta, sex self-identification 79, 102
#ManFriday 110 n.16
Manne, Kate 47
masculinity, norms of 3
materialist feminism 40
Matsuda, Mari 176
Maya Forstater v GCD Europe, 2019 177–8 n.15
McCready, Elin 164–6, 168
McKinnon, Rachel 53, 58 n.13, 150, 154
Mendelberg, Tali 197
Mikkola, Mari 54
Millet, Kate 92
Minshull, Kellie-Jay (aka Posie Parker) 205
misgendering 69
misogyny 47–8, 49, 135–6 n.24
moral/political category 'woman', and gender justice requirements 55–7
Murphy, Megan 153, 175 n.11
Murrow, Gail 176
Murrow, Richard 176
Muscato, Danielle 108 n.11

New Zealand 8
  inclusion of transwomen in CEDAW 82 n.8
  public consultation over inclusion of transwomen in women-only spaces 133
  sex self-identification 8, 79, 102
nonbinary, as pathway to ending sex-based oppression 12–16
Norway, sex self-identification 79, 102
Nunberg, Geoff 157–9

ontological oppression 59 n.15
oppressed groups, need for spaces of their own 24

paedophiles 203
Parker, Posie 205
Payton, Dee 47
perlocutionary effects argument for 'trans women are women' 60–3
Pettit, Philip 70–1
pornography 32
Portugal, sex self-identification 79, 102

privacy of women:
  assurance in women-only spaces 107
  female-only bathrooms 129–30
  as rationale for women-only spaces 9, 86–7, 94
public bathrooms:
  accommodating women's and transwomen's interests 144
  councils and companies as stakeholders 140
  debate over inclusion of transwomen in female-only bathrooms 123–5
  gender non-conforming people (who are not trans) 138–9
  men's perceptions of 138
  reasons for segregation 126–30
  safeguarding of children 139–40
  tradeoffs between stakeholders 140–3
  transwomen's interests in using women's bathrooms 135–8
  women's interests in having women's bathrooms 130–5

racist abuse 206
racist dogwhistles 199–201
racist political speech 196
radical feminism 14, 33, 63 n.21, 154–5
recognition respect argument for 'trans women are women' 69–70
Reddit 175
Reilly, Wilfred 187–8
respite for women:
  assurance in women-only spaces 107
  as rationale for women-only spaces 88, 96–7, 107
'Reverse Voltaire' 125 n.8
Richardson-Self, Louise 164
Rowling, J. K. 204, 205

safety of women:
  assurance in women-only spaces 107
  female-only bathrooms 129–30
  as rationale for women-only spaces 85–6, 94, 96, 107
Sankaran, Kirun 66
Saul, Jennifer 60–1, 62, 135–6, 137, 150, 194, 196, 198–200, 209
second wave feminism 32
self-determination of women:
  historical violation of 186 n.28
  as rationale for women-only spaces 92–3, 94, 97
self-inclusion, by males in women-only spaces 111–12
Serano, Julia 18, 47 n.31, 47–8, 71

sex, distinguished from gender 9, 32–3
sex-based oppression:
    gender abolition pathway 23, 24
    third gender pathway 23, 24
    transgender pathway 23, 24–5
sex-based oppression, ending of:
    gender abolition pathway 9–12
    hybrid pathways 22–5
    nonbinary pathway 12–16
    third gender pathway 16–17
    tradeoffs between pathways 22
    transgender pathway 17–22
    transitional pathways 5–9
sex-based rights 195
sex caste, gender as 33–9, 41, 43, 45–6, 47, 48–9
sex class, physical cues for membership 108–9
sex differences:
    debate over 32
    importance of acknowledging and accommodating 103
    moral and political significance 96
sex/gender recognition under law:
    debate over 8
    departure from biological sex 102–3
    diagnosis of gender dysphoria 115–17
    gender dysphoria 114, 115–17
    implications for access to single-sex spaces, services, and provisions 94–5
    liberalization of category of legal sex 103, 104–5
    living as acquired gender for specific period 114–15
    need for protection of biological sex 82–5
    requirements to provide assurance to women 112–19
    sex-reassignment surgery requirement 107, 113–14
    sex self-identification 8, 79, 81 n.7, 102–3, 119, 125 n.9, 210
    stakeholders 103
    third sex/gender category 115
sex inequality, justifications for 4
sex-reassignment surgery:
    and change of biological sex 113–14 n.22
    as requirement for legal change of sex 107, 113–14
sex self-identification:
    legal recognition 8, 79, 81 n.7, 102–3, 119, 125 n.9, 210
    and women's interests 25, 107, 119
sex stereotypes 35
sexual harassment 57–9, 129–30
sexual objectification 57–8, 106–7
sexual subordination 59–60

signaling:
    costly signals 103–5
    physical cues for sex class membership 108–9
    presentational cues for femininity 108, 109–10
    to provide assurance to women 108–12
    self-inclusion 108, 111–12
    speech acts 108, 110
Simpson, Robert 176, 181 n.22
slurs:
    as allegiance to a derogating perspective 166–7
    contemporary philosophical accounts of 156–7
    as cues for harmful ideologies 160–2
    dehumanizing function 162–4
    general features 151–4
    as markers of in-group allegiance 157–9
    as offensively chosen over neutral counterparts 159–60
    pragmatic accounts 157–62
    semantic/expressivist accounts 162–7
    socio-political importance 158
    as subordination by privileged group members 164–6
Snyder-Hall, Claire 41
socialization, see gender socialization
social media 110, 199, 204, 211
social norms 3–4, 44
social position theories of gender 13
speech acts, to signal one's sex class 110
sport 79, 83, 86, 87, 88, 94, 96, 118
Stanley, Jason 208
Star of David argument for 'trans women are women' 67–8
Stevens, Aimee 62
Stock, Kathleen 178
Stoljar, Natalie 55
suicide 39, 60, 61, 61 n.19, 69 n.32
Swanson, Eric 160–2, 168
Sweden, sex self-identification 102

Tasmania:
    public consultation over inclusion of transwomen in women-only spaces 133
    sex self-identification 79, 102, 125 n.9
TERF:
    contested status of term 154
    gender identity activists use of term 158–9
    as merely descriptive term 154–6
    neutral counterpart of term 156, 159–60
    original meaning as an acronym 10, 149
    partial reclamation of term 149 n.1
    as slur 159, 160, 162, 164, 165, 167, 168, 169
    status as a slur or derogatory term 10, 149–51
    use of term to derogate or dehumanize 152–4

third gender:
  categories 16
  as pathway to ending sex-based oppression 16–17, 23, 24
third wave feminism 41
trans equality norm 197
trans-exclusionary radical feminist, *see* TERF
transgender, as pathway to ending sex-based oppression 17–22, 23, 24–5
transgender activism, as a feminist movement 18
transmisogyny 47 n.31
'trans panic' defence 62 n.20, 187
trans people:
  homicide rate 187–8
  negative stereotypes 202–4
  percentage of UK population 12 n.11
  violence against 187–90, 209
transphobia, use of concept 201–2
transphobic dogwhistles 202, 204, 208
transphobic violence and oppression 60
trans resentment 197–9
transsexuals, percentage of UK population 12 n.11
trans women, versus transwomen 54, 54 n.2
transwomen:
  male puberty 79–80 n.3
  masculine socialization of 45
  as threats to women's saftety 85–6
  versus trans women 54, 54 n.2
  violence against 212
'trans women are women' arguments:
  aspirational argument 66
  existing arguments in philosophical literature 53–4
  first-personal authority argument 65
  hermeneutical injustice argument 57–60
  by Jenkins 42–3
  libertarian self-determination argument 63–4
  mere insistence on claim 53
  moral equality argument 70 n.34
  moral/political not metaphysical argument 54–7
  new arguments 54, 66–7
  ontological oppression argument 59 n.15
  perlocutionary effects argument 60–3
  recognition respect argument 69–70
  Star of David argument 67–8
  success of 72
  violence argument 42–3, 60–3
  war argument 68–9
  woman-izing argument 70–2
trendsetters 44, 45
Twitter 152, 174, 175

United Kingdom:
  gender-critical movement 211
  public consultation over inclusion of transwomen in women-only spaces 133
  sex self-identification 8, 10, 79, 81 n.7, 102, 114–15
United States:
  protections for trans people 211
  sex self-identification 102
Universal Declaration of Human Rights 179 n.17

Victoria:
  public consultation over inclusion of transwomen in women-only spaces 133
  sex self-identification 8, 79, 81 n.7, 102, 125 n.9, 202–3, 210
violence:
  against trans people 187–90
  against women 105–6
violence argument for 'trans women are women' 42–3, 60–3

Waldron, Jeremy 176, 178
war argument for 'trans women are women' 68–9
Wellman, Christopher 90
White, Karen 203
Willoughby, India 204
Wollstonecraft, Mary 3, 31
woman:
  dictionary definition as harmful speech 205–8
  Jenkin's revision of concept of 41–4
woman-izing argument for 'trans women are women' 70–2
women:
  biological sex as common feature 56
  female nature 30–1
  inferiority of 30–1
  respect for women's boundaries 133
  sex-based marginalization 82–3
  treatment as objects 32, 57–8, 106–7
  violence against 105–6
women-only spaces:
  intent of the creators rationale 93, 94
  intimate association rationale 90–1, 94
  justice/fairness rationale 87, 94, 96
  likelihood of shared bodily experiences 89–90, 94, 96
  moral rationales for 81, 84–5, 94–5

women-only spaces (*cont.*)
  privacy/dignity/comfort rationale 6, 86–7, 94, 107
  public consultation over inclusion of transwomen 133–4
  respite rationale 88, 96–7, 107
  safety rationale 85–6, 94, 96, 107
  self-determination rationale 92–3, 94, 97
  sex or gender identity? 95–8
  see also public bathrooms
Wynn, Natalie 153

Yaniv, Jessica 203
Yogyakarta Principles 69
Yong, Caleb 176